THE ESSENTIAL
Cross-Country
Skier

A
STEP-BY-STEP
GUIDE

PAUL PETERSEN AND
RICHARD A. LOVETT,
WITH TWO-TIME OLYMPIAN
JOHN MORTON ON RACING

RAGGED MOUNTAIN PRESS / McGRAW-HILL
Camden, Maine • New York • San Francisco • Washington, D.C. • Auckland • Bogotá
Caracas • Lisbon • London • Madrid • Mexico City • Milan
Montreal • New Delhi • San Juan • Singapore • Sydney • Tokyo • Toronto

Ragged Mountain Press

A Division of The **McGraw-Hill** *Companies*

6 8 10 9 7 5

Library of Congress Cataloging-in-Publication Data

Petersen, Paul, 1958–
      The essential cross-country skier : a step-by-step guide / Paul Petersen
and Richard A. Lovett with John Morton on racing.
         p.   cm.
     Includes index.
     ISBN 0-07-049625-0 (alk. paper)
     1. Cross-country skiing.   I. Lovett, Richard A.   II. Morton,
John, 1946–   . III. Title.
GV855.3.P48   1999
796.93'2—dc21   99-23369
                                           CIP

Questions regarding the content of this book should be addressed to
Ragged Mountain Press, P.O. Box 220, Camden, ME 04843
www.raggedmountainpress.com

Questions regarding the ordering of this book should be addressed to
The McGraw-Hill Companies, Customer Service Department, P.O. Box 547, Blacklick, OH 43004
Retail customers: 1-800-262-4729, Bookstores: 1-800-722-4726

The Essential Cross-Country Skier is printed on 70# Citation

Design by Tim Seymour
Illustrations by Tom Frost
Project management by Janet Robbins
Page layout by Deborah Evans
Production assistance by Shannon Thomas
Edited by Tom McCarthy and Kate Thompson
Skier silhouette courtesy Swix

This book is dedicated to Dianne, who has been very patient and resourceful through the lengthy birthing process of this project.
—Paul

For Dave and all the gang in Minnesota. May you be blessed with endless-powder winters.
—Rick

CONTENTS

© DAVID MADISON

Part 2 Cross-Country Skiing 201: Expanding Your Skills

ACKNOWLEDGMENTS

It's impossible to acknowledge all the great people and industry organizations and suppliers that have made possible what I know and have experienced. With apologies for omissions, the following were significant contributors to my professional development: My parents and particularly my ski instructor father Reidar Petersen. Professional Ski Instructors of America and particularly the past and present members of the PSIA Nordic Demo Team. Cross Country Ski Areas Association, Rossignol, Salomon, John King, David Madison Photography, *Cross Country Skier* magazine, Casey Sheahan, the North Face, Swix, Bollé, all of the Bear Valley Cross Country Staff, Bear Valley Ski Area and all other ski areas that have comped me skiing privileges, Don Pattison, Jimmy Katz, Tony Forrest, Vladimir Smirnov, the Diehls, and Bill Koch. Without the support and motivation of all the aforementioned I can't imagine having the tools to educate that I today possess. Thanks.

—Paul

There is a myth that authors work by locking themselves into snowbound cabins, far from the rest of humanity. If I ever tried that, I'd need lots of extra bunk space for friends. Thanks to all the people who taught me skiing techniques or commented on the manuscript or outline. Specifically, thanks to Vera Jagendorf, Richard Scheideman, Linnea Nelson, Rick Rust, Einar Traa, Georgeanne Schultz, Robin Rolfe, Paul Mattson, Kelly Scott, Robert Grott, Dave Gustafson, Don Gustafson, Lori Nagel, the Portland chapter of the Oregon Nordic Club, Al Matson, Dick and Pat Lovett, David Lovett, Denise Robinson, Sonja Kindley, Laurie Wong, Bryan Bashin, Mary Vorhies, and Bob Jensen for encouragement, support, good ideas, proofreading, or simply being there through the writing process. Thanks also to my coauthor Paul for his experience and encyclopedic knowledge and for reading endless technical e-mails during the process of long-distance collaboration. Finally, thanks to Alex Barnett, Jonathan Eaton, and all the other good folks at Ragged Mountain Press who helped bring this book to life.

—Rick

INTRODUCTION

We live in a golden age for cross-country skiing. Compared to skis of only a few decades ago, modern equipment is unbelievably light, strong and easy to use. In the United States alone, an estimated 4 to 8 million skiers have discovered how the sport opens the winter landscape to people of all ages and abilities. It has been said that if you can walk, you can cross-country ski, and on today's equipment that's literally true.

Even a low-key stroll across a snowy city park or golf course is enough to make you wonder why our ancestors ever complained of cabin fever. Each new snowfall transforms even the most familiar terrain into something new and different, where you expect magical discoveries at every turn. Floating across this snow on skis turns the everyday motion of walking into a rhythmic dance, full of joy and a sense of boundless well-being. With practice, the joy deepens. Remember how it felt as a child to run into the kitchen and slide across the linoleum floor? Even as a beginner, skiing on flat surfaces, you'll find moments when both feet are sliding at once. The feeling may be unfamiliar at first, but soon it induces a euphoria of effortless, perpetual grace matched by few other sports.

High-tech clothing has also helped open the winter to all comers. Not long ago, if you wanted to venture forth on skis, you needed bulky, itchy wool or expensive silk. Today, a multitude of light-weight synthetics keep you warm even if they get wet. Because moving under your own power also generates body heat, cross-country skiing has been called the "warm" winter sport. The biggest problem most beginners face is a tendency to overdress.

If getting out of the house to slide around the winter landscape sounds like fun, this book is for you. In a series of simple lessons, we'll teach you the basics and get you out exploring on your first outing. How much further you want to develop your skills is up to you. It might be that just getting out for a few hours a few times a year is enough. Or you might find yourself drawn to longer outings or to experimenting with other styles of skiing such as skating, citizens'

racing, backcountry exploration, or nordic downhill skiing. Whatever your taste, we'll provide you with a range of techniques and tips to be sampled at your leisure.

KNOW YOUR AUTHORS

John Morton, whose chapter on racing (chapter 11) will take you beyond the basics to one of the sheer joys of the sport, competed on the U.S. Biathlon Team for two Olympics (1972 and 1976), after which he became assistant coach and then Olympic Biathlon Team Leader. He has also been Head Coach, Dartmouth College Men's Skiing Team. Morton still races competitively as one of the top-ranked Masters competitors in the nation. He is the author of *A Medal of Honor: An Insider Unveils the Agony and the Ecstasy of the Olympic Dream* and articles on skiing.

Paul Petersen and Rick Lovett bring their own different but complementary perspectives to the sport. Paul is a veteran ski instructor and served twelve years as a member of the National Nordic Team of the Professional Ski Instructors of America. He has also been the instruction editor for *Cross Country Skier* magazine. His passion for skiing has taken him around the globe and drawn him to all aspects of the sport, from Norwegian ski marathons to first free-heel descents of 20,000-foot peaks. He lives at the 7,000-foot elevation in the Sierra Nevada and has spent the last twenty-two winters in a snowbound house, skiing to and from the nearest plowed road. Paul has been active in equipment design as well as trail-system development through his many years operating the Bear Valley Cross Country Resort. Describing himself as a recovering skiaholic, he blends technical skiing expertise with a sense of fun and adventure.

Rick is a professional journalist and travel writer who's written about outdoor topics for numerous magazines and newspapers in the United States and Canada. A one-time university professor, he discovered skiing in graduate school, when a friend invited him for a cross-country ski weekend. Later, Rick moved to Minnesota, where he encountered powder snow, groomed trails, and a culture where winter was a reason for celebration rather than hibernation. Mostly a recreational skier, he took up racing for the distance challenges, completing several 50- to 60-km races with respectable, middle-of-the-pack finishes. He now lives in Oregon, skiing mostly on the lower slopes of Mt. Hood.

Most of this book is a joint effort drawn largely on Paul's expertise, but when our perspectives differ we'll pop up from time to time in sidebars to offer individual suggestions or anecdotes.

WHO CROSS-COUNTRY SKIS?

Cross-country skiing isn't just for natural athletes who grew up on skis. It's for anyone with a sense of adventure and a desire to glide across a dazzling, Norman Rockwellesque landscape. All you need is to be in generally sound physical condition (if in doubt, ask your physician) and the willingness to learn new skills. If you have these, it doesn't matter if you're 15, 25, 45, or 65. Skiing is a multigenerational

family sport. Even more than adults, children often take to it naturally, led by their intuitive sense of play. You don't even need to be all that athletic because you can select terrain and paces that suit your own levels of skill, confidence, and conditioning.

The Essential Cross-Country Skier is designed to be beginner-friendly, providing a full course of instruction for people with no prior experience. But it will also be useful to intermediate skiers who want to hone their skills as rapidly as possible—or diversify into new forms of skiing. No book, however, can replace the hands-on experience of taking a lesson from a qualified instructor. The two modes of learning are complementary. You'll get the greatest benefit from both if you read the book first, take a lesson, and then return to the book to reinforce what you learned.

USING THIS BOOK

Like a year-long university course, this book is divided into parts. Part 1, Cross-Country Skiing 101, covers

© MIKE ROTHWELL

beginner and low-intermediate skills, ranging from those you'll need for your first cross-country stroll to more advanced techniques that can carry you efficiently over fairly rugged terrain. Because we strongly recommend renting skis, poles, and boots for your first several outings, this section begins with instruction in basic skills (as well as dressing for the winter weather) and waits until chapter 5 to discuss equipment purchase—an action that can mark your graduation from beginner to intermediate. As a graduation exercise, chapter 6 suggests ways to apply your growing skills to an ever-broadening scope of ski activities.

Part 2, Cross-Country Skiing 201 moves on to more advanced skills, including skating, telemark turns, and backcountry skiing. Because of the popularity of skating, this section leads off with that skill, but each chapter stands on its own, and you generally need not have mastered any one skill to attempt the others (although telemarking is useful for the more advanced types of backcountry skiing epitomized by ski mountaineering). This part also covers several other advanced skills, including winter survival, ski backpacking, citizens' racing, structured training regimens, and the art of ski waxing.

THE ESSENTIAL
Cross-Country
Skier

Part 1

Cross-Country Skiing 101:
Getting Started

© VERA JAGENDORF

Chapter 1

Enjoying the Winter Environment

© PAUL PETERSEN

The trail curves through a birch forest where mist blends the landscape into a surreal mix of white on white. It seems to extend forever—which is good, because you feel as though you could ski forever in this primordial forest whose only sign of civilization is the ski trail, rising and falling into the distance. The thermometer reads 25 degrees, but you're comfortable in polypropylene tights and a thick, long-sleeved shirt. Suddenly, the trail rounds a bend and swoops down a hill, leaving fog and birches behind. Sun sparkles diamond-sharp on snowbanks threaded by the crystalline waters of a small creek. Another bend, and the creek swells to a frozen lake backed by pine-studded cliffs. It's a scene straight out of a winter calendar, but you're in the middle of it, your skis whispering feather-light across the snow.

This is cross-country skiing at its finest: a ticket to winter beauty and solitude, a wonderland that can be as close as your doorstep or as remote and adventurous as Yellowstone National Park or northern Minnesota. Visiting it doesn't require the grueling work you may have seen in television broadcasts of the Olympics, where skiers collapse at the finish line, exhausted. You can work that hard if you wish, but you can also choose not to break a sweat, strolling, exploring, and soaking up the natural beauty —pushing yourself no harder than on a summer hike.

VARIETIES OF CROSS-COUNTRY SKIING

There are, in fact, as many approaches to skiing as to walking. Some are athletic excursions, others far more relaxed. It's even possible to mix skiing with rustic lodges, fine food, and blazing fireplaces suitable for a baronial manor—the type of resort experience more commonly associated with downhill skiing. Here are some possibilities. The list isn't complete, and there is some overlap among the categories:

- **Recreational touring.** This is the most popular form of skiing. Nobody's holding a stopwatch, and finding a pretty spot for a winter picnic is more important than being the fastest skier in the group. It takes two primary forms: track skiing and back-country skiing.
  - **Track skiing.** Commercial cross-country ski areas and some government agencies and ski clubs use snow-grooming machines to create thousands of miles of track throughout the

United States and Canada. Properly maintained, this track offers an ideal surface for skiing.

- **Backcountry skiing.** This simply means venturing away from the groomed trails. Technically, skiing down an unplowed road or across fresh snow in a city park is backcountry skiing, although most people associate the term with adventuring more deeply into the winter wilderness. Except for the need to break trail, it can be very similar to track skiing. But venturing into deep powder or hilly, mountainous, or remote terrain requires a greater range of tactics and more self-sufficiency.

Skiing the Yosemite backcountry.

- **Recreational racing.** All-comers' ski races, also called *citizens' races*, let you test your abilities against the clock or other skiers. Like a runner, you may find yourself pursuing "personal best" times or measuring your standing against age-group competitors. Or you may simply enjoy the adrenaline-fueled energy of a mass start or the challenge of completing a ski marathon. Recreational races can also be tours. With groomed track, food stops, helpful support personnel, and shuttle buses, they open up point-to-point routes that would otherwise pose logistical difficulties. Many people ski the races not as speed challenges, but as once-a-year paths to areas that aren't normally accessible.

Groomed tracks and skating lanes have transformed cross-country skiing from a walking sport to a gliding sport.

- **Classic skiing.** This is more a style of skiing than a type of outing. The easiest method to learn and the foundation for all other techniques, it is closely related to walking. As in walking, the skis move forward one at a time as you stride with first one leg and then the other. The poling motion is much like a walker's arm swing. Because of this "cross-lateral" synchronization of arm and leg motion, classic skiing is also known as the *diagonal stride*, a term we will use frequently in this book.

- **Ski skating.** Modeled on the hockey player's or speed skater's ice skating technique, this is best done with specialty equipment on groomed snow. It is a vigorous form of skiing in which you use the edges of your skis as though they were oversized ice skates. It is extremely fast, popular among racers, and harder work than beginner-level classic skiing.

- **Telemarking.** The telemark turn is an elegant way of converting a steep, powdery downhill into

4

A Note about Terminology

Cross-country skiing is sometimes called *nordic* skiing because of its strong historical link to the Nordic countries of Finland, Sweden, and Norway. Downhill skiing is called *alpine* skiing because of its association with mountains, particularly the Swiss Alps. Because you'll hear these terms regularly, we'll use them all in this book.

a series of slow, elegant S-turns. Some people view it simply as a way of traversing otherwise impassable terrain—just one more method of getting from here to there. Others pursue it for its own sake, riding the ski lifts at downhill resorts to get in as many descents as possible.

- **Nordic downhill skiing.** Any form of cross-country skiing at a downhill ski area is nordic downhill. The border between it and traditional downhill skiing is becoming increasingly vague because specialty nordic downhill skis have come to look more and more like their alpine cousins. Just as wide and with metal edges, their chief distinction is that nordic downhill or telemark skis have bindings that attach only at the toes, not along the entire sole of the foot. This allows your heel to lift away from the ski, leaving only the toe bound. Such free-heel bindings—now nearly as stable as downhill skis—give you access to a range of techniques, including the diagonal stride and the telemark turn, unavailable to downhill skiers.

Where to Ski

As long as there's enough snow to keep you from damaging your skis or yourself, any snow-covered patch of terra firma is fair game for a cross-country ski jaunt. But different locations offer different brands of experience.

- **Commercial cross-country ski areas.** The best places to begin your nordic career, these offer services for expert skiers as well. In addition to good snow and groomed trails, the package typically includes convenient parking, restrooms, rental equipment, lessons, food, maps, well-marked routes

Rick Says

The types of skiing available to you will depend on where you live or where you head on winter vacations. Winter in Sun Valley, Idaho, offers almost every type of skiing imaginable. Minnesota has some of the finest snow in the United States and an extensive network of groomed trails, but telemarking and ski mountaineering opportunities are limited. New England offers a nice mix of woods and mountains, although snow cover is more reliable inland than in coastal areas.

I learned to ski in southern Michigan, where some winters served up crisp powder snow that offered delightful skiing for weeks at a time, while others regularly ruined the snow with half-inch freezing rains. Now I live in Portland, Oregon, where I rarely find skiable snow at my doorstep—but it piles up 10 and 20 feet deep at trailheads less than an hour's drive away in the Cascade Mountains. The trick is to make the most of what you have available and not to procrastinate when you do get exceptional snow. Skiable snow can fall even in Hawai'i, atop 13,800-foot Mauna Kea. When it does, skiers turn out in surprising numbers—although finding rental skis in Hilo might be a challenge.

(showing distances and difficulty levels), and a ski patrol. Some areas have trailside huts and cafes, lights for night skiing, groomed areas for practicing downhill turns, special events, and children's trails. A few even have ski-in lodging.

- **Other groomed trails.** Increasingly, groomed trails can be found at places other than commercial ski areas. Provided by state or county parks or the U.S. Forest Service, they typically are free or have a nominal parking fee or donation. The quality of the amenities varies. In some places, track is set almost to the standards of the most exacting commercial trail systems. And parks, particularly in ski-happy states like Minnesota or Wisconsin, may have warming lodges and food service. Elsewhere, groomed trails may be all that's provided—and grooming may be infrequent. Ask locally, or be prepared for a quasi-backcountry experience. Be sure you know the parking rules before driving into the country—some states require "snow park" permits that cannot be purchased at the trailhead.

- **Unplowed roads.** These can serve as good cross-country ski routes, although you may share them with snowshoers, hikers, dogs, and snowmobiles. In addition to providing wide, treeless paths into the backcountry, roads have the advantage of not being very steep—although some are too steep for beginners. Snow conditions can vary from deep powder to ice, requiring better than beginner skills at turning and stopping, except in the most gentle terrain. Other than the possible need for a snow-park permit for trailhead parking, ungroomed roads are almost certain to be no-fee and are available for thousands of miles, providing good avenues for endless exploration. They're also good places to learn backcountry techniques that will later take you off-road.

- **Ski trails**. Increasingly, national forests and state parks are marking ungroomed ski routes in lengths ranging from easy, hour-long outings to strenuous, full-day circuits. Some trails follow unplowed roads, but wherever the terrain permits, they plunge cross-country—perhaps following a summer hiking trail or going across snow-covered brush on routes that are invisible after the snow melts. Although signing methods vary, such trails are often marked by small squares of blue plastic or wood, nailed to the trees far above the maximum snow depth. If you're not the first skier, you can simply follow the tracks of your predecessors. For scenery and solitude, these routes are among the most rewarding, but even in flat terrain they usually require intermediate skiing skills and route-finding confidence. Again, beware of snow-park permit requirements.

- **Snowmobile trails.** The groomed surface of snowmobile trails can be pleasant midweek, non-holiday, or early or late in the day. All other times, cross-country skiers and snowmobilers are best

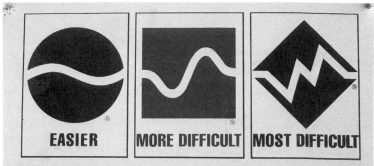

These national standard signs indicate relative difficulty of cross country ski trails at each area. Remember to observe all warning signs and always ski within your ability. Be Safety Conscious!

separated. The exhaust from snowmobiles is noxious, emitting 200 times the concentration of carbon monoxide of a car. Be cautious and courteous when using multiuse areas.

- **Hiking trails.** If you can find them, hiking trails not marked for skiing also offer cross-country ski opportunities. Just remember that these trails are built for hikers. Trees, creek crossings, steep descents, and switchbacks must be approached with caution and a willingness to turn back if conditions are beyond your ability.

- **Skiing from the back door.** If you live in snow country, this represents the essence of cross-country skiing's winter freedom. Housebound while waiting for the snowplow to clear away yesterday's blizzard? No need for cabin fever. Pull on your ski boots, grab your skis and a friend, and take advantage of the mobility that only cross-country skis can provide. If you're determined to get to work after a big snowfall, it's even possible to ski commute.

- **Golf courses.** Snowfall converts city golf courses into open beltways of billowy white. Because the fairways are generally free of rocks and logs, it doesn't take much snow to make them skiable, and each new snowstorm tends to bring out local skiers in droves. Just stay off the greens—and check first that skiing is permitted.

- **Downhill ski areas.** In the last decade, these have gained considerable popularity among cross-country skiers. It's best to have metal-edged skis and at least intermediate skiing ability. In addition, the ski area might require that you use safety straps to keep your skis close by if a binding releases. Most, but not all, also frown on skiing uphill along the side of the slope. It's best just to buy a lift ticket and do it the easy way: skiing downhill and riding the lifts back up (if you're unfamiliar with lifts, ask for assistance). Recognizing the growing interest from cross-country skiers, many downhill ski areas now offer rental equipment and telemark lessons.

HISTORY OF SKIING

You don't have to know anything about cross-country ski history to enjoy the freedom skis give you to explore winter. But it's interesting to know that the sport you've taken up has a history stretching back nearly to the end of the last Ice Age.

No one knows where cross-country skiing was invented. But when the Roman Empire expanded into northern Europe nearly 2,000 years ago, the Romans were intrigued to encounter a winter-mobile people called *skridfinar* (sliding Finns)—skiers. The skridfinar appear to date back well before the Romans. Archaeologists have found a 4,000-year-old petroglyph in a Norwegian cave north of the Arctic circle, depicting a skiing hunter. Other northern cultures invented similar devices. In Siberia, reed snowshoes have been carbon dated to 2,500 B.C., and in Korea, a skiing variant called *solmae* dates back at least 2,000 years. So, regardless of who did it first, the people of Scandinavia and northern Asia have been sliding across the snow for at least 4,500 years.

Skiing was useful for warriors as well as hunters. In the most famous early cross-country ski military mission, two Norse scouts in 1206 rescued a kidnapped infant king by slipping into his captors' camp, then skiing 55 kilometers up and over a mountain to return the boy to his home village. Because the scouts wore birch-bark gaiters to keep the snow out of their shoes, they were known as *birkebeiner* (birch-legs). Today, thousands of Norwegian skiers honor their achievement in the annual Birkebeiner ski race, which tours the original 55-km course from Lillehammer to Rena. Norwegian immigrants to the United States have brought the tradition with them in the annual American Birkebeiner, which draws more than 5,000 skiers to a 55-km course from Hayward to Cable, Wisconsin.

Although Scandinavian immigrants have undoubtedly been skiing in the United States since their first winter snowfall (one theory is that the first North American skier was Leif Eriksson), skiing didn't make a major impact on this side of the Atlantic until the California Gold Rush, when Norwegian miners used it to enliven mining-camp winters. At the time, there was no true distinction between cross-country and alpine skiing, and in the northern Sierra Nevada mountains, daredevil miners raced downhill at speeds clocked as high as 88 miles per hour on 12-foot-long skis weighing up to 25 pounds a pair. In an effort to achieve higher speeds, these racers lubricated the bottoms of their skis with concoctions of vegetable oil, animal fat, and tree sap—thereby inventing the art of ski waxing.

The most famous of these skiers was Jon Luras Varkaasa, better known as Snowshoe Thompson. Wearing a pair of these heavy "Norwegian snowshoes," Thompson found there was more gold to be had in the snow than in the mines. Beginning in 1855, he hauled 100-pound packs of mail across the mountains on a 90-mile, three-day traverse for which he charged as much as $2 a letter—at the time a staggering fee. Perhaps inspired by Thompson, an Oregonian named John Craig attempted the same feat in the central Oregon Cascades but perished in his first attempt, when a blizzard soaked his matches and left him unable to light a fire.

At the same time U.S. miners were discovering skiing, another Norwegian, Sondre Norheim, revolutionized ski design and used it to pioneer a new form of turning that later came to be called *telemark turning* for Norway's Telemark district, where Norheim first introduced it. Prior to the 1880s, cross-country skis were held to the foot with a broad strap that snugged tightly across the toes. This sandal-style design made them cumbersome to steer and easy to step out of accidentally. Norheim realized that skis could be more firmly attached if the binding included a strap that ran behind the heel. These *cable bindings*, whose descendants are still in use, allowed more aggressive steering, permitting him to invent the telemark turn. Norheim is also credited with inventing the sidecut in skis (the hourglass shape, with the middle of the ski narrower than the tip and tail) as well as the *christiana* or *christie turn* (see page 36) familiar to downhill skiers. The telemark turn, however, languished in obscurity until it was rediscovered by Colorado ski mountaineers in the late 1970s and early 1980s.

Prior to the 1970s, cross-country skiing was a minor sport in the United States, even though it was virtually the national pastime of Norway and other Scandinavian countries. In the States it had been eclipsed by downhill skiing, which boomed from the end of World War II through the early 1970s. During the 1960s, cross-country skiing was an oddity, pursued by a few enthusiasts who put up with equipment that by today's standards seems hopelessly inefficient: heavy, cumbersome, and requiring finicky attention to using precisely the right wax for each day's snow conditions.

But the fitness boom that produced the 10-speed-bicycle craze of the 1970s and the running boom of the 1980s indicated tremendous potential interest in a self-powered winter sport. Cross-country skiing

was the obvious candidate. Ski manufacturers rose to the challenge by inventing the first no-wax skis, opening the sport to people who wanted to hit the trail instantly, without fussing with wax. At the same time, wax manufacturers developed easier-to-use waxes for traditional skis, and lighter, stronger fiberglass models replaced heavy wooden skis.

As millions of people take to the outdoors to glide through winter landscapes from Maine to Minnesota and from Fargo to Flagstaff, the millennia-old sport has continued to advance with amazingly youthful vigor. In the past 20 years, skating and telemarking have opened new frontiers of technique, speed, endurance, and terrain. Simultaneously, equipment continues to improve. For people with a craving for speed, there is essentially nothing downhill skiers can do that can't be replicated on modern free-heel telemark skis. And in the years since Snowshoe Thompson's 12-foot boards, skis have continued to get shorter and lighter. The current generation of skis are barely taller than the skier, which makes them easy to learn and easier to master than longer skis. In the ensuing chapters we'll take you from your first tentative shufflings to a confidence of style that only a generation or two ago would have amazed even the experts.

Chapter 2

First Strides

© RICHARD A. LOVETT

Once they've decided to give cross-country skiing a try, most people feel an overwhelming urge to head outdoors and immediately start exploring.

It's a lot easier to do this cross-country skiing than downhill. After all, it's simpler to shuffle across flat terrain without tutoring than to stand at the top of a downhill run with 2,000 vertical feet of snowfield falling away before you. So if you're the type who hates to read instruction manuals until you've experimented on your own for a while, don't worry—you won't develop any lifetime bad habits in those first few minutes.

What you will do is discover that cross-country skis are long, narrow contraptions that move relatively easily in a straight line but require patience to steer around corners. You may wonder how to put on the brakes other than by falling down, and you'll find that even a slight downgrade can be a source of uncertainty.

That's when you need help. Although it won't substitute completely for live instruction, this chapter will tell you how—with a few hours of practice—to advance from shuffling to purposeful skiing. Combined with a ski lesson from a professional instructor or a skilled friend, it will help cement what the instructor tells you—and may even help later on, if you teach a friend.

Don't worry if, on your first few outings, your technique isn't perfectly smooth or you're timid about hills; both of those take practice. Your first goal is simply to become comfortable on skis, see the sights of winter, and fall in love with skiing. The learning process is cumulative. Even if there's a delay of weeks or months between your first and second outings, you're unlikely to lose skill. With each outing, your skiing will become more comfortable and dynamic.

RENTAL EQUIPMENT

Wherever you choose to ski on your first outing, renting rather than buying equipment is your best bet. You can rent an entire package of decent equipment—skis, boots, and poles—for a weekend for less than the cost of a good dinner, and you should practice a few times on rental equipment while you build skills. Later, when you're ready to buy, you may want considerably different equipment from that on which it is easiest to learn. Many ski shops offer "demo"

Paul Says

Whether you're looking at the first cross-country ski outing of your life or getting back into the sport after a long layoff, my advice is to visit a professionally groomed trail system and take a lesson. Many cross-country ski areas offer packages that include rental equipment, a one- to two-hour lesson, and a trail pass—for as little as $25 to $35. It's a wise investment in what could become a lifetime passion.

The trail pass is your ticket to the ski area's groomed trail system, which can comprise anywhere from a dozen to hundreds of kilometers of interconnected routes. Typically the pass is a gummed sticker you wrap around a ski pole so it's obvious from a distance that you've paid the fee. Although it may seem odd to pay to ski at an area surrounded by vast stretches of no-fee terrain, what you're paying for is the groomed trail, which will make your first few outings a great deal more enjoyable. You'll also get such amenities as bathrooms, plowed parking, rentals, instruction, hot food, ski patrol, trail maps, huts, picnic sites, and well-marked routes.

Rick Says

I learned to ski from a neighbor on 6 inches of snow on the University of Michigan campus, far from the nearest cross-country ski area. In subsequent outings I continued to learn by the do-or-die method of dodging trees on snow-covered hiking trails never intended for skiing. Later, I moved to Minnesota and discovered a whole new world of broad, treeless, groomed trails (now common in other states as well), but still had no lessons. Yet the lack of formal training never affected my interest in the sport.

It's great to take advantage of professional instruction if it's available; otherwise, find a patient friend and gentle terrain such as a meadow or golf course and put into practice the techniques outlined in this chapter. Early instruction will help you improve more quickly, but that first outing will still introduce you to a winter world that will make you feel like a 10-year-old, playing in the snow and wondering why so many adults grumble about winter.

packages that allow you to rent high-quality equipment, then deduct the rental fee from the price if you decide to buy. This is an excellent way to try a range of equipment before you buy.

When renting, be wary of inexpensive packages that can give you a poor first taste of the sport. Ask for supportive, higher-than-the-ankle boots and "midlength," "light-touring" skis. For the moment you don't have to know what these terms mean; we'll discuss that in chapter 5. For your first outings you'll probably prefer the "no-wax" skis—they're the easiest to find, anyway (we'll talk about waxable skis in chapter 12).

Boots should fit snugly, not loosely, with just enough room to wiggle your toes a bit. Loose boots make it much harder to control the skis. Most boots snap into the binding simply by stepping down firmly, but a few require you to bend over and use your hands or the tip of a pole as well. Ask for a demonstration when you rent the skis, and if possible practice a few times indoors, on a carpeted floor.

Ski length for adults and kids varies with the type of ski. Trust the shop to pick an approriate length for you.

Selecting the ideal pole isn't as important as getting the best fit in boots and skis, but poles should be of at least armpit height.

Winter Parking

Parking at a winter trailhead or cross-country ski area isn't as easy as leaving your car for a summer hike. You may have to pay to enter a state or county park in order to park in a plowed parking area where you won't be blocking traffic or snowplows. If you're not parking in a public lot, beware of driveways and no-parking signs.

Your best bet is to ask about local parking rules at the shop where you rent your skis. Some states, particularly in the West, use a "snow park" system; these daily, weekend, or annual passes usually have to be purchased at sport shops miles from the trailhead, so be prepared for snow-park signs and heed them; trying to get away without a permit is a good way to get a parking ticket. In a few states, parking permits are even required at commercial cross-country ski areas, although here they will be available on site.

ANATOMY OF A SKI

Skis look simple, and inherently they are. But they have several parts, and it's hard to talk about using them without knowing those parts' names and basic purposes.

The curved-up point at the front end is the tip, although *tip* can also refer to the ski's entire front portion. The rounded, upward curve helps the ski ride over the top of loose snow. The opposite end is the *tail*. The length (and width) of ski in between helps spread your weight across the snow so you don't sink in too far.

The bottom of the ski is the *base*. It's made of plastic and is either smooth or has a molded pattern or *tread* designed to allow the ski to slide forward easily but not backward. If there is a tread, it is concentrated in the *grip zone*, which covers about half the bottom of the ski, centered under your foot. Smooth-bottomed skis are *waxable*

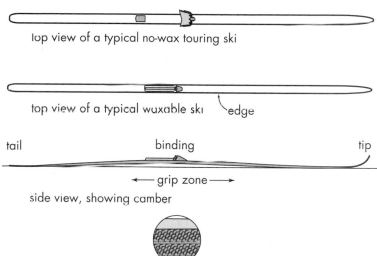

Parts of a ski.

top view of a typical no-wax touring ski

top view of a typical waxable ski — edge

tail — binding — tip

← grip zone →

side view, showing camber

kick zone of no-wax ski, showing tread pattern

skis, substituting snow-gripping waxes for the tread. For the moment we'll assume that if you have waxable skis, they're already properly waxed (this process is discussed in detail in chapter 12).

The top of the ski is called just that. Centered there, at the ski's balance point, is the gadget that attaches your boot to the ski. It's called a *binding* and includes a locking mechanism that snaps to your boot. The binding may also include molded ridges, grooves, pins, or plastic plates designed to mate with matching shapes on the sole of the boot, increasing your control of the skis.

The corners where the sides of the skis and the base meet are the *edges*. When the skis are on your feet, they are either flat on the snow or tilted onto their edges to some degree. The ability to control the amount of tilt, or *edging*, is an important skill that we'll discuss later. Light touring, track, and skating skis have plastic edges; most backcountry and telemark skis have metal edges.

Poles have five parts: *grip, strap, shaft, tip,* and *basket.* The terminology is pretty obvious. The grip is what you hold onto; the strap goes around your wrist; the shaft is the straight section in the middle; the tip is the business end; and the basket is a plastic ring or *hoof* that keeps the tip from spearing half-way to China, allowing you to push against the snow.

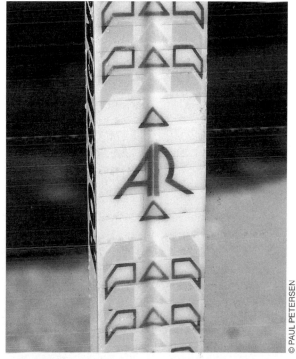

A "waxless" ski with the patterned base instead of grip wax providing the traction.

© PAUL PETERSEN

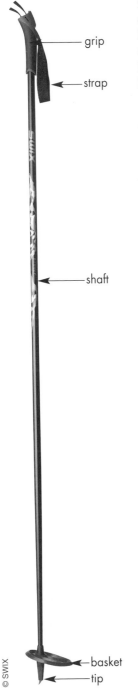

Parts of a ski pole.

grip

strap

shaft

basket

tip

© SWIX

Cross-country ski boots have the same parts as hiking boots, cowboy boots, or dress boots, except they have a tab or metal bar protruding from the toe, allowing them to attach to the binding.

GETTING STARTED

Once you've rented equipment and driven (or if you're lucky enough to live near good snow, walked) to a ski area or suitable stretch of flat terrain, it's time to put on your skis. To begin,

- Find a nice flat spot where you won't slide forward or backward before you're ready.

- Stick your poles upright in the snow on both sides of your skis. Don't put your hands though the wrist straps; at this point you merely want your poles handy if you need to grab one for balance. A steadying hand from a friend can also be helpful.

- Make sure your boots and bindings are free of packed snow. Fresh, near-freezing snow is particularly prone to forming frustrating snowballs on your feet. Use your pole's tip or basket to scrape it away rather than taking your gloves off and doing it with cold fingers. If you're not good at standing on one foot, you may

Five different types of boots, each requiring a different binding. Rent boots and skis as a package to ensure that the boots and bindings match.

© PAUL PETERSEN

RICK SAYS

If your first ski outing is of the golf-course or city-park variety, make sure the snow conditions are adequate for a pleasant excursion. Conditions are ideal when there are several inches of *base*—snow that's firm enough so you don't sink into it but soft and thick enough to cushion falls—topped by one to three inches of fresh snow. In rough country you need more base, to safely cover logs and rocks. Too much fresh snow over the base (more than five or six inches) isn't ideal for a first outing either, because skiing through it is too much of a test of stamina and balance.

If your first outing is at a commercial ski area or on other machine-groomed trails, you'll probably encounter good snow conditions whenever the area is open for business—even if nature is uncooperative, grooming machines can do much to make conditions acceptable. Other types of ski routes aren't maintained and can become tailbone-bruising ice if a cold snap follows a long thaw. When renting skis, feel free to ask what the rental shop employees know about conditions at your destination. Ski shop workers typically are avid skiers and will generally give you good advice.

have to repeat this procedure every time you accidentally put your foot down on the snow before you get your boot attached.

Attaching boots to skis on slippery snow isn't as easy as it was on that carpet back home or in the shop, but soon it will be second nature. For most bindings, point your toe downward, as though you're wearing high heels, so you're pushing the metal bar on the boot straight into the binding's slot. If the boot flexes rather than snapping into the binding, you may be holding it at the wrong angle. If you're skiing with small children, you'll probably have to help them. They may not be strong or dexterous enough to do it themselves.

If you rented equipment with *three-pin bindings*—which have three small pins that fit matching holes beneath the boot toe—make sure you have the skis on the right feet (for other bindings, it doesn't matter). If the skis aren't marked R and L, match the skis so the wider edges of the bindings are on the outside (just as your feet are wider on the outside). A clamp, called a *bail*, lifts to let you insert your boot toe into the binding. When you think the pins are in place, wiggle your heel back and forth a bit to ensure they're engaged properly, then snap the bail down firmly for a secure attachment.

Taking skis off is simpler than putting them on. Some have a button on the binding that you push with the tip of your pole to release. Others have a clamp that you open with your hand. Either way, it's best to do this on flat terrain, lest the ski glide away without you. Also, don't ski all the way out onto bare ground or into a parking lot before removing your skis. Even a small pebble can put a nasty scratch in the base.

One other piece of advice: when you take your skis off at rest breaks, don't jam the tails into firm snow like you're planting a flag pole. This is okay in soft snow—and often unavoidable to keep skis from sliding away from you—but in firm snow it will cause the tails to fray or delaminate. When possible, use a ski rack if one is available, lean the skis against a wall or tree, or leave them flat on the snow.

Once you have your skis on, it's time to make sure you're holding the poles correctly. There are two

Toe bar snaps in here

© PAUL PETERSEN

To latch the binding on this outfit, step onto the ski and roll your foot forward. The arrow shows where the boot's toe bar snaps into the binding.

ways to hold them, so it's 50/50 you'll get it right the first time.

Begin by making sure you know how to tighten or loosen the wrist strap. There are several designs, but the simplest uses a plastic device recessed into the grip. Popping it loose allows you to control the length of the strap. Make sure the strap is long enough to allow your gloved hand to slide easily through the loop. We'll tell you how long is "long enough" in a moment. Now, stretch the strap out from the pole, making sure it's free of twists. Reach through the loop from the bottom side and grasp the grip, with the ends of the strap passing between your thumb and forefinger. A loop of strap will pass across the back of your wrist. A simple mnemonic for children also works for adults: pretend your hand is a rabbit and the strap is the rabbit hole. The rabbit comes out of its hole, looks around for a carrot (the grip) and seizes it. This gives you a firm, supportive, but flexible grip on the pole—a lot better than the loose, wobbly grip you get if you start by reaching downward into the rabbit hole. Be aware that it's possible to twist the pole to an incorrect grip position without removing your wrist strap. Check your pole grip periodically to make sure it's right, until the correct grip becomes second nature.

To grip the pole, slide your hand through the strap loop from the bottom (left)*, pull down on the strap* (middle)*, and grip the pole and strap* (right)*. Here, the strap length is just right.*

Now it's time to check the strap length. Ideally, it should be adjusted so that when you lean down against it with your hand comfortably positioned on the grip, the web of your thumb and forefinger rests against the strap just at the point where it emerges from the grip. If there's slack, tighten the strap. If you find yourself wishing for grease to get your hand through the loop or if your hand is too high on the grip, loosen the strap.

Getting Comfortable

Now that you've put on your skis and picked up your poles, you're almost ready to explore. But before you hit the trail, taking five minutes to try a few simple practice maneuvers will add a lot to your confidence.

Begin simply by standing in place. Planting your poles firmly in the snow for balance, shuffle one foot forward and back to get a feel for how the ski glides. Now, standing on one foot, pick the other ski up completely off the ground, keeping it as level as possible. Do the same with the other ski. Notice how rocking your ankle forward and back makes the tip and tail bob up and down. Try raising the tail off the snow while leaving the tip on the ground. Do the same with the tip, leaving the tail on the ground.

Standing on both skis, tilt your ankles slightly so the skis rest partially on their outside edges. First do one ski at a time, then both at once. The goal isn't to sprain an ankle, only to experiment with the tilt of the skis. Do the same with the inside edges, then return the skis to level, trying to get them as flat on the snow as you can.

With a stepping motion that lifts one ski off the ground, point your toes outward to make a V shape with the skis, without letting the tails cross behind you. Broadening your stance (i.e., moving your feet farther apart) allows you to make a wider V. Return to your original position, skis parallel, then make a V by stepping with the other foot. Try using smaller

Paul Says

Take your time at this point to get to know your "long feet" and your new environment. These little movement patterns are specific to skiing and aren't developed by other activities like hiking and cycling, so now's the time to play with them and see what they feel like. If you don't want to do these practice drills at the trailhead, you can do them equally well on a carpeted floor at home. A little stretching at this point is a great way to start the day.

*To move your skis into a V shape,
lift the tip of one ski and move it slightly away from parallel to the other
ski (left). Lower your foot so that your skis now form a V (middle).
Lift and bring the other ski over to close the V (right).*

© PAUL PETERSEN

steps to make a V by moving both feet, then return to your original skis-parallel stance. Now reverse the angles of your feet to point your toes inward in an inverted V, which we'll call an A (the cross bar of the A is your body, centered above the skis). The ski tips are together and the tails splayed apart.

These drills may not seem like skiing, but they involve important basic skills. The A shape, for example, is useful in braking and turning on descents. Digging in the edges (called *edging*) is useful in turning or traversing slopes without slipping sideways. Flattening the skis helps you go faster and straighter. Pointing them outward one at a time, as you did in forming the V, is a precursor to what is called a *step turn*, which is

*Start the A with the tip of one ski remaining on the snow. Move your
heel out slightly so that your ski tips are pointed toward each other.*

© PAUL PETERSEN

V-stepping around your ski tails.

make a V and close it, make a V and close it, until you've turned as far as you want.

Next, put your skis in the A position and try tromping out a "snow-daisy" by wedge-stepping in circles—clockwise and counter-clockwise—with your ski tips glued to the center.

Getting anxious to ski? You have two more basic skills to learn: falling down and standing back up, and we're going to ask you to fall down, deliberately.

Falls are part of skiing, but the good news is that unless the snow is very firm or you're out of control heading for a tree, they rarely hurt. Furthermore, a deliberate fall is often the surest way to stop. Think of it as "bailing out" rather than crashing and never hesitate to do so *before* you lose control of your speed.

It's best to not fall directly on your buttocks. Instead, you want to land somewhat to the side, although not so much so that you land on the point of your hip. Find some reasonably soft snow and try it now, with a motion that feels a bit like sitting down, with a sideways roll to one side or the other. Don't land on your ski tails. Ideally, you'll hit about 45 degrees off-center from your buttocks, midway between falling directly backward and directly to the side, then roll completely to your

the easiest way to change direction in flat terrain. Finally, you've practiced shifting your weight from one ski to the other in a controlled setting where you're unlikely to fall down. This will help when you start to move and turn.

After you've practiced each of these drills a few times, it's time to learn how to turn around on skis—a useful skill for getting back home.

Arrange your skis in a V shape, with their tails close together. To turn clockwise, pick up the left ski and set it down beside the right one, parallel to it, so both skis are pointing slightly to the right. You're now facing a slightly different direction. Repeat the process enough times to rotate 180 degrees, then reverse course until you're facing the direction in which you started. Fine-tune the drill by trying to step in a circle that pivots as precisely as possible about your ski tails. In other words, with each step, your ski tails stay in approximately the same location as you rotate around them; in fresh snow your tracks would produce a daisy pattern, with the tails at the center of the daisy. Reverse directions and V-step the other direction until you've "unwound" completely. In all of these drills, it's important to practice left and right turns equally, because you'll need both. Remember: the process is to

A-stepping around the tips is a great warm-up drill.

side. Standing on level snow for your first practice fall, this might not be easy. It's easier to make a controlled fall when you're moving, and it will feel more natural with practice.

You're about to discover that falling is easy. Getting up with your skis on is tougher, which is why it's useful to practice a few times before you actually start skiing. First, get organized. From your fallen position, roll to your side, making sure your skis aren't crossed, and bend your knees to draw the skis close to your buttocks. You're going to try to get up from the side of the skis, rather than from behind, as many beginners want to. If you try the latter approach, the skis will slide out from under you and you'll be back in the snow in a glorious tangle of skis and poles. If you're on a hill (and you shouldn't be at this point), your skis should be downslope from your body, lined up perpendicular to the slope to keep them from taking off downhill the moment you're half-way to your feet.

Don't be in a hurry to stand up; it's easier to get hurt floundering around after a fall than in the fall itself. Use your hands to scoot your body toward the skis in stages, until you're squatting over them if possible (or kneeling if that won't work). Use your hands, not your poles, because poles can break. Once you have your face over the ski tips, slide one ski forward and stand up, using your poles to help you balance but not to lever you upright. If the snow is soft, form an X with your poles to create an unsinkable platform to push against.

If you have trouble crouching over your skis or if you feel strain in your knees, simply remove one ski, stand up normally, and reattach the ski.

With practice, the motion of standing up will become fluid and effortless—at least on reasonably firm

snow. And when you start doing hills, you'll find that standing up on a slope is easier than doing so on level snow. When you fall on a descent, in addition to falling toward one side, try to keep your knees bent and your skis perpendicular to the slope, downhill from your body. Using the slope to your advantage this way makes it a lot easier to stand up.

You won't be venturing onto steep hills on your first few outings, but learning to automatically get

Getting up from a fall is easy if you follow these steps.

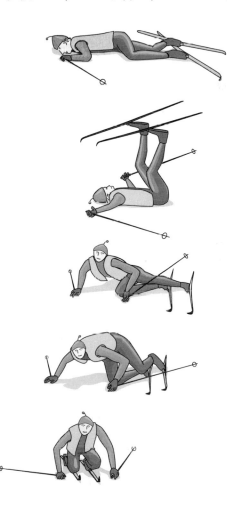

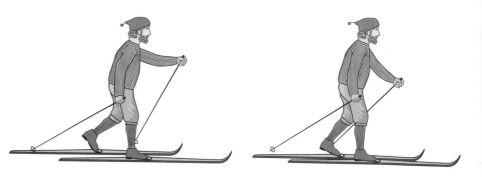

The basic diagonal stride (right). Putting it all together for a more energetic diagonal stride (bottom).

Try to avoid a "face-plant" fall.

into this sideways crouch position will help you maintain control of falls even on steep, icy hills. This skill also allows you to stop quickly by digging your ski edges into the snow as you slide on your side. An unexpected fall may send you sprawling face forward, but "bail out" falls should automatically put you in this position, allowing quick, controlled stops.

STROLLING ON SKIS: INTRODUCING THE DIAGONAL STRIDE

Now you're ready to hit the trail. The technique you'll start with is called the *diagonal stride,* and the motion is a lot like walking, as you move from ski to ski, swinging your arms in counterpoint. The main difference from walking is that you'll slide your feet instead of picking them up off the ground. You'll also experience a momentary pause on each foot as

you slide (or *glide*) across the snow. Kids will probably get the idea quickly, because most likely they've already learned to do something similar, stocking-footed on linoleum floors.

To start with, simply shuffle across the snow. Don't worry if you feel wobbly—most people do at first. Use the poles primarily for balance and try to add a brief hesitation between steps as you glide. As you gain confidence, you'll find you use the poles less for balance and more to push yourself forward for added speed.

This walkinglike movement is best done without thinking too much about it. The quickest way to get confused is to concentrate on specifics, such as how you're using your poles, or precisely what your legs should be doing. Part of what makes the diagonal stride fun is that it feels very natural; the less self-conscious you are about arm and leg motions, the more likely you are to do it right.

Nevertheless, it's impossible to talk about the diagonal stride without dissecting it into component pieces. There are four: *kick, glide, poling,* and *weight transfer*. The first two are so integral to the technique that many skiers refer to it as *kick and glide* skiing.

The kick is the rough equivalent of taking a step. But instead of pushing off forward as in walking, it begins with a downward tromping onto the snow that more or less glues the ski in place so it can serve as a platform for launching yourself forward, to glide on the other ski. As you tromp down, you bend your leg to sink downward a bit over the kicking ski, then straighten it in the push-off that is the heart of the kick. Done with just a moderate amount of effort, this should induce a bit of glide on the other ski. At a more relaxed shuffling pace, there will be little to no glide, but at this stage that's okay.

While one foot tromps down, the other swings energetically forward so the ski is in position for gliding. Again, this feels natural—until you start thinking about it too much. As your diagonal stride improves, you'll view yourself as "launching" off the kicking ski onto the gliding ski, and you'll concentrate on rolling most of your weight over the front of the kicking foot onto the gliding ski—the "weight transfer" we mentioned earlier. This weight transfer maximizes both kick and glide. But for now, all you need to realize is that you don't just push the kicking foot backward; the downward aspect of the push not only keeps the

ski from slipping when you complete the kick, but also gives you the opportunity to swing the other foot forward into position for the glide.

Your arm swing should come from your shoulders, not your elbows. Think of your hand as moving forward, gently pulling you down the track, as opposed to popping up, sending energy into the sky. Arm swing and hand position can be more important than precisely what you do with the poles. As the hand passes backward, behind the hip, relax your grip on the pole, allowing the tip to retain contact with the snow. If you have a death grip on it, you'll wind up with the tip in the air, pointing uselessly backward. While you're poling, you should feel some of the weight of your arm and body accumulate on the strap as your wrist leans against it. You're truly leaning on the strap, not just pushing on it with your arms.

Proper body position also helps. For a smooth diagonal stride, tip forward at the ankles as though you were leaning into a moderate wind. Your head should be up, scanning the trail ahead, instead of gazing at your ski tips. It's just like driving a car; if you aim high in your steering, you're less wobbly. Keep your shoulders and upper body relaxed, not tense.

With practice, the diagonal stride is a fluid, rhythmic motion, but it may be a bit jerky at first, punctuated by random pole thrusts to keep you from toppling sideways. Don't worry about it: that's just part of the learning process. When you hit the rhythm it

will feel so natural you'll know you have it right. Concentrate on these rhythmic moments and don't waste mental energy fretting about the times you're not finding the rhythm.

In addition to rhythm, a core element of the diagonal stride is balance. This comes mostly with practice, but there are a few tips that can help speed your progress. Some we've mentioned before, but we'll list them all here for handy reference:

- Make sure your boots are tight.

- Bend your ankles and knees slightly.

- Resist the temptation to stare at your skis. Instead, keep your eyes on the trail 5 to 15 feet ahead. If you look at your feet you're inherently wobbly.

- Keep your skis, particularly the weight-bearing ski, flat to the ground by centering your weight on it,

Swing your arms from your shoulders in the diagonal stride arm swing. Doing it without poles is a great drill. It helps your balance, too.

side to side. This will reduce the ski's tendency to wobble sideways or unexpectedly dig into the snow.

- When gliding, center your weight fore and aft on your foot. This will not only improve your balance, but it will give you a stronger kick—automatically improving your glide as well.

There are some simple drills that can help improve both balance and glide. Some involve balancing on a single moving ski. Although that's difficult at first, it's an important skill because one-ski balance is key not just to your glide, but to all future skiing improvement.

- Ski without using your poles.

- Remove one ski and "scooter kick" on the other, as though you were using a skateboard.

- Ski with both skis on a gentle downhill, raising one a few inches above the snow and gliding briefly on the other.

- Take a few quick strides, then g-l-i-i-i-d-e on the forward ski.

- Experiment with the amount of weight you transfer to the front ski as you glide. Try putting 100 percent of your body weight on it, then 75 percent, and then 50 percent. Which feels most comfortable to you? There's no right or wrong answer at this stage.

Paul Says

Work on developing proper skiing posture from the start; the habits you form on your first outings will stay with you as you gain experience. Try to lean forward a bit and round your back slightly. Let your arms swing with only a moderate bend in the elbow, and keep your hands low.

Depending on how much background you've had in other sports, you may be able to effect a good forward lean and weight transfer to the front ski as you glide—or you may initially feel comfortable only with less forward lean and a minor weight transfer. The difference affects how fast you go—something like the progression from walking to jogging to

sprinting. Begin with what feels comfortable and seek that elusive rhythm. At this point, Brownie points go more for rhythm than for energy output.

Proper pole plant is also helpful. The pole should angle backward, with the tip well behind your hand, so you can push off against it. If the pole contacts the ground with the basket in front of your hand, it's creating extra effort by putting on the brakes at the start of every stride. This is why it helps to think of the hand and elbow as driving forward, not upward, on the arm swing—perfecting that arm swing keeps the hand ahead of the basket at the time of pole plant.

Use a slight forward lean when skiing slowly (left) *and more of a lean when moving quickly* (right).

- Ski with your body very stiff. Then relax and ski "loose."

- Curl your toes up inside your boots. Then relax and flatten them. Ski both ways, noting the difference in your stride.

Patience is the name of the game. At first you may feel uncomfortably out of control when both skis are sliding at once. That's fine: go at whatever pace is comfortable. You can still enjoy the winter outdoors at a slower pace. And with time and mileage you'll find that gliding becomes the fun part.

Climbing Hills

When you're going uphill, technique becomes more important. Not getting enough grip is a potential problem; your skis may want to slide backward each time you try to step forward—at best breaking your rhythm and possibly making you fall to hands and knees. There are several ways to avoid this. Which one you'll need depends on the steepness of the slope and the slipperiness of the snow, as well as your athletic abilities, skill level, and ski design.

On gentle hills, just shorten your stride so your weight is more firmly over the grip portion of the ski base. Take shorter, choppier strides, with a quicker tempo, and make sure the poles angle well backward, allowing you to catch yourself on them in case you slip a bit. With practice it's possible to jog up surprisingly steep slopes this way, right on the edge of slipping but never doing so. Or take it easier and bend your knees and ankles a little more (but don't jackknife at the waist).

On steeper hills, you'll need to learn the *herringbone*. So-named because it leaves tracks in the snow like the skeleton of a fish, this technique involves splaying your tips apart into a V position, tipping your skis securely onto their inside edges, and waddling uphill like a duck.

It's not as difficult as it sounds. Before the hill gets steep, get your skis into the V shape you practiced earlier. How broad or narrow a V will depend on snow conditions and the steepness of the hill—on particularly steep hills your skis may form more than a 90-degree angle. Walking up a hill with your skis splayed out like this, you have two problems: not

stepping on the tails (which are crossed behind you), and not sliding backward and falling to your knees.

To reduce the problem of stepping on your ski tails, try narrowing the V or taking bigger steps. This minimizes the amount of tail crossing you have to deal with. If the slope is gentle and you're in a narrow V, you may be able to keep the tails from crossing at all. If you're not so lucky, you're going to have to take an exaggeratedly careful step each time you move, making sure each step carries the tail completely over the top of the other. It's kind of like walking with untied shoelaces—if you always know where the laces are and are careful enough, you won't trip. With practice, this becomes automatic, but it feels a little strange at first.

To keep from slipping backward, you have to use your inside edges and poles. Keep the pole baskets behind your hands at all times, so the poles are leaning

© PAUL PETERSEN

The herringbone, jokingly called the "Norwegian fish maneuver."

somewhat forward (but still securely planted in the snow), and feel free to lean or push on them as needed. As for your edges, dig them firmly into the slope with each step. The ideal amount of edging depends on the slope, the firmness of the snow, and your ankle strength. Experiment.

If you start to slip, you can take any or all of six remedial actions:

- go straight up the slope (not at an angle) making sure neither ski is pointed directly parallel to the fall line (the path a snowball would take rolling down slope)

- dig in the edges more firmly by actively rolling your ankles into the hill

- tromp down harder with each step, to plant the ski's tread more firmly in the snow

- push harder on your poles

- take shorter steps and quicken your tempo or

- widen your skis into a more exaggerated V.

Some hills are too steep to herringbone. You probably won't encounter many of these on groomed trails (unless you venture onto more difficult routes before you've sufficiently honed your skills), but off-trail they abound. Even a three-foot embankment can present a major obstacle if it's steep.

The way to get up these really steep hills is to *sidestep* (you can also do this on less steep hills if you're tired of herringboning). The technique is easy. Simply step sideways up the slope, skis parallel to each other and perpendicular to the fall line of the slope. Dig in your uphill edges to keep the skis from skittering sideways out from under you. Keep one pole on the uphill side, the other downhill. The foot motion is obvious: lift one ski and move it sideways, then lift the other and bring it back close to the first, taking lots of little steps until you reach the top.

The sidestep is a simple if painstaking way to get up surprisingly steep slopes. But botched attempts to sidestep can generate falls. If you don't keep your skis perpendicular to the fall line, they're going to take off downhill, fast—sometimes forward, sometimes back. If you slip at all, something is wrong. Make sure you really are perpendicular to the fall line, which can

RICK SAYS

When you're herringboning up a narrow trail or unplowed road, your route is dictated by the path you're following. But on a broader hill, you have choices, and often you can work them to your advantage.

Few slopes are absolutely uniform. Most have dips and swells that form miniature ridges or gullies—often quite pronounced. If you have the option, seek out the ridges and avoid the gullies. Straddling the crest of even a minor ridge reduces the amount by which you have to point your skis uphill—reducing slippage and easing your ascent. Trying to climb a gully has the reverse effect, compounding the ascent's difficulty.

I stumbled onto this fact on my first attempt at low-key ski mountaineering on an 11,000-foot peak in southern Utah. For a flatland skier like me, the thought of herringboning up a 2,000-foot slope was daunting. And the first 500 feet gave me serious second thoughts about the wisdom of my proposed course of action. But then I struck a ridgeline and rode it all the way to the summit like a giant highway, doing an easy ridge-straddling herringbone the entire way.

© PAUL PETERSEN

The sidestep works well on steeper hills.

change direction a bit with each lump or depression in the hillside. If you slip sideways rather than forward or back, you're not edging hard enough. Try getting the ski bottoms horizontal and digging those uphill edges in, hard. In firm snow you may actually have to stomp down with each step, and on an extended slope your ankles may get tired, just as they would ice skating. If you're still slipping sideways, perhaps you need to tighten your boot laces for better edge control. If nothing else works it's also possible to take off the skis and walk up (good advice if you encounter a downward slope that's too steep, too!).

Stopping

When you're beginning, the simplest and most foolproof way to stop is often to "bail out" by deliberately falling down, using the controlled, feet-first fall we described earlier in this chapter. Or, on obstacle-free, level terrain, you can usually glide to a halt within a few feet. Another stopping method you may discover on your own is to plant your poles in front of you and lean forward against them. This is inherently unsafe, so use it only at very slow speeds to avoid breaking poles, spraining your wrists, or bashing yourself in the chest or face with a pole.

Other than the bail-out, there are two basic techniques for stopping on firm snow or groomed trails: the *half-wedge* and the *full wedge* (or *snowplow*).

The half-wedge is easier to master but works well only if you're in a track. It's a particularly good maneuver if another skier stops suddenly or falls down unexpectedly in front of you. First, you have to get one ski out of the track. This is your braking ski, and it can be either the left or right one (unless there's an obstacle in the way, such as a snowbank close to one side of the track). We'll assume you're braking with the right ski, but you should practice equally with both.

To get the ski out of the track, simply lift the right ski high enough to clear the lip of the track and set it on the adjacent groomed surface, with the tip angled toward the other ski. Rock it sideways so the inside edge scrapes a bit on the snow, and put some weight on it to dig in the edge. The angled ski may now want to run in the direction it's pointed, toward the tip of the other.

Allowing your ski tips to cross will stop you, but the stop will be more abrupt than you intended (although unlikely to be painful). If this starts to happen, it means you're digging in the edge too hard. Relax the ankle and take a little weight off it to reduce the amount of edge pressure, but continue to apply sufficient outward pressure to the angled ski to maintain your half-A orientation. As you slow down, the angled ski will scrape sideways across the snow with its inside edge digging into the surface. Varying the angle of the ski and the pressure on the inside edge (plus the compensating outward pressure on the ski) will allow you to stop quickly or slowly, as desired.

The full wedge is similar, but this time both skis are out of the track and both are angled, in the full-A pattern you practiced earlier. Both skis are *edged* (i.e., rocked onto their inside edges) with equal pressure. This gives you double the stopping power of a half wedge but requires you to control the motion of both skis to keep them scraping across the snow properly, rather than crossing. Experiment with the amount of edging by controlling how much you tip the skis onto their edges. Experiment also with the angle of the A: twist your tails apart widely for extra braking power; use a narrower angle if all you want to do is slow down a bit. Practice this on your first outings, even if you're skiing mostly on flat snow where there's no need for quick decelerations. The full wedge is such a valuable stopping tool that you need to have it in your arsenal before proceeding from beginner to intermediate terrain.

Be aware, though, that the full wedge doesn't work under all conditions. In heavy, loose snow or breakable crust, the skis are going to want to cross rather than move sideways, and no amount of outward pressure will prevent this. We'll tell you more about such snow in later chapters, but for the moment, just try not to pick up too much speed if you encounter these conditions. If you do, your best beginner stopping method is to step turn or simply bail out.

Descents

What goes up generally comes down, so once you've climbed a hill be prepared for the descent. Again, there are a variety of techniques, depending on the grade.

The half wedge.

The full wedge or snowplow.

Basic Athletic Stance

Before descending, you should assume what we call the basic athletic stance. It's the skiing equivalent of the position assumed by a basketball player on defense or an Olympic wrestler sizing up an opponent before grappling. This catlike stance keeps you balanced, mentally focused, and ready to respond to whatever happens. For the basketball player that's the opposing player's unpredictable actions; for you it's whatever bounces and wobbles the hill may have in store. You're also in proper position to use whatever braking or turning maneuvers will be needed.

The stance isn't exactly a wrestler's crouch, but it has similarities. Your knees and ankles are comfortably flexed for shock absorption on bumps and to lower your center of gravity. Your hands are to the front, your torso is in a relatively upright position, and your head is up, eyes looking well beyond your ski tips. But unlike in the wrestler's or basketball player's stance, your boots remain flat on the skis (not up on the balls of your feet), and your hands aren't spread wide apart like you're trying to hug a bear.

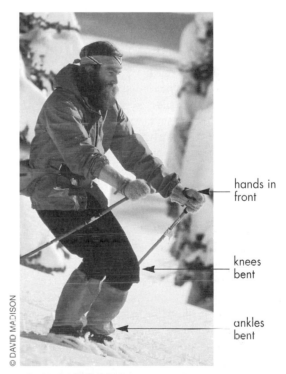

hands in front

knees bent

ankles bent

The basic athletic stance.

On short or gentle slopes, you can just run straight and fast, enjoying the effortless speed. Remember to keep those knees bent while keeping your torso upright. Keep your poles out to the sides, ready for use, not tucked uselessly under your armpits. The basic athletic stance isn't a downhill racer's tuck; its purpose is to keep you stable and ready to react to the hill, not to cut wind resistance.

To shed a little speed and improve your balance, you can drag your poles in the snow beside you. It's not highly recommended, but at this stage, who cares. How much to bend your knees depends on how comfortable you are with the slope, which is a very personal thing. Advanced skiers may sail down an intermediate hill with a barely perceptible bend of the knees; beginners may need to crouch much more deeply. Most people, when they're learning, don't bend their knees sufficiently. What feels like a deep knee bend is probably only a moderate crouch. If you're stiff, with locked knees—which is how most people tend to act if they're afraid of the hill—you're more likely to fall.

Gliding Wedge

After you've taken a few straight runs on moderate slopes, you're ready for the gliding wedge (another form of *snowplowing*). It's a lot like the wedge technique described earlier for stopping, only this time use it merely to control your speed, rather than coming to a halt.

First, you need to find a hill on which you can generate a little speed. Nothing life threatening is needed; walking speed is fine. But it's actually easier to practice these maneuvers at three miles an hour than at a "Gee, I'm scared" crawl.

Let your skis glide while you pick up speed. That means keeping the bases flat to the snow. Bend your knees enough to feel a bend in your ankles, and hold your hands in front of you, poles angled behind, ready to steady your balance but not dragging in the snow.

Once you're up to speed, twist and point your skis into the A-shaped wedge position you've already practiced on flat terrain. Your legs should be well apart, knees still bent. As you move in a straight line, your skis are now scraping at an angle across the snow, already slowing you a bit. Dig in the inside edges, and they'll slow you a lot. If you come to a complete halt, edge a little less strongly or find a steeper hill.

The gliding wedge does two things. First, it serves as a way to slow you down, as well as setting you up for turning, which we'll describe in a moment. But its more important function is to create a wide, stable platform on which to stand. Even if you don't slow down much, the mere act of moving into a wedge will allow a more stable descent than if you simply ran straight down the hill.

As you discovered earlier with the braking wedge, the ski tips may tend to want to cross—something you need to prevent. The goal is to keep the skis in the A-shaped wedge as you apply the brakes evenly to both of them. With practice, this becomes automatic. Always edge strongly enough to the inside to make sure the wrong (outside) edges don't accidentally dig in and send you sprawling face forward. Don't worry if the skis tend to jump around a bit, especially on uneven snow, as you learn the art of fine-tuning your edge control for minor terrain variations.

Paul Says

It can be difficult to come to a complete halt with the wedge. Your goal on descents shouldn't be to stop midway down but to keep your speed under control. Furthermore, creeping slowly down the slope isn't ideal because that makes it much more difficult for you to twist to brush your skis into the desired positions. At the same time, you don't want to pick up so much speed that your only resort is to bail out. Hitting this happy medium is called *maintaining speed control*.

Paul Says

Want to really hone your wedging skills? Try what I call the *wedge change-up*. Start with your skis pointed straight downhill. Twist them so the tails brush outward into a wedge, then guide them back to parallel so they're again pointing straight down the hill. If you have a long enough hill, try doing this several times in one run.

Wedge Turn

Once you feel semicompetent in the gliding wedge, you're ready for the wedge turn—the easiest way to change direction when you're descending on firm snow.

Begin in a gliding wedge with the ski tails not too broadly spread apart. (In a broad wedge, the edges dig more firmly into the slope, which is great for braking but makes turning difficult.) Once you've achieved a shallow, gliding wedge position, simply coax your ski tips in the direction you want to turn by twisting your hips, feet, and knees. You'll probably feel your weight shift to the outside (downhill) ski as you turn. This is normal; in chapter 3 we'll tell you how to take advantage of it for even better turning control (see page 36).

Don't lean into the turn as you would on a bicycle—that will take too much weight off the outside ski. You also want to continue to engage the *inside* edges of both skis. If a ski rolls over onto its outside edge, you'll probably trip over it and fall face forward. Or it might suddenly shoot cross-slope in a straight line, a phenomenon called "railing an edge" because the ski acts like it's stuck on a railroad track. Here are a few exercises to help you execute turns.

- If you're getting into a nice wedge but can't seem to make it go any direction but straight downhill, pretend you have flashlights strapped to your knees, and try to turn them to illuminate your desired path.

- If you can't seem to shake the habit of leaning into the turn, touch your hand to the knee that's on the outside of the turn as you round the bend. You can't do that while leaning strongly in the wrong direction.

- To keep from standing too straight and stiff (a common beginner fault), put both hands on your knees while keeping your torso more-or-less upright (as you should in the basic athletic stance). This will force you to bend your knees.

These exercises are intended for training specific skills, not for permanent use. Once they've done their jobs, give them up. You don't want to spend the rest

In this exercise to help you learn how to avoid leaning into turns, touch your outside knee, and you will naturally remain more upright.

of your skiing career cruising downhill with your hands on your knees!

Once you've completed a successful turn, stop (or find another hill) and try again. This time, try turning in the opposite direction. Do a few of these single turns, then try "linking" them in a serpentine path in which one turn flows smoothly into the next. This is a fun and easy way to shed unwanted speed, and it will lead naturally into more advanced hill-descending methods to be discussed in later chapters. In linking turns there's no need to make broad, sweeping curves that take up half the hillside—there's plenty of room to make a series of shallow wiggles down a trail or path that's only a few feet wide.

As you practice linking turns, seek a cadence that involves bending and straightening the knees and ankles with each curve. Rise as you approach each turn, then sink and steer through it. Rise to the new turn, then sink and steer. That's the cadence: *sink and steer, sink and steer.* Let your upper body "flow" down the hill with your feet and knees turning beneath it as you focus your attention on the rising and sinking motion.

Wedge turn.

© PAUL PETERSEN

❸ ❷ ❶

Linked turns are the ultimate in speed control. Not only are they fun and challenging, they're the most efficient way to control speed—much less taxing than the constant strain of doing a braking wedge all the way downhill. How many corners you do on a particular grade depends on your interest, the steepness of the slope, and the width of the trail. Each turn gets you out of the fall line; that's what slows you down. With the start of the next turn, you accelerate back into the fall line, which at first is scary but soon becomes fun. It's a continual rhythm of acceleration and deceleration—and once you've practiced it enough, you'll gain confidence that the deceleration will indeed happen as you angle away from the fall line at the end of each turn.

Sidestepping

You can use the wedge and wedge turn to inch your way down fairly steep slopes, but occasionally you may encounter a grade that's steep or icy enough you're afraid to wedge down it. Don't despair: the sidestep technique you used for ascending hills also works for descending them. You may also need to sidestep in soft snow if the skis sink so deep that you can't twist them into the wedge shape without stopping too abruptly. And don't forget: there's no disgrace in taking off your skis and walking down

steep grades. Just stay to one side of the path to avoid making bootprints in the middle of the trail.

TURNING ON THE FLATS

On gentle turns in machine-set track—or simply the deep-set tracks of numerous previous skiers—you don't need to do anything special to turn. The track will do it for you by guiding your skis in the right direction.

But when you're not skiing in groomed tracks, you have to execute the turn on your own. One way is simply to stop and V-step until you're facing the right direction; another is to V-step while gliding slowly. In chapter 3 we talk about some more athletic turning methods (see page 35), but they merely allow you to keep up your speed while zooming around corners—not much use until you've moved on to an intermediate level where you may *want* to zoom around corners.

TRAVERSING

Generally, beginner ski trails either stick to flat terrain or cross mildly rolling hills. But sometimes you may find yourself on a *sidehill*, where the trail runs across the slope, either climbing, flat, or descending.

The first time you attempt a traverse, you may find yourself drifting inexorably toward the downhill side of the trail, unless you have a well-set track to keep you in place. Combat this by edging as firmly as necessary with the uphill edges. Ascending, you can sometimes use a lopsided herringbone, with one ski angled more to the side than the other. Descending, try a gliding wedge in which you're constantly putting excess pressure on the downhill ski to keep you going diagonally across the slope.

On a gentle, gliding descent—where you don't need to either put on the brakes or kick to maintain speed—your skis should be parallel, with the uphill one leading by 4 or 5 inches. Your uphill hand should also be significantly ahead of the downhill one. Unless you're following a firm track, your uphill edges will be engaged sufficiently to keep you from slipping sideways down the slope. Center your weight between your feet and assume the basic athletic stance, as always, to maintain balance. Ideally, you should twist slightly at the waist so your upper body is facing a bit toward the downhill side. This will become more important when we get to intermediate maneuvers in chapter 3.

Traverse position, with uphill hand and ski leading.

The techniques discussed in this chapter are all you need to be comfortable on gentle terrain, opening the door to a wide range of winter-draped landscapes. Under good snow conditions, they'll also work on many unplowed roads and golf courses. Your assignment now is to get out there, log some mileage, and have fun. Congratulations: it's one of those "tough jobs" you hear about in all those "somebody has to do it" jokes.

Beyond the Basics

The skills discussed in chapter 2 are the foundation on which all other skiing techniques are built. They'll serve you well on many outings, but there are refinements that can allow you to ski farther, faster, and more efficiently over a greater diversity of terrain and snow conditions, while giving you more control on turns and descents. The skills discussed in this chapter will move you firmly from beginner to intermediate status.

Learning these skills comes most easily on groomed trails or in backcountry settings with similar firm-packed (but not icy) snow. Wilder backcountry and its potpourri of snow conditions are discussed in chapter 9.

IMPROVING YOUR DIAGONAL STRIDE

As an intermediate skier, you'll find that the diagonal stride is still your mainstay. But you can pick up speed and improve efficiency with simple enhancements to your rhythm, poling, kick, and glide. As you accumulate mileage, your balance will also improve.

Rhythm

Rhythm, as we said in chapter 2, can be elusive. It's better to enjoy it when you get it right than to fret when you don't. Try chanting "one, two, one, two," as you stride. Or hum a few bars of a favorite tune with approximately the right cadence. The goal is to relax, allowing your creative "right brain" to take control, freeing you from worrying too much about mechanical details. When you hit a good striding rhythm, you'll know. Concentrate on that experience, and ignore the wobbles. They'll become less frequent with time, mileage, and perhaps a good tune under your breath.

Poling

You can improve your poling greatly by making sure you're not holding the pole in a death grip. Grip the handle loosely, with a relaxed grip that makes it easier to follow through with a little extra push as your hand passes behind your hips. Gripping the pole loosely will also keep your forearms from tiring.

Liberty Bell looms over a North Cascades playground.

As you swing your arm forward between pole plants, envision yourself tossing a softball underhand, without much bend in the elbow. The pivot should be mostly at the shoulder. As the arm swing ends and the tip of the pole reaches for the snow, continue driving your hand forward to avoid the high hand position that plagues most beginners. If you raise your hand at the end of the swing rather than driving it directly forward, you're likely to plant the pole at the wrong angle, reducing the effectiveness of your poling. To be efficient, the pole basket needs to hit the snow behind your hand, not in front of it or even directly below it. That way the pole is angled so you can push firmly against it from the moment it hits the snow, rather than having to wait until you've moved far enough forward for your arms to catch up with it.

Rick Says

I'll never forget the moment I discovered what cross-country skiing rhythm was about. It was my third or fourth outing, on a snow-covered jogging path beside a frozen river on a cold, sunny day. Dozens of other skiers had passed before me, leaving a smooth track almost as good as a groomed trail, and a brisk wind at my back urged me along. Prior to this, my skiing had been mostly shuffle-walking, but encouraged by the wind I began to lengthen my stride, slow down my cadence, and stretch out the glide.

The result was magical. I was flowing across the landscape in seven-league strides. The kick-glide, kick-glide rhythm dominated my senses almost to the exclusion of all else, and for a few brief moments, I thought I could ski forever. Then, of course, I lost the rhythm and the magic moment evaporated. But from then on I knew what I was looking for and found it more and more frequently, until wobbles and missteps were increasingly rare exceptions to a process that became so natural that I could leave my body on autopilot while my mind ran its own course, relaxed and free.

Kick

In chapter 2, we analogize the kick to taking a step. It's time to move beyond that. Rather than simply being a step, the kick is the portion of your stride where you push off on one ski, preparing to glide on the other. Kick and glide are inextricably linked. It is the kick that produces the forward momentum that allows you to glide, and the glide that allows you to gather your energy for a powerful, rhythmic kick. Furthermore, the two motions aren't jerky or stop and go. Rather, they are a seamless blend of fluid, perpetual movements that merge into each other like the pedal strokes of riding a bicycle.

Nevertheless, the kick is a mystery to many beginners. It helps to remember the physics of how your skis operate. The purpose of the kick is to push downward so the patterned base (or the wax, on waxable skis) bites into the snow while simultaneously propelling you forward. An effective kick begins by

As a training exercise for developing a stronger kick, let your upper body sink and rise significantly with each stride, moving smoothly up and down. This exaggerated up-and-down motion may also help you kick up gentle upgrades, rather than resorting to the more time-consuming herringbone. If you're doing this drill correctly, you'll feel more knee and ankle bend than you're probably used to, and the muscles of your upper and lower legs would tire if you tried to do it all day.

A properly executed kick is also well-timed: the kicking foot should be firmly smashed to the snow when the other foot is passing it on its way forward. You're more likely to kick too late than too early, so try beginning the kick's downward pressure when the kicking foot is still (however briefly) the leading ski. If you feel your ski slip backward at the end of the kick, you're probably kicking too late.

You may hear your skis go *flup, flup, flup* against the snow (called *slapping*) with each kick. This indicates that you are starting to execute a powerful kick—as well as fully shifting your weight from ski to ski—but it is also a sign that your balance is a bit off, you're a bit late with your kick, or your hips aren't rising up and forward enough with each stride. Slapping robs you of energy. To eliminate it, first review the one-ski balance exercises in chapter 2. If they don't work, try pretending that your rear foot, as it swings forward, is an airplane about to land on a runway. Make sure the airplane lands smoothly, right next to the other foot, rather than crash-landing early, significantly behind the other foot. This usually solves the causes of ski slapping so automatically it's almost magical, without the need for complex analysis of your stride.

Former World Champion Vladmir Smirnov demonstrates proper pole plant. Note that, at this speed, the basket lands just behind the skier's hand.

© PAUL PETERSEN

pushing straight down on the middle part of the ski, directly beneath the arch/heel part of your foot, compressing the ski tightly against the snow. To prepare for a good kick, lower your body slightly, bending at the ankle and knee, then assertively transfer your full body weight to the kicking ski. Now, launch yourself forward, shifting your weight to glide on the other ski once it has moved to the front.

A strong, well-executed kick is crucial for skiing at a fast pace. You can liken a strong kick to energetically climbing a flight of stairs, two at a time. For slower touring, the kick can be less intense, but proper execution still increases your efficiency and the distance you can cover in a day.

PAUL SAYS

Most ski instructors say ski slapping is bad. I regard it as a milestone in a skier's development, because it shows you are achieving complete weight transfer to the forward, gliding ski. So, if your skis are starting to slap, congratulations: you've moved from shuffling with two skis always firmly planted on the snow to truly gliding from ski to ski. Fixing the slap is merely the next stage in your advancement.

© DON PORTMAN

For the optimum diagonal stride, the kick begins when the feet come together and ends when the rear foot lifts off the snow.

Glide

As we said earlier, kick and glide are so closely associated that the separation between them is largely semantic. Nevertheless, there are things you can do separate from your kick to enhance your glide—things that are arguably more important than refining your kick. The key is committing yourself to transferring 100 percent of your body weight onto the gliding ski—something that gets easier the more confidence you have in your one-ski balance. Here are four simple tricks:

- With each stride, center your body weight sideways over the gliding ski. Think in terms of placing your head and belly button directly over it. Or line up the zipper of your jacket over the top of the ski. This helps keep the ski flat, so it glides freely.

- Strive for a dynamic arm swing. Imagine pitching a softball underhand—energetically so the ball would go in a flat, fast arc.

- Get a good leg swing going by pretending you're kicking a soccer ball as you bring the trailing leg forward to become the next gliding ski. Like the arm

swing, this will transform into extra forward momentum just when you want it for the next glide.

- When you transfer your weight to the front (gliding) ski, you should feel it centered on the arch/heel of your foot—not toward your toes.

- Lean slightly forward, rounding your back rather than arching it backward (see photo on page 34).

If you're tired or simply don't want to move quickly, you can still earn style points (and conserve energy) by doing milder versions of the same arm and leg swings. Good technique is nearly as useful if you're going slowly as it is when you're skiing quickly, and there's nothing wrong with cruising along easily as you talk to friends or just soak up the scenery.

To speed your progress, ski as often as you can. Mileage is vital to rapid progress. Another aid to progress is being able to see yourself in action. The next time you're out with a video camera, taking pictures of your new winter playground, have a friend take a few shots of you, skiing, from in front, behind, and to the side. Looking those over with a critical eye will do wonders for helping you figure out which portions of your stride could benefit from fine tuning. Off the snow, do other balance-oriented sports that help train the small muscles in your legs and torso that are vital to good balance. Ice skating and in-line skating are ideal balance sports, but virtually anything that has you constantly shifting position will help.

Remember that although we broke down the diagonal stride into components for purposes of discussion, the real goal is to combine these movements into a fluid diagonal stride, without getting hung up on details. So go ahead and isolate the skills. Perform the drills and tune yourself up where you need work. But don't forget that favorite tune and the relaxation

PAUL SAYS

Don't worry if you don't master all of these refinements immediately. The diagonal stride is easy to learn, but you can spend a lifetime perfecting it. Even Olympic skiers receive striding pointers from their coaches. And part of the fun of mastering it is that the only way to practice is by getting out on the snow!

Vladmir Smirnov demonstrates nice, rounded back and good forward lean.

that allows your body to naturally and unconsciously synthesize the components into a sensuous motion that will gradually feel as natural as walking.

DOUBLE POLING

Spend a few minutes at any popular ski area, and you will see enough people double poling to know how it differs from conventional poling. Instead of swinging one arm at a time, double poling involves planting both poles at once and using them to propel yourself forward. There's no kick, as your legs concen-

trate on keeping the skis flat to the snow for maximum glide.

If you're built like Arnold Schwarzenegger you may be able to double pole from a standing start or even uphill. Otherwise, the first time you attempt it, you're better off on snow that can give you better-than-average glide—what skiers call *fast* snow. Use your diagonal stride to get up to speed, then swing both poles forward and plant them simultaneously. Now, transfer lots of body weight onto the poles by leaning forward onto them and bending—*compressing* more accurately describes what it feels like—the upper body down so it's nearly parallel to the ground. If you have enough glide, hesitate ever so briefly in this bent-over position as the poles lose contact with the snow behind you and you continue to slide forward. Then, before you lose too much speed, straighten up for the next pole plant. Think of your upper body as an oil derrick going down and up with each double-pole stroke and subsequent recovery.

The most common beginner mistake is to swing the tips of your poles too far forward with each pole plant. Just as with single poling, the basket should not be planted in front of the hand—although in double poling it's okay if the pole lands vertically or nearly so. If the pole lands too far forward, you're putting on the brakes rather than pushing yourself forward. Don't bend your legs too strongly, and don't do all the work by pushing backward with your arms. In a strong double-poling stroke, you're leaning heavily on the poles, not only with the strength of your arms and shoulders, but also with much of the weight of your upper body. As you swing the poles, maintain this pressure by adding the strength of your abdominal muscles as you bend forward at the hips.

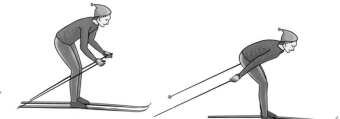

Double poling.

Rick Says

The basic double-poling motion isn't all that complex. But it takes practice and thought to use the move to its full potential. If you just stab the poles backward with your arms, you may get some forward impulse, but it will be minimal. Really leaning on the poles is important because it greatly multiplies the strength of your push, and it lifts weight off your skis so they'll glide that much better. And it won't tire you out as quickly as trying to do it all with your arms.

The *kick double pole* is a variant on double poling in which you add a well-timed kick before each pole plant. This gives you enough extra impulse that you can do it uphill or on snow too slow for ordinary double poling. Some people do each kick with the same leg; others alternate legs with each stride. Sometimes you may simply want to throw in one or two good kicks if you start to lose speed doing an ordinary double pole.

The timing of the kick is critical. It needs to come near the end of your glide, just as you're swinging your poles forward for the next pole plant, but before they hit the ground. It does *not* come in the middle of the double-poling stroke. Properly executed, the kick can save you quite a bit of time and energy. Poorly executed, it interferes with your glide and may be slower than simple double poling.

The timing goes like this: *kick, pole-plant, compress, glide. Kick, pole-plant, compress, glide.* Imagine your body as a giant clam shell, opening and closing with each kick double pole. At the end of the double-poling stroke, the shell is tightly closed, as your torso is bent over and your hands are behind your knees. Then you kick, while simultaneously standing up and reaching forward with your hands, preparing for the next pole plant. The clam shell is open, stretched out. Then it snaps closed again, as you plant the poles, compress the upper body, and draw the trailing leg forward until you're gliding on side-by-side skis.

If you've already got a good double pole, the kick isn't all that hard to learn. If you're having trouble timing it correctly, get an experienced friend to ski along beside you, so you can mimic the timing of your friend's kick. Once you get it right, you're unlikely to forget it.

Corners and Downgrades

Now that you're beginning to pick up speed, you're going to find yourself wanting to make higher-speed corners, so you don't have to slow down each time you approach a bend. Furthermore, you're going to need to know how to dodge quickly around obstacles (people, dogs, trees, *sitzmarks*—where somebody fell down and left a hole in the trail).

For turning or dodging stationary obstacles without slowing down too much, the *step turn* is the easiest to learn. It consists of lots of little V-steps, much like what you did when you were practicing snow daisies in chapter 2, but now done while maintaining forward momentum. The technique is simple, but the balance is more challenging because each step leaves you briefly standing on a single ski—although that should no longer be all that intimidating.

Practice first while stationary on a flat surface. V-step around your ski tails, opening the V by angling one ski into a half-V. Close the V by stepping parallel

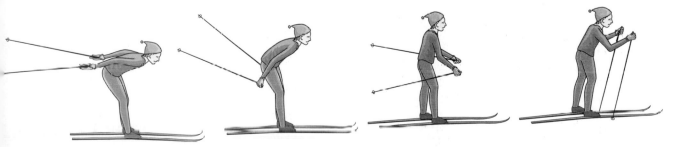

Kick double pole.

to the original ski. Do this a few times in one direction, then in the other.

Once you're comfortable with that, it's time to do it on the move. Get up to speed with the diagonal stride, then bring your skis side by side, adding a few double poling strokes to center your weight and steady your balance. When you're ready, angle one ski into the half-V and step on it (see photo on page 15). As you begin to move off in the new direction, bring the other ski around parallel to the first and transfer half of your weight back onto it. Double pole if necessary to keep from losing too much speed. Repeat this maneuver as many times as necessary to make the turn. Lots of little steps are easier to control than a single huge one.

Passing People

Passing slower skiers is a bit more difficult. Simply yelling, "Get out of the way," might work, but it's rude, as is the once-acceptable "Track, please!" unless there's a whole gaggle of people blocking every conceivable line of progress. Generally, it's your responsi-

bility to pass slower skiers, not theirs to get out of your way. How you do this depends on snow conditions, the slope of the trail, and your diplomatic skills. Try whatever combination of step turns, straight downhill gliding, and turning on the double-poling afterburners that works at the time.

Skate Turn

If you want to corner more quickly, there's a better maneuver than the step turn. Called the *skate turn*, it can also help you maintain speed when stepping out of the track to pass slower skiers.

The skate turn is similar to the step turn but more vigorous, allowing you to accelerate and turn at the same time. In the step turn you pick up one ski and set it down angled in the new direction. Then you step the other ski around parallel to it. For the skate turn you do the same basic thing, but instead of merely stepping off one ski as you round the corner, you push strongly off of it, launching yourself onto the angled ski for a nice glide in the new direction. The pattern of foot and leg movements is similar to the step turn, but the propulsion is much more vigorous and correspondingly speedier.

To get a good push-off, start with a deep flex of the ankle and knee. This will also make it easier to dig in the ski's edge, so it won't slip sideways when you push off.

Wedge Christie

Sometimes speed isn't what you want—particularly on long downhills. You already know how to bleed off unwanted energy with the snowplow, but that works best at slow to moderate speeds. Sometimes you want to run more quickly—but not *too* quickly. A fun way

to shed unwanted speed is by skidding your skis around a series of "linked" turns.

You've learned to do this by making linked wedge turns, as described in chapter 2. But a better move is the *wedge christie*, sometimes mistakenly called a "stem christie" or "stem turn." Whatever you choose to call it, it's a turn that starts out like the familiar wedge turn but ends with your skis parallel to each other, skidding a bit sideways across the snow.

Sounds scary? It isn't all that difficult if you practice under the right conditions. Find a broad, shallow slope where you don't have to worry about running into trees or other skiers. A bunny hill at a downhill ski area is perfect, as is a wide golf course hill that trampling, sledding, or repeated freezing and thawing have converted into something similar to a machine-groomed surface. You may even find a wide enough groomed hill at a cross-country ski area. What you don't want is snow that's so soft your skis sink into it and won't slip sideways when you want them to. An inch or two of loose powder atop a firm base is ideal.

Using the wedge christie, you're going to tack down this hill in a series of gently descending traverses, linked by turns. But first, let's polish your traversing skills.

In a descending traverse you glide down the hill at a shallow enough angle to keep your speed comfortable.

Paul Says

The wedge christie is my favorite turn for skiing steep terrain while carrying a heavy pack. It also works on moderate terrain with a light pack. It's versatile, stable, and fun.

Remember that the uphill ski leads, as does the uphill hand. To be prepared for turning, twist at the waist slightly, so your upper body faces a bit away from the hill. This twisted traverse position is what you should strive for at the start and end of each turn.

To start the turn, brush the skis out into a wedge position, while pointing, guiding, and steering them toward the fall line (downhill) just as you would for an ordinary wedge turn. You'll feel yourself start to accelerate downhill, but don't panic. Just keep steering your feet, knees, and skis around the turn. After the skis have passed through the fall line and continue to turn toward the opposite traverse, start exerting

Rick Says

My first couple of seasons, I skied with the gliding wedge and wedge turn as my principal downhill tools. On good snow, even the most wicked hills can be conquered with these techniques, combined with the kamikaze approach of simply riding them out and bailing out if you start to lose control. But even on tree-lined hiking trails only a few feet wide, a couple of quick little wedge christies are another good way to shed speed, especially if you're shooting gaps between trees that are too narrow for a full-blown snowplow. They can also help you skid around those annoying right-angle bends you sometimes find at the base of a big hill.

It wasn't until I moved west and discovered hills that can take more than a few seconds to descend that I began to seriously experiment with turning and braking techniques. I was surprised to discover that many were things I'd already learned dodging trees on Midwestern hiking trails.

steering pressure on the inside leg, to complement the strong steering you'll be feeling on the outside leg. This should produce two results: the inside ski and foot will move forward a few inches, and that ski will tip in the direction of your little toe, engaging what is now the new uphill edge. Unless you're creeping around the turn very slowly, both skis will also slide sideways a bit as their uphill edges scrape against the snow. The skis will settle into a new traverse, completing the turn. On steeper terrain you may feel the urge to make the inside ski come around the bottom half of the turn more quickly by picking it up and stepping it around parallel to the outside ski. Do this if you must, but try to keep that ski on the ground.

Once you've done one wedge christie, try another in the opposite direction. Then link them together one after another. To keep your skis from slipping sideways more than you want, face more strongly down the hill and avoid leaning toward the hill or facing into it. Try going faster, "working" those turns as you feel your skis dig and slide as you come around the bottom half of each turn. Then move to steeper terrain and use the same turning method to keep your speed comfortably under control.

PAUL SAYS

You now have the tactics to ski increasingly challenging terrain. As you venture farther from the trailhead you'll find better views, more exciting downhills, and fewer people. Have fun, and remember the proper order for assimilating new skiing moves: safety is first, fun is second, and technique comes last. Except on well-traveled trails, always ski with a friend, take a map, and don't overextend yourself or your friends.

The wedge christie begins with a wedge and ends with the skis parallel.

© PAUL PETERSEN

Hockey Stop

As long as you're working on the art of skidding your skis sideways in a wedge christie, you can adapt that skill to the flashy *hockey stop*, which is simply a way to come to a quick, controlled stop on flat or gently sloping terrain. The technique is simple: quickly twist both skis to one side or the other, winding up with them still parallel to each other but perpendicular to your direction of progress—just like a hockey player would do for a fast stop on ice skates. A little bit of a hop to unweight the skis makes this easier. Keep your head and torso facing in the direction you're moving. Dig in the trailing-side edges of the skis to come to a quick, snow-spraying halt. It's lots of fun, a great way to practice important skills, and quicker than the snowplow if you need to stop in a hurry.

© DAVID MADISON

Three quarters of the way around a hockey stop.

© ALPINA

Dressing for Success

Earlier in this book we called cross-country skiing the "warm" winter sport. Many beginners, in fact, tend to overdress so badly that their first experiences are more reminiscent of a sauna than a winter snowfield. On the other hand, if you dress too lightly, you'll find that rest breaks or photo stops turn into "freeze" breaks if you linger more than a few minutes. Ironically, you have the same problem if you dress too warmly, as all that sweat you've been generating turns to ice water.

Dressing properly for cross-country skiing is a skill like any other—just as important to your total enjoyment as a rhythmic diagonal stride, a well-honed kick-and-glide, or perfect poling. In this chapter, we'll teach you how to dress to stay warm and dry from head to toe, in any conditions. And we'll discuss such often-glossed-over essentials as eye protection and sunscreen.

UPPER-BODY LAYERING

If you're a backpacker, cold-weather cyclist, or winter jogger, you probably already know the basics of cross-country dress. The principal difference here is that ski-

ing generates so much body heat—especially if you ski quickly and energetically—that the difference between moving and resting is magnified. If there is a single basic principle for staying comfortable while skiing, it is to dress in layers. *Layering* allows you to fine-tune your clothing to weather conditions and your energy output, without having to stuff your pack with an entire wardrobe. If you have enough layers to choose from, it's easy to add a new one or *peel* an unneeded one without going from overheating to shivering. A lightweight shirt and thick parka do not make a good layering system. Several thinner layers is the key.

For maximum comfort, arm yourself with at least three layers, each either stretchy or loose fitting to allow uninhibited motion, but each serving a different function. The inner layer (preferably synthetic) wicks moisture away from the skin, avoiding that cold, clammy feeling that can easily set you to shivering. Once you've warmed up and are actively skiing, this may be the only layer you wear. Make sure it's lightweight enough you won't overheat, no matter how warm the day gets. Only experience, though, will tell you what *lightweight enough* means for you. Your needs will change as you gain experience. As you

Chapter 4

It's not what you wear, but how you layer.

progress from "walking" to "brisk walking" or "jogging," the potential for overheating increases.

The next layer is your "bulk" or insulation layer. Wool, synthetic fleece, or other warm synthetics are the fabrics of choice for the bulk layer, which provides the majority of your warmth during rest breaks. For extended outings, it's best to divide the bulk layer into two thinner layers of unequal thickness. That gives you maximum flexibility, since you can wear either or both.

The final layer should be windproof and moisture resistant to keep cold breezes, snow, or rain from robbing your bulk layer of its warmth. A light nylon shell is usually adequate.

No matter how warm the weather, at least one upper-body layer needs to be long-sleeved. All you have to do is fall once on coarse, abrasive snow to know why.

Beyond these basic principles, how to dress is greatly affected by the type of ski trip you've planned. On groomed tracks with an easy return to a warming lodge and the reassuring presence of ski patrols, most intermediate and advanced skiers travel lightly. Why carry all those extra clothes if you

Avoid Cotton

Experienced backcountry skiers have a slogan: "cotton kills." Cotton has no place in cold, damp weather (e.g., on snow) or in cool-weather conditions when you're going to be working up a sweat.

The reason is simple: when wet, cotton loses most of its warmth—up to 90 percent according to some estimates. In addition, it traps moisture and takes forever to dry. This means a cotton T-shirt is worse than useless. Instead of wicking moisture away from your skin, it traps it, chilling you badly. Unchecked, this chilling can lead to hypothermia—a fancy term for a dangerous loss of body heat—producing uncontrollable shivering, loss of coordination, impaired judgment, and even death. Wear cotton on hot summer days, never on snow.

A few years ago, the only alternatives to cotton were silk (expensive) or wool (itchy). Today, there are a plethora of synthetic fibers that are not only warm but comfortable. Examples are Lycra, Thermastat, Capilene, Thermax, polypropylene, synthetic fleece (a form of polyester), and Coolmax.

Finally, the ban on cotton includes not only the aforementioned layers but, ideally, underpants and bras. Cotton underwear may not give you hypothermia, but if it gets wet it can be uncomfortable and may chafe.

can be back to civilization in 20 to 30 minutes? But anytime you're beyond range of a ski patrol or on an extended loop, you need to be more conservative about what you pack.

Lower-Body Layering

Proper layering for the lower body is trickier, because adding or shedding layers typically requires removing not only your skis but also your boots. That puts a premium on getting it right the first time. Again, long pants are critical for abrasion protection. Tights are often best. Even the lightest-weight Lycra will protect against scrapes, and it's remarkably tear resistant.

Unfortunately, if you overheat it can be a lot more difficult to change pants than to shed an upper-body layer. If you're skiing in a popular area and wearing long underwear under your tights, for example, you're going to have to either find a bathroom or not mind being an exhibitionist to get rid of it—and even exhibitionists may balk at standing stocking-footed in

Paul Says

Practically speaking, blue jeans and a cotton sweatshirt may work for a skier who never falls or breaks a sweat. Mere mortals should beware: if you wear cotton, all it takes to ruin your day is bad weather, wet snow, harder going than anticipated, or an injury. If you venture far from a trailhead wearing cotton, dangerous hypothermia lurks even on sunny days.

Rick Says

I've skiied mostly in the Oregon Cascades or the upper Midwest, often on ungroomed routes an hour or more from the trailhead. In the Cascades, where temperatures hover around the freezing mark and strong winds are uncommon, I typically carry three layers for my upper body: a long-sleeved polyester undershirt, an old wool sweater, and a fleece jacket. Skiing, all I'll typically wear is the undershirt. The other layers are for rest breaks, with the fleece jacket serving as a combination bulk layer and partial breeze protection. In colder weather I add a cheap nylon windbreaker and possibly a second undershirt.

My legs aren't as sensitive to temperature changes, and I rarely change layers on my lower body. Typically I'll wear cycling tights—lightweight Lycra ones in mild conditions, a heavier polypropylene pair (designed for cool-weather cycling) at colder temperatures. For emergencies, I carry a pair of fleece pants, but I can't remember ever using them. In addition to the clothing, even on short trips I carry a backpacker's foam sleeping pad. I can roll this out on the snow and sunbathe for an hour without getting cold, even at 20-degree temperatures.

On the other hand, as a former Minnesotan, I've skied at temperatures down to –10°F and at wind chills well into the –40s. In fact, one of my favorite

the snow while they change. It's particularly painful to watch experienced downhill skiers make their first attempts at cross-country skiing in long underwear and insulated bib overalls. There's nothing they can do but sweat.

There are two solutions to the pants-changing problem. The most straightforward is to make sure your inner layer is something you wouldn't be overly embarrassed to wear in public. Some skiers hit the trails in polypropylene long underwear and running shorts. Others find that lightweight cycling tights offer an acceptable alternative without breaking the budget. For maximum flexibility, try wearing midthigh-length Spandex shorts under your tights— similar to cycling shorts but without the seat padding. Substituting these for cotton underwear can eliminate

cross-country ski memories is a January, full-moon ski when the mercury was hovering around –10°F.

At those temperatures, there are special considerations. First, you may want extra socks, but they probably won't fit into boots sized for skiing in warmer temperatures. Cutting off circulation by trying to squeeze in an extra sock that doesn't really fit merely makes your feet colder, with possible risk of frostbite. If you do much skiing at those temperatures, you may need a second pair of boots, sized to allow for two pairs of thick socks.

Second, the massive amounts of body heat generated by skiing can mask the danger of frostbite to exposed, poor-circulation portions of the anatomy, such as ears. It's insidious—you can get frostbite without even knowing it's happening. The principal warning is that the affected area goes numb. Dressed lightly for skiing, you need to check occasionally to make sure exposed areas aren't losing sensation, especially if the temperature is below 15 to 20°F.

Finally, men need to beware that vulnerable portions of the anatomy include the genitals. If you're wearing thin pants or tights, it is possible to freeze solid certain sensitive portions of the male anatomy—especially if you're heading into a brisk wind. Try wearing two layers of underwear or buy "wind panel" briefs, made for the purpose.

a source of chafing, while allowing you to peel off your long underwear in public.

The other major problem—the need to remove skis and boots—can also be solved. Look for nylon wind pants or fleece pants with half- or full-length zippers on the outside of each leg so they can be put on or taken off over your boots, quickly and conveniently, without getting your socks wet. If you can't find them in a ski store, try a mountaineering shop—climbers face a similar need for pants that fit over climbing boots and crampons.

Socks

Socks are easy to take for granted until they cause problems. Then we tend to blame our boots. But socks have a lot to do with foot comfort. They provide warmth, wick moisture away from the feet, and help prevent blisters. Until recently, most skiers

Paul Says

For track skiing on short loops, my favorite choice at near-freezing temperatures is a lightweight, synthetic long-underwear shirt and a synthetic, zip turtleneck. I top this with a fleece vest and on windy days add a thin nylon jacket I can tie around my waist or tuck in a fanny pack. In colder weather, I replace the vest with a long-sleeved jacket. If it's really cold (which in my California mountains means single digits), I add a second long-underwear layer beneath the turtleneck.

For the lower body, I use tights (either loose fitting or skin tight, depending on my mood) or synthetic sweat pants and nylon wind pants. I prefer wind pants with at least a half-length zipper so I can get them on or off over my boots. For backcountry skiing, when deep snow may make it inconvenient to remove skis, I use wind pants with a full-length zipper.

The tights/wind pants combination is about right for most low-intensity skiing situations, while allowing me to shed the outer layer if it gets too warm. In colder weather, I wear the tights over long underwear.

always wore two pairs, but a new breed of sock designs has made it possible to get away with one.

The two-pair approach is still favored by many hikers and may save you the chore of buying new socks if you already have a good supply of hiking socks. The concept is to wear a thin "liner" sock on the inside, with a thick wool or synthetic one over it. The inner sock wicks moisture away from the skin; the outer provides warmth and cushion. In theory, using two pairs allows rubbing to occur between the layers, rather than against your skin, but the latest breeds of synthetic socks don't require a liner. Bearing brand names such as Thorlo or Ultimax, they also feature beefed-up padding under the heel and ball of the foot. First introduced for joggers in the late 1970s and early 1980s, they are thinner than old-fashioned wool and are the first choice of many skiers.

Whatever socks you use, make sure they are free of folds or wrinkles that can cause blisters. Also, avoid cotton and carry a spare pair in case your feet get wet. And when buying or renting boots, try them on with the socks you'll be wearing on the trail, so you're sure they'll fit.

Gaiters

In the skiing world, gaiters aren't toothy reptiles that live in swamps. They're nylon ankle covers, typically extending up to mid-calf, designed to keep snow out of your boots. They'll also help keep your socks dry. If you're a hiker, you can get double duty from them in summer to keep dew or rain on tall grass from running down your legs into your boots.

Gaiters are a luxury, a necessity, or useless, depending on the type of skiing you're doing. On groomed trails or packed snow, you don't need them. In the backcountry, especially in deep powder, they're essential unless you have very tall boots or specially designed pants with built-in gaiters.

Gaiters come in several styles, designated as short, long, and full overboot. "Short" and "long" relate to how far the gaiters come up the calf. Which you want depends on whether your pants are waterproof, the depth of loose snow, and what feels comfortable. It's mostly a personal decision, but realize that if you get your tights wet above the top of the gaiter, they'll conduct a remarkable amount of moisture down to your feet.

Full overboot gaiters are for backcountry or telemark skiing, where many boots are made of leather and resemble hiking boots. They cover the boot's entire leather upper and are designed to prevent wet snow from soaking through. They're a specialty item for this type of boot and aren't necessary for the new plastic boots, which are inherently more waterproof.

Although there are variations in designs, gaiters typically wrap around the ankle and lower leg, closing with a zipper and/or snaps. This means you don't have to take off your skis and boots to put them on or take them off. To tell left from right (for styles that distinguish), make sure the zipper is on the outside, where it can't snag the other gaiter, tripping you. The front of the gaiter has a metal hook near the bottom that attaches to your boot's laces or Velcro closing strap. At the top, an elasticized band around the calf keeps the gaiter from falling down like a big sock.

© PAUL PETERSEN

Gaiters protect your leg from knee to ankle from snow and ice. These gaiters snap at the rear, with no difference between left and right.

The metal hook isn't enough to fully secure the gaiter. There's also a strap running around the boot, beneath the arch of your foot. The first time you put on the gaiters you may have to tie it into place; after that, you can just slide your toe through the loop. Inexpensive gaiters use a simple nylon cord that ties to eyelets on each side of the gaiter. (When purchasing gaiters, make sure the cords are attached; sometimes they fall off during shipping.) These cords tend to wear out and have to be replaced from time to time. More expensive gaiters substitute a reinforced strap and buckles.

HATS, MUFFS, AND NECK GAITERS

The biggest single source of heat loss for the human body is through the head. Estimates vary, but it is often said that the head and neck account for one half to two thirds of the body's total heat loss.

This means that if your toes are cold, putting on a hat may help; if you're overheating, the first thing to remove is your hat. Skiing in mild conditions, in fact, many people find they seldom need a hat, although you should always carry one for rest breaks and emergencies.

The type of hat is pretty much up to you. Favorites for most skiers are thin wool or polypropylene stocking caps or simple headbands that cover the ears. If that's not enough, try ear muffs. If it's cold and windy or snow is blowing down your neck, you can add a pull-over neck warmer called a *neck gaiter*. For near-Arctic conditions, try a ski mask or its cousin, the balaclava. These items cover the entire head, face, and neck with holes for eyes and breathing. Some backcountry skiers, extreme telemarkers, and ski mountaineers now use ski helmets for both warmth and safety. These are highly recommended if you're skiing fast in the trees.

GOGGLES, GLASSES, AND EYE SHIELDS

Sunglasses aren't optional. Sunlight on snow can be dazzling, and you need good glasses to avoid the risk of serious eye injury. Even if it's cloudy, sunglasses are important, especially at high altitudes.

A neck gaiter is a good idea on an especially cold or windy day.

For the average skier, standard drugstore sunglasses with good UV protection are all that are needed, possibly combined with a retention strap such as those made by Chums or Croakies. If you want better eye coverage, you may prefer a type of partial goggle called a *shield*. In addition to being a fashion statement, shields are useful in bad weather.

Eye shields, which extend around the sides toward your ear, provide more protection than standard sunglasses.

They deflect wind better than sunglasses and can serve double duty for bicycling, mountaineering, or hiking. Shields are less prone to fogging than sunglasses, which in certain ranges of temperature and humidity have a nasty tendency to fog up the moment you start breathing hard.

A full goggle offers the ultimate in sun and snow protection while shutting off the last traces of eyeball-searing drafts. Also, young children tend to tolerate them better than they do sunglasses. That makes goggles worth the price if your child has a tendency to pluck off sunglasses and throw them in the snow when you're not looking. The downside of goggles is that they are hot and fog up much more easily than sunglasses. Some people also think they are a fashion "don't," as they can make you look like a bug-eyed monster or a World War I trooper in a gas mask.

Goggles are well-suited for kids or telemark skiers.

45

Any form of eye protection is compatible with contact lenses, but eyeglass wearers have special problems. Clip-on sunglasses are inexpensive but fall off easily, can scratch plastic lenses, and don't offer much protection from light coming in from the sides. Custom sunglasses are better, especially because they can be designed in wraparound styles that offer a good deal of side protection. They can also be equipped with plastic or leather side protectors to block light coming in from an angle.

Another solution is Photogray lenses, which darken automatically in bright light. The super-dark Photogray Extra is satisfactory for skiing, although the Photogray system requires glass lenses rather than plastic—a disadvantage for people who prefer lightweight plastic.

Eye shields don't tend to be compatible with eyeglasses, but many brands of goggles fit nicely over glasses. Some brands of shields and goggles (Bollé, for instance) are designed so an optician can equip them with custom lenses, although this can be expensive.

Gloves

Beginning skiers tend to wear gloves that are far too warm or bulky. In cross-country skiing, unlike down-

hill skiing, your arms and hands are constantly in motion, pumping warm blood through your fingers. Most days, thick gloves or mittens designed for downhill skiing will be much too warm—and probably won't fit into your poles' wrist straps.

If you value the skin on your palms and knuckles, gloves are essential when you fall. For spring skiing, make sure you find a pair that is lightweight enough that you're not tempted to take them off when you overheat.

Sunscreen

View sunscreen the way old-fashioned Hollywood leading ladies used to view makeup. Unless you're skiing in January in a far-northern climate, you shouldn't consider yourself fully dressed without it. Even if it's cloudy, sunscreen is important, because skin-cancer inducing ultraviolet (UV) light can penetrate all but the thickest cloud layers. If you're skiing at high elevations, the risk is magnified.

Use a sun protection factor (SPF) of at least 15 and buy a water-resistant brand that won't run in your eyes when you sweat or leave thin spots when you wipe your brow. Reapply sunscreen at least once or twice a day. You should also carry—and use—SPF 15 lip balm.

In addition to lips, sensitive places are the ears, neck, and face. Don't forget the part in your hair or a bald spot. A baseball cap can help shade your face, but UV light reflecting off the snow can still get under it. One sensitive spot first-timers often overlook is the bottom of the nose, which is also exposed to reflected light.

PAUL SAYS

For warm days, I use gloves like Rick's, technically called *spring gloves*. As it gets colder, I shift to *lobster gloves* or *split mitts*, followed by thick downhill ski gloves or mittens with nylon overmitts.

Putting on a hat can help your hands, just like it helps your feet. So can pulling up zippers or putting on ear muffs or a neck gaiter. Wet gloves are no good, and failing to eat or drink enough is also a factor in causing cold hands. Always carry a water bottle and a snack such as a Clif Bar or Powerbar.

DEALING WITH RAIN

Skiing when it's snowing is fun. The snow collects on your hat and coat, but it's easy to brush off before it melts. Cold snow is less likely to get you wet than warmer, wetter snow, though both raise safety and route-finding issues that we'll discuss later (see page 104).

Most people find that skiing in rain, on the other hand, is ghastly. If you live in the Midwest, New England, or the Central Rockies, the best solution is to avoid it by not going out on damp, near-freezing days. There'll be plenty of better weather. In the Pacific Northwest and parts of California, though, "damp" and "near-freezing" are too often the norm. Sometimes you can move higher into the mountains, above the magic *snow level*, where precipitation comes as white flakes rather than rain. Other times you just have to be prepared to get wet. That typically means either not venturing too far afield or having adequate rain gear.

The design of rain gear is a tradeoff between waterproofing and breathability. And when purchasing rain gear, price is also a factor. Coated nylon is inexpensive, lightweight, easy to stuff in a pack, and about as close to 100 percent waterproof as you can get. But it won't breathe and can be uncomfortably warm. You may get just as wet from your own sweat as you would have from the rain. Some jackets, particularly those made for runners or cyclists, have air vents in the back or under the arms. These are an improvement over unvented jackets and are only moderately more expensive.

RICK SAYS

Even living in Oregon, the rain capital of the cross-country ski world, I seldom ski in heavy rain. Off-and-on showers or light mist are one thing; an all-day soaker will send me back to my car in a hurry. If an equipment failure or injury strands you miles from the trailhead, it's a lot more dangerous in the rain. But the snow-line effect is amazing. Sometimes it can be drizzling at the bottom of a 300-foot hill, dropping wet, fluffy flakes halfway up, and producing fine powder at the top. In these conditions, skiing on groomed trails, unplowed roads, or easy trails, I don't find rain to be much of a threat. I own a lot of rain gear, but usually all I carry are a couple of extra bulk layers and a nylon shell, making doubly sure everything is made of fabrics that will keep me warm when wet. Since I'm going to sweat anyway, I figure a little rain won't make much difference. (But I was the type of kid who never understood when my mother insisted I bundle up on a winter day.)

I wouldn't recommend this approach when you're starting out. You have to have a lot of outdoor experience to know what fabrics will keep you warm and how many layers are enough for you.

PAUL SAYS

I seldom let rain stop me. In addition to a raincoat, for a full day in the rain I take several extra pairs of gloves, as well as two or three extra sets of socks. I also take an extra hat and extra long underwear, leaving all of this in my car for periodic quick changes if I can or carrying it with me if necessary. But I'm a ski addict. Other people may decide days like that are made for sitting at home by the fire.

Most expensive are waterproof-breathable fabrics such as Gore-Tex and its family of imitators. These fabrics, however, aren't alike; the physics of their construction requires that the more waterproof they are, the lower their breathability. Gore-Tex is on the high end of the waterproofing scale, lower in breathability (although still a major improvement over coated nylon). This means Gore-Tex is great for low-level exercise, but it's easy to work up enough sweat to overload its ability to breathe, particularly in the high-humidity, freezing-point temperatures at which rain is most likely. Other fabrics, called *micropore* or *durable water repellent* (DWR) fabrics, are more breathable but less effective at shedding rain. Ultimately, the trade-off is personal, often made with an eye to the price tag. If you have only a limited budget to spend on breathable rain gear, invest it first on

upper-body clothing, and get less expensive rain pants. Hooded jackets are preferred.

When skiing in the rain you also have to worry about getting your head wet—especially since that can be a source of extremely rapid heat loss. Even if you're one of those people who seldom wears a cap, carry one made of wool or a warm-when-wet synthetic, just for safety. To keep rain out of your eyes, try wearing a baseball cap under the hood of your rain jacket.

TRANSPORTING SKIS

Transporting your skis to the trailhead can be as easy as sliding them into the passenger compartment of a hatchback automobile or as complex as checking them as airplane baggage. At the trailhead, you may also need to carry them around by hand.

Carrying skis by hand is easier if you clamp the tips and tails together. This also helps protect the bases from scuffing. Big rubber bands will work, but for a nominal price you can buy durable ski straps with buckle or Velcro closures. For added protection of the base, try Ski Bones or padded straps designed to space the ski bases apart, or use socks or rags. Fancier hand-held ski carriers exist but are seldom necessary.

If you can't—or don't want to—get your skis into your car's passenger compartment, a roof rack is the alternative. Specialty ski racks can cost more than your skis, although some come in modular units that easily adapt to bicycle, kayak, or canoe carriers. The chief disadvantage of ski racks is that they leave ski bases exposed to the elements and road salt. You could also put your skis in a modestly priced nylon ski bag and lash it to a standard roof rack, such as the one that may have come with your vehicle. Weigh convenience, price, and grit protection to make the decision that's right for you.

To ship skis by public transportation, you'll need

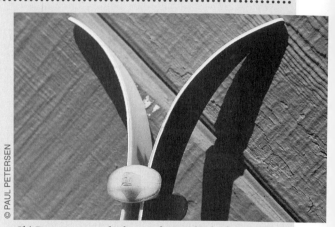

© PAUL PETERSEN

Ski Bones protect the bases of your skis by keeping them from scraping against each other.

a ski bag, although some airlines supply free plastic ones at check-in. Strap the ski tips and tails; your poles go in the bag with the skis. You may want to protect them with cardboard or foam "pole tubes," obtainable from ski shops. Flying with skis is remarkably easy. Although rules are always subject to change, airlines seeking to curry favor with skiers have traditionally exempted skis from oversized-baggage fees. Skiers may even be allowed to treat skis and a boot bag as a single item of luggage.

Chapter 5

What Skis to Buy?

© PAUL PETERSEN

Any sport is more fun if you have the right equipment. But the problem with skiing is that there are so many types of skis. Worse, to the uninitiated, they all look pretty much the same.

If you look closely, though, you'll start to see differences. Some types of skis are longer than others. Others are relatively wide or narrow. Some are edged with metal to cut into hard snow. Most have repetitive wedge or fish-scale patterns imprinted on the bottom; a few don't.

Poles, boots, and bindings also vary. With poles it's primarily a question of length, but poles intended for different purposes can also have different compositions. With boots and bindings, the differences are more obvious. Boots can be high-top or low, leather or plastic, conventionally laced or fastened with quick-close Velcro. Boots designed for one type of binding won't fit another.

All this equipment, though, can be separated into three general categories, according to primary purpose:

• track skiing–light touring,

• skating, and

• backcountry touring–telemarking.

Your first skis will almost certainly be in the track skiing–light-touring category, which is the only type of skiing previous chapters have discussed in any detail. Skating will be discussed in chapter 7, backcountry touring and telemark skiing in chapters 8 and 9. For ease of comparison, all three types of equipment are discussed in this chapter.

Skis, boots, bindings, and poles are frequently sold in discount packages. Typically, the package allows

PAUL SAYS

Each type of equipment has strengths and weaknesses. Addicted "skiaholics" like me often have at least one full set of equipment—skis, boots, poles, and bindings—in each category. After all, skiing's important. Fire the baby-sitter, mow the lawn yourself—do what it takes to save up for that next set of skis. That's the ski-addict motto.

49

RICK SAYS

Although there's no such thing as an all-purpose ski (you wouldn't want to do ski mountaineering on skating skis), there is some flexibility among the categories. I have a pair of inexpensive track skis I've taken down intermediate runs at a downhill resort and used in my first experiments with skating. They're far from ideal for either purpose, but they allowed me to stretch my limits while I debated whether I was interested in specialized equipment. Similarly, a single well-chosen pair of boots can serve more than one set of skis, particularly if the skis aren't radically different.

Remember also that it isn't just beginner equipment that can be rented. The first time I went overnight touring I did so on equipment I rented for an entire week at less than a tenth the cost of purchase. Even if you never plan to buy more than one pair of skis, this chapter will help you decide what to rent.

you to mix brands of equipment, with the only constraint being that you must buy everything at the same time.

To Wax or Not to Wax

With the exception of skating skis, nordic skis come in two broad categories: waxable and waxless. Waxless skis can be identified by the fish-scale or wedge patterns on their bases. Each of the little wedges allows the ski to slide forward easily but digs into the snow (or *grips* it) to prevent it from slipping backward. This is what allows you to alternately kick and glide when doing the classic diagonal stride. Waxable skis have smooth bases that glide beautifully but provide no grip. Instead, grip is provided by ski waxes that

hold to the snow when pressed firmly against it but don't provide much resistance when gliding. Different waxes are needed at different temperatures and on old versus fresh snow. Climbing skins are often used for grip on waxable telemark skis.

Approximately 80 percent of the cross-country skis sold in the United States are waxless, and rental skis are almost always waxless. This doesn't mean waxing is archaic, but it is a skill most people prefer not to learn. We'll discuss the subject in greater detail in chapter 12. For the moment, you only need to know that you should consider waxable skis for your first pair only if you live in an area where temperatures are consistent—and below freezing—throughout the day. The colder and more consistent the temperature, the more advantages waxable skis have.

Track Skiing/Light Touring
Skis

Skis for use on groomed track are frequently referred to as *track-skiing* or *light-touring* skis. If you go into a ski shop and ask to see equipment in this category, the sales people will know exactly what you're seeking, even if you don't.

Light-touring skis can be used equally well in groomed track or off-track on gentle terrain such as golf courses or alpine meadows. The middle-of-the-road versatility of this class of skis makes them the most popular, especially for beginners; they'll even function in powder if the terrain isn't too steep. But they are not usable for ski mountaineering and are only marginally better for nordic downhill (where their plastic edges won't get enough bite on steep, icy slopes) and skating (for which they are too slow).

Skis in this category (as in the other two) must be selected based on the combination of your weight, height, and ability. Of these, the most important are weight and ability. Improper selection will result

The camber (upward bow) of the ski can easily be seen by placing the ski on a flat surface.

tail

tip

shovel

grip zone

either in poor glide or poor grip (i.e., they'll feel too slippery when you kick).

Stand a pair of skis on end, holding their bases together, and you'll understand why. When the tips and tails are touching, there is a gap in the center. This gap, called the *camber*, results from the fact that skis are slightly bowed. When you're gliding, the skis bow upward so your weight rests largely on the tips and tails, where there's little or no waxless pattern to create drag, which slows you down. When you kick, the wax or tread pattern beneath your foot squashes firmly onto the snow, preventing the ski from sliding backward. Waxable skis work the same way waxless skis do because you apply sticky "kick" wax beneath your feet and "glide" wax to the tips and tails.

The combination of length and camber is important in choosing a ski. Too much camber for your weight, and you won't be able to make firm contact with the snow when you kick. Too little camber, and you'll wonder why everyone glides past you on descents. The length of the tread pattern is also an issue, although you generally can leave this to the manufacturer's engineering department.

Skis vary in camber to accommodate different levels of ability and people of different weights. If you are thin for your height you'll want less camber than if you're heavy. If you buy stiff-camber skis, you're going to have to kick like a mule to make them go anywhere, and you'll have to herringbone up every molehill. But they'll glide like a charm. Highly athletic skiers and racers can take advantage of this extra glide and prefer more camber than the average touring skier.

Camber is typically described in terms of the firmness or springiness of the ski's arch. A ski with a lot of camber is described as *firm* or stiff; one with relatively little is *soft*. When sorting through skis to find a camber suitable for your first pair, a useful rule of thumb is to reject any pair you can't squeeze completely together with two hands. If you can do it with one hand, they're too soft and will glide poorly (unless you're a featherweight or have extraordinarily strong hands). If no amount of hand strength will close the gap, leave it to the racers. Individual pairs of skis vary, even if they look identical. Sort through the ones in the shop, squeezing each pair. Shift to a slightly larger or smaller size if necessary.

Checking camber by squeezing skis.

© PAUL PETERSEN

Ski shop employees can help you fine-tune your choice. One method they may use is to have you stand on the skis on an uncarpeted floor or a special device made for the purpose, with a piece of paper beneath the center of the ski's arch. If your weight is equally distributed on the skis, the paper should slide easily along the length of the tread pattern—demonstrating that the tread won't drag significantly when you're trying to glide on both skis. When you shift most to all of your weight to a single ski to mimic the effect of a kick, the entire length of the ski should flatten firmly against the paper. If you're already an advanced skier with a strong kick, you may want more camber. Pick skis that allow the paper to slide freely beneath the entire length of the tread pattern or waxing zone (the *grip zone*, see chapter 12) even when your full body weight is on a single ski. This allows the ski to grip only during a vigorous kick.

Ski length is more confusing, because light-touring skis are designed in two length categories: *midlength* and traditional (or *long*), with a wide range of lengths in both categories (a third category, *micro*, is no longer available). First choose a category, then a specific ski, making sure you don't accidentally cross category boundaries when fine-tuning your choice of lengths. A midlength ski designed for a tall person can look similar to a traditional-length ski for a short person, but it will have very different handling characteristics, including camber and tread pattern. Within categories, camber is more important than length; if you have to fudge a bit on length to find the right camber for your weight, do so. All skis are measured in metric units, so you might as well get used to thinking in centimeters.

Traditional skis typically run 180 to 215 centimeters for adults. They have better *flotation* in soft snow than midlength skis (i.e., their larger surface area keeps them from sinking in as deeply), but they are harder to maneuver. A rough rule of thumb for picking the right length in this category is to raise your arm over your head and pick a ski whose tip comes approximately to your wrist. Midlength skis, on the other hand, are generally about head height. For most people they're the better choice. They turn easily, glide well on packed snow, and allow a little venturing off the packed trail.

In addition to varying in length and camber, light-touring skis also vary in width. Extremely narrow skis are designed for racing. They have thin, pointy tips and may be 20 or 30 percent narrower than medium-width models. The thinness is primarily to cut weight, reducing the effort of skiing around all day and making them particularly well suited for groomed tracks. They usually have stiff cambers, though, and if you take them off track you'll sink to your knees in all but ideal snow conditions. Buy these as a first pair only if you intend to spend almost all of your time on groomed track and can find a pair with a relatively soft camber. Unusually wide light-touring skis are designed to provide better flotation on loose snow. They're heavier, harder to tip on their edges, and may not fit perfectly into machine-set track. Pick them if most of your skiing will be off-track. (Often there's not much difference between wide light-touring skis and entry-level backcountry skis.) Medium widths, like medium lengths, are compromise designs intended to provide the widest range of uses. That makes them a good choice for your first ski.

Beginners often expect there to be a difference between left skis and right skis, but this is not the case. They're interchangeable unless you later attach an asymmetric binding such as the three-pin bindings discussed on page 53.

Ski prices range from $110 to nearly $300. For your first set, you can get away with equipment near the lower end of this range. Cross-country ski areas and shops often sell used gear at the end of the ski season; spring is a great time for bargains on equipment.

Midlength and traditionally sized skis of appropriate length for this skier.

Boots

Boot shopping is simpler than ski shopping but potentially more time consuming if you have trouble with fit. Light-touring boots range from low-cut styles similar to tennis shoes to high-top varieties rising above the ankle like hiking boots. They're much more lightly constructed than downhill ski boots but less flexible than running shoes. Generally, the binding clips to a horizontal bar near the toe, and indentations on the sole mesh with ridges in the binding to help give you firm control over the ski (see illustration on page 53)—don't forget that your boots and bindings must be compatible (see Bindings, below).

Boot material varies. Leather was once traditional, but has largely been replaced by plastic and synthetic leather combinations. Some light-touring boots have hinged plastic cuffs or other types of firm ankle support. These boots, sometimes called *combination boots* because they work well for both light touring and skating, give maximum control (and prevent ankle twists) while still allowing forward-and-back flex.

With light-touring boots, only two factors matter: fit and ankle support. If you're blessed with fit-anything feet, you'll have a plethora of choices. Otherwise you'll be constrained by the shape of your feet. Since most manufactures produce only a single width of boots, you'll have to shop around if you have narrow or wide feet.

You're looking for a boot that comes up over the ankle and fits snugly without crowding your toes. Snug fit and firm ankle support are important because the boot is the critical link between your body and the ski. If that link is loose and wobbly, you won't have good control. Longtime skiers who have honed their technique can use their balance skills to compensate for lightweight boots, but low-cut boots are for racers who want to reduce weight, not for beginners. Avoid them. Recently, women have begun to see an increasing range of choices in boot fit. If you have a narrow heel and normal-to-wide forefoot, it's getting easier to find women's models that fit.

Combination boots are wonderful if you can afford them; they're the first choice for beginners. Otherwise, get the sturdiest high-top boot you can afford. Economize on other portions of the ski package if necessary. You can get inexpensive boots for as little as $80, but when it comes to improving control of your skis, you'll get the biggest bang for your buck from the boot. A boot with good ankle support will cost $125 to $200—about half that if you can find a used pair.

Bindings

There are three basic types of bindings. Fifteen years ago, virtually all skis used the three-pin or 75-millimeter style, which has three metal pins that fit matching holes under the toe of the boot. Such bindings are still used for backcountry skis, but good-quality three-pin bindings are hard to find for light

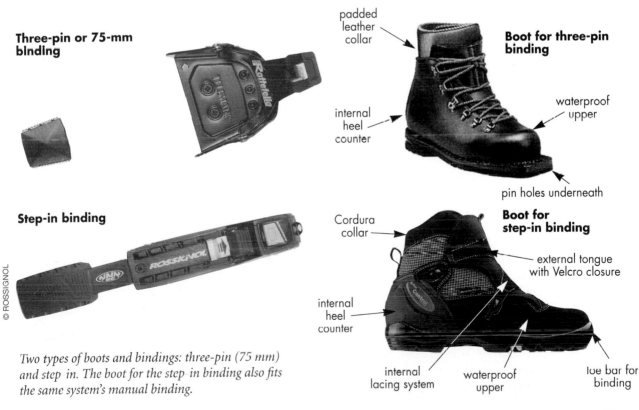

Three-pin or 75-mm binding

Step-in binding

© ROSSIGNOL

padded leather collar

internal heel counter

Boot for three-pin binding

waterproof upper

pin holes underneath

Cordura collar

internal heel counter

Boot for step-in binding

external tongue with Velcro closure

internal lacing system

waterproof upper

toe bar for binding

Two types of boots and bindings: three-pin (75 mm) and step-in. The boot for the step-in binding also fits the same system's manual binding.

RICK SAYS

I bought my first pair of combination boots in 1994 and was stunned by the difference from my old high-tops. Descents that once were challenging became trivial, and suddenly I found myself experimenting with skating, just for a change of pace. The rigid plastic materials also made the boots lighter in weight than my old leather high-tops. It was an all-round improvement that was well worth the cost.

touring, as are good light-touring boots to fit them. If you've inherited old touring skis with three-pin bindings, plan on replacing the bindings with a new boot/binding package.

Modern track and light-touring bindings have slots designed to fit a thin metal bar that protrudes from the toe of the boot. They come in two main styles, called *SNS Profil* (for Salomon Nordic System) and *NNN II* (for New Nordic Norm). They're about equally popular. Both are slightly narrower than the ski, and differences in performance are minimal. Unfortunately, boots that fit one binding won't fit the other. Choose the boot first, then get the binding that goes with it: there are ridges on the binding that must match the boot sole.

The only real choice you have in bindings is between *step-in* (sometimes called *automatic*) and manual. Step-in bindings allow you to put on your skis in a single motion. You just point the toe and push the bar on the front of the boot into the binding until it clicks. Practice this a few times in the shop—balanced on one foot in soft snow, it's not quite as easy as it sounds. To remove your skis, simply press the prominent button in front of your toe, and the boot pops free. Manual bindings require you to fasten a latch over the top of the boot's toe bar. It's not hard, but it's a little less convenient than the step-in style. Manual bindings offer a bit better ski control than automatic ones, but unless you ski a lot you're unlikely to notice.

Once you've bought bindings, they'll need to be mounted on the skis. If you're handy, you can do this yourself, but it's risky. Pay the shop and have it done by an expert for a nominal fee. The bindings themselves will cost about $45 to $70.

Poles

As a beginner you don't need fancy, hyper-expensive poles. The $20 variety will work just fine. You can spend up to $200, but these designs are for high-mileage skiers who want to cut pole weight for that extra edge in speed and endurance. Make sure you get poles designed for cross-country skiing: downhill poles have differently shaped grips and baskets that will hinder you if you try to use them for light-touring or track skiing.

You do have a couple of choices to make, however. One is the type of basket design you like. The most common is a relatively small, asymmetric style called the *hoof* design because the print it leaves in the snow is shaped a bit like an animal's hoof. It's best for groomed trails or firm snow. The other, intended to give greater support in loose powder, is larger and round or asymetric. Both types are adequate for light touring.

The second choice is pole length. This depends not just on your height, but also on your skill level and the type of terrain you expect to encounter. The less experience you have or the hillier the terrain, the shorter your poles should be. Good skiers on flat terrain like their poles a little longer. For all-purpose use, look for poles that stand somewhere between your shoulder and armpit height, and remember that a couple inches one way or the other is a *big* difference. Poles that are too long are awkward to swing; overly short poles won't let you stride out to the full extent of your abilities. Although most people don't find themselves at war with their poles, remember that poles are relatively inexpensive—if one pair doesn't work, don't be afraid to get another.

Pole baskets can look quite different: a hoof basket is on the left; a round basket is on the right.

LIGHT-TOURING CHECKLIST

- Use the phrase *light touring* (or *track skiing*) when talking to sales people. This is the "open sesame" to the proper department of the store.

- Choose between midlength and traditional.

- Choose a width. Use the terms *narrow*, *medium*, and *wide* rather than worrying about specific measurements.

- Determine the approximate length in your chosen category that is proper for your height, but don't be wedded to it.

- Check the available options for camber. Individual skis vary, so just because one pair isn't right, don't ignore the others on the same rack.

- Buy a snug-fitting boot with maximum ankle support. Spend as much as you can afford.

- Buy the binding that fits the boot. You'll probably want the step-in style.

- Pick poles suitable for your height, skill, and terrain plans.

SKATING EQUIPMENT

If you've experimented with ski skating but never tried it on equipment designed for the purpose, you're in for a treat. Skating skis have no tread pattern (because you don't need grip), blunt tips (to save weight), and are stiffer against twisting (torsional) motions than are touring skis to give you greater edge control. You have to wax them (see chapter 12), but waxing is relatively simple because you're waxing only for glide, not grip. The boots rise above the ankle and have stiff soles and hinged plastic cuffs to allow desired ankle motions without sacrificing stiffness. Poles are long—chin height or taller. (For extensive coverage of skate skiing, see chapter 7.)

Skis

Skating skis come in only one length category. Like midlength touring skis, they should be approximately head height. Prices range from $180 to more than

PAUL SAYS

Do you have an old pair of skis with bindings that don't fit a new pair of boots? No problem. It's okay to remove the old bindings and replace them with new ones. Because this means plugging up the old screw holes and drilling new ones, some people argue there's a risk of not getting the binding firmly secured. But I've done it a hundred times and never had a binding pull out on light-touring skis.

$400, with higher price tags bringing skis that are lighter but easier to break. For many people, the best compromise is a model that is one step down from the top of the line. But good skis are now available in the entry-level price range. To truly understand which ski is right for you, try renting demo skis from a cross-country ski area or ski shop.

Just as individual touring skis vary in camber, individual skating skis vary in stiffness. There are no easy rules of thumb for determining what's ideal for you, but luckily, as a beginning or intermediate skater, it's not as important as the choice of camber in a touring ski. If possible, try to let a good ski shop's trained sales people pick a pair with the right amount of flex for your skill level and expected snow conditions.

Boots

Skating boots must fit snugly and have lots of ankle support. As discussed in chapter 7, skating requires you to tip the ski and roll its edge into the snow. Good boots make it easier to do this with precision. Top of the line (about $300) is a good way to go if

"COMBI" SKIS

Some manufacturers produce *combi* skis (the ski equivalent to *combination boots*) that can be used for both skating and diagonal stride. It's a compromise for people who want to skate and stride on the same pair. These skis generally have the length, torsional stiffness, and blunt tip of skating skis but the camber of touring skis. Junior racers and skaters who occasionally stride love them. Unfortunately, as of this writing, no manufacturer has figured out how to make a no-wax variety.

you can afford it. The best skating boots are lightweight and stiff-soled and have nicely designed laces, zippers, or Velcro closures and a lot of ankle support. The stiffness and ankle support make the boot more sensitive to minor changes in snow conditions and ski movement.

Combination boots (see page 53) are a good money-saving alternative. They're not quite as stiff as dedicated skating boots and may be a bit heavier, but for many people the slight loss in skating performance is a small price to pay for not having to buy separate boots for skating and light touring. Combination boots are a particularly good option for children and for adults with small feet, because small-sized combination boots are inherently stiffer than the larger sizes.

As with light-touring boots, once you've selected the boot, you have to buy the style of bindings that comes with it. Historically your only choice has been between manual and step-in varieties. Because many manual bindings are specifically designed for skating, most skaters prefer them. In 1998, however, a new skating boot-binding system called SNS Pilot bindings appeared on the North American market. These bindings attach at two points, one at the toe, the other under the ball of the foot, for added control. It is too early to tell if they're the wave of the future or destined to remain a high-end specialty item.

Poles

Skating poles are easy to spot because they have the small "hoof" baskets designed for use on track (see page 54), and are very long. The ideal length is a subject of debate among ski coaches, but your best bet is

Some straps are designed to allow you to relax your grip on the pole completely.

to get poles that stand as high as your mouth. Go a little longer (nose height) if you ski mostly on flat terrain, shorter (to the chin) if you like hills.

With skating poles, the more you spend, the less you get—and the more you get. You get less because the poles are lighter and more likely to break. You get more because they are stiffer, keeping you from wasting energy flexing them with each plant. They also have fancier straps designed to hold your hand in ex-

SKATING EQUIPMENT CHECKLIST

- Pick a price range you can live with
- Length of ski is about head height
- All skating skis are narrow, so width isn't much of an issue
- Have a trained professional select the right ski flex for you
- Shell out the dough for stiff, snug-fitting boots
- Get the skate binding that fits your boot
- Poles are mouth height, plus or minus

actly the right position, even when it's relaxed. Good poles begin at about $90 a pair.

BACKCOUNTRY AND TELEMARK EQUIPMENT

Although backcountry skiing and telemark skiing are different, there is a good deal of overlap in equipment—enough that many skis will easily serve double duty.

Technically, any departure from groomed trails is backcountry skiing, although easy routes on firm snow don't require special equipment. Telemark skiing is nordic downhill, ranging from machine-tended slopes at downhill areas to deep-powder descents in remote backcountry. The necessary skills are discussed in chapters 8 and 9.

Skis

Skis for both purposes are wider than other classes of cross-country skis. For nordic downhill skiing on groomed alpine trails, the extra width gives you greater stability for high-speed turns; for backcountry skiing it gives you much-needed flotation in deep powder. Most backcountry and all telemark skis also have metal edges for greater control on steep, hard snow or icy slopes.

The first question is whether you need metal edges. There's no sense in spending the extra money if you don't need them, especially because they add significantly to the skis' weight. As with all equipment choices, begin by evaluating the conditions you expect to encounter. If you see yourself traversing a steep, firm snowfield, as at a downhill ski area, then

you definitely need metal. Also, if you have a downhill skier's lust for aesthetically pure, rounded turns on steep terrain, you should say *yes* to metal edges. But if all you want is to ski on golf courses or meadows without sinking knee deep, metal edges are unnecessary. The ski you want is called a *touring backcountry ski* and will look a lot like a light-touring ski, only wider. Prices range from $100 to $300.

If you're undecided, you may want to opt for a partial metal edge ($130 to $280). These edges run three quarters of the length of the ski (excluding the tip and tail), helping it to snowplow down a firm trail or bite into an icy traverse. But you'll miss the full edge if you try serious nordic downhill skiing. Cost for full edges: $200 to $450.

Regarding lengths, you have three choices. As with light-touring equipment, ski design is dominated by a tradeoff between ease of maneuvering and glide. All other factors being equal, longer skis glide better; short skis are easier to turn, especially in less than ideal conditions. The short end of the market is occupied by a category appropriately known as *short*, ranging in length from 160 to 190 centimeters. Midlength skis are 170 to 200 centimeters, and *traditional* long skis are 180 to 210 centimeters.

Short skis are a specialty backcountry design intended for a fairly narrow range of difficult conditions. They usually are wide (80–85 mm) and look pudgy compared to other skis. They are sized several inches below head height, with the optimum length depending on your weight and desired tradeoff between glide and traction. They're an unusual type of ski, filling a niche somewhere between conventional skis and snowshoes, although they glide and turn far better than snowshoes. That means they're not what most people want for a first pair of backcountry skis. They work in soft snow and powder that's not too deep but are difficult to handle on ice or hard-packed snow. Nordic downhilling at a ski area on these is pretty much out, but they're great in snow with the consistency of mashed potatoes, which is common in the Pacific Northwest.

Midlength backcountry–telemarking skis, like their touring and skating counterparts, are approximately head height. Most are wide, from 85 to 95 millimeters at the tip, and are just now becoming available in no-wax varieties. Waxable models are far more common.

Just as new *super sidecut* skis are revolutionizing alpine skiing, midlength super sidecut telemarking skis are doing the same for nordic downhill and telemark skiing. *Sidecut* refers to the narrowing of the ski beneath your foot, which on older skis isn't very noticeable. The super sidecut models have a distinct hourglass shape, improving your ability to turn at slow speeds and to carve really tight curves. Not everyone likes them, and it takes a big boot to drive them (we'll get to that in a moment), so rent before you buy.

Traditional-length skis—designed like their light-touring counterparts to be approximately wrist height (see page 52)—are becoming an endangered species for nordic downhilling. With modern materials and ski designs, nordic downhillers or telemarkers simply don't need skis significantly taller than their height. But long skis are still the most popular length for run-of-the-mill backcountry use. The backcountry varieties are relatively inexpensive (under $250), versatile, and work with many types of boots and bindings. Their principal weakness is that they don't turn easily, particularly in crud (inconsistent snow), crust, and moguls. You can find them in both waxable and no-wax styles, although no-waxes haven't dominated the backcountry market as they have the light-touring market. Metal edges are favored by many skiers under the perception they will improve turning ability. In hard, icy snow, this may be true, but a good boot does more for your ability to turn than the ski itself.

Once you've chosen a category of skis, you need to think about the ski's desired stiffness. For traditional backcountry skis, choose camber much as you would for touring skis, but select a softer camber than you would for track skiing; you'll want it to get grip in deep, soft snow. Camber isn't as much of a factor for telemark skis because they're designed primarily for going downhill rather than striding. Climbing, you'll probably be riding a lift, hiking up spring corn snow, or ascending with climbing skins (see page 95). But overall flex is still important. Choose it based on expected snow conditions. Stiff skis are for going very fast on hard snow; softer ones are for powder, crud, or moguls.

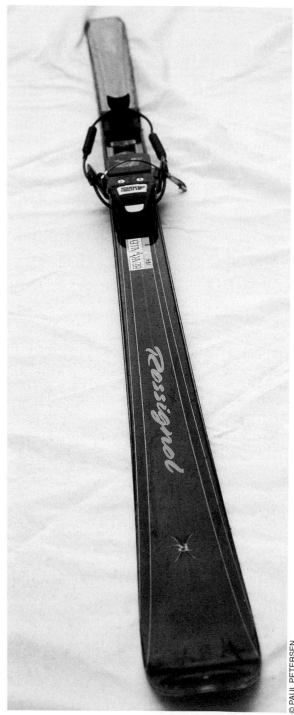

Super sidecut or "shaped" ski, where the ski is significantly narrower under the foot.

© PAUL PETERSEN

Boots and Bindings

Backcountry/telemarking boots come in enough styles and materials to make it difficult to summarize current models, let alone anticipate what next year's market might bring. A decade ago, most were leather affairs that looked like heavy-duty hiking boots. Today you can choose from leather, plastic, synthetic fabrics, or any of these in combination. All are high-top, reaching over the ankle like a hiking boot or alpine ski boot. Prices range from $200 to $500.

Backcountry boots are the only category of ski boot for which it pays to think about bindings, rather than just buying the one that comes with the boot. Your choices are between three-pin (75 mm), cables, and two boot-binding systems.

Three-pin bindings have a trio of metal pins that fit matching holes on the sole of the boot, which extends a half-inch forward from the toe in order to allow room for the binding to engage. The binding fastens by manually clamping a metal plate, called a *bail*, onto this toe lip. Because the binding is designed to accommodate the entire toe of your boot, left and right bindings are different and are generally marked "L" and "R." Skis are removed by releasing a catch on the bail, allowing it to swing free.

Putting on skis with three-pin bindings isn't as easy as stepping into an automatic light-touring binding, but it's generally simple enough unless the pin holes on the boot become worn or clogged with snow. A pocket-knife awl is invaluable for curing the latter

problem; new boot soles or pin-hole reinforcing plates are the only answer to the former. Because the tightness with which the ski attaches to the binding is dependent on how firmly you press down on the bail, it pays to check it by picking up your foot and wiggling the ski after fastening the bail. It's a nuisance to have a loose ski fall off in the first 100 yards.

All of this means that three-pin bindings are a bit more inconvenient to fasten than automatic bindings. But they are strong, and their width gives better control of the ski in difficult terrain or for nordic downhilling. Price: about $60.

Cable bindings are the most popular among hardcore telemark skiers but least popular among beginners because they're the most complicated to attach to your boot. With these bindings, your toes are typically secured by a bail, while a cable wraps around your heel to provide additional stability. A notch in the boot heel holds the cable in place. These bindings have two major advantages: they don't allow the heel to lift as high as other bindings do, increasing your cornering and edging control; and they can pop completely free in a wicked fall without ripping out the pin holes of a three-pin binding. Price: about $115.

Your third alternative is a system-type binding (in which boots and bindings were developed as a matching "system"). Two backcountry styles exist: Profil BC and NNN BC, which are the backcountry equivalents of the similarly named light-touring

The three-pin binding, also known as the 75-millimeter binding, and the corresponding boot.

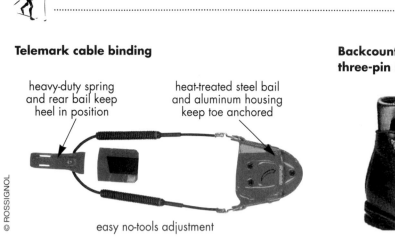

Telemark cable binding

heavy-duty spring
and rear bail keep
heel in position

heat-treated steel bail
and aluminum housing
keep toe anchored

easy no-tools adjustment

© ROSSIGNOL

Cable bindings are 75 millimeters wide but don't have the pins.

Backcountry boot to go with cable or three-pin binding

© KARHU

bindings. The Profil BC isn't strong enough for heavy-duty telemarking. The NNN BC is stronger but still doesn't rival the three-pin binding for heavy-duty use. It is available in both manual and step-in styles. Price: about $80.

Boot fit and stiffness, of course, are even more important than binding styles. Get a boot that fits comfortably but snugly when you're wearing your skiing socks—and spend as much on it as you can afford. Plastic boots can offer several advantages over leather. They are sometimes less expensive and are generally warm and waterproof. Some boots have a locking, hinged cuff that allows the boot to serve a wider range of functions. You can leave the cuff unlocked for diagonal stride or hill climbing, fastening it for rigidity on descents.

The wide variety of styles and evolving science of boot design make specific recommendations difficult. The best approach to boot shopping is to seek the counsel of ski instructors or ask for advice at well-run ski shops. The boot you choose will have a tremendous influence on your ability to deal with terrain and snow conditions. One thing you should know is that the wider your skis are, the more torque it takes to control them, whether it's for traversing, sidestepping, or holding a snowplow on hard snow. Super sidecut skis are like wide skis because their tip widths can be 100 millimeters or more, requiring substantial turning leverage. Wide skis need a big boot, made of plastic or a leather/plastic combination that will flex fore and aft but not sideways.

Poles

Pole choice for backcountry skiing is also more complex than for light touring or skating, because you'll be dealing with a wide variety of conditions with differing ideal pole lengths. For nordic downhill at a downhill ski area, the best poles are those designed for alpine skiing. To find the right size, turn the pole upside down and grab the shaft in the position that is

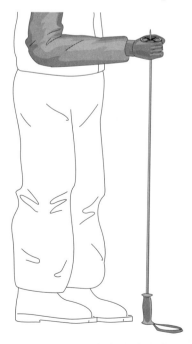

Choosing pole length for nordic downhilling.

now immediately below the basket. With your elbow at your side, your forearm should be parallel to the ground. Price: about $40.

You can also use such poles for backcountry touring in variable terrain. In terrain where the pole feels too short, eke out a few inches of added length simply by pushing on the top of it with your palm rather than using the grip. Another option is an adjustable pole ($80), which telescopes from downhill ski pole length to armpit height or anything in between.

Strength is more of an issue with backcountry poles than with other types, because you're putting a lot of stress on them—and you may be far from the trailhead if one breaks. Opinions vary, but aluminum is probably strongest, followed by epoxy-resin fiberglass, then cheaper fiberglass.

If you're using alpine poles, palm the top of the pole to eke extra length from the pole.

© PAUL PETERSEN

TELEMARKING/BACKCOUNTRY EQUIPMENT CHECKLIST

- Choose a category: backcountry or telemarking.

- Decide if you want metal edges.

- For traditional backcountry skis, pick between waxable and no-wax. For midlength telemarking skis, choose between conventional (little sidecut) and super sidecut.

- Ski length varies with different ski types; consult expert sales people or a ski instructor.

- Flex or camber should suit your weight (for backcountry skis) and expected snow conditions (for telemark skis).

- Choose a binding type.

- Pick boots sturdy enough for adequate steering control over your chosen ski.

- Make sure the boot fits; change binding types if necessary.

- Size poles, such as light touring, with the forearm test or buy adjustables.

- Rent before you buy or try out equipment for free at a manufacturer-sponsored "demo day."

PAUL SAYS

Good equipment makes skiing a joy. Inexpensive or outdated equipment may work on favorable terrain or in good snow conditions—or if you have unusually good balance. But trying to get away with inadequate equipment in more difficult conditions is a prescription for frustration that leads too many people to abandon the sport for good. Cross-country skiing can be a lifetime pleasure, with tremendous physical, mental, and spiritual benefits. Invest accordingly.

Adding Adventure to Your Skiing

Even in its most basic form, skiing is a way to escape housebound winter for a fairyland that feels like a cross between wilderness and a Currier and Ives print. If you're like many skiers, you'll develop favorite routes you return to again and again, reveling in the way familiar landscape is transformed by every shift in weather or snow.

But many cross-country skiers are explorers at heart. Occasionally we crave a change of pace—and variations in routine often create the best memories.

This chapter presents a few suggestions for new ways to experience winter by ski. The fundamental rule is simple: within the confines of safety and your abilities, be as creative as you like.

Try a New Type of Skiing

Do you normally ski on groomed trails? Try venturing off track. Breaking trail in loose snow can be hard work, but the moment you start carving your own tracks you know you're going somewhere no one else has ever been—at least since the last snowfall.

Have you always skied only in the backcountry? Groomed trails may offer less of a wilderness experience, but you'll be stunned by how much easier it is and how much more distance you can cover in a day.

Go by Moonlight

Moonlight transforms everyday terrain into a magical realm of boundless possibilities tinged with an aura of the wild and remote. Also, the evening chill augments even the best powder conditions, allowing you to glide through the night silently, seemingly without effort. Unless you venture into pines or the moon goes behind a cloud, moonlight on snow provides more than enough light to see where you're going, particularly on groomed trails or unplowed roads, where route finding is simple.

The moon is ripe for skiing two or three days before it is full, when sunset finds it high enough in the sky to provide good light. Each day after that, it rises 50 minutes later, forcing you to delay your departure accordingly.

Chapter 6

Carry a thermos of hot chocolate, take a group of special friends, and enjoy more solitude than you will find on even the least crowded days. Even beginners needn't pass up a full moon. Just look for flat terrain with few trees and no dips or creeks you could fall into unawares. The choices range from golf courses to alpine meadows or groomed trail systems in parks or resorts. Trail systems that are normally open only for day use often have extended hours or even guided tours during the full moon.

Although you probably won't need a flashlight while you're on the move, carry one for putting on skis, fishing goodies out of your pack, and the never-to-be-neglected risk of clouds. A headlamp is best, because it's a lot easier to use if you need it to ski out. Make sure you have spare batteries (they don't last long at winter temperatures) and a spare light, just in case.

SKI WITH YOUR DOG

Dogs love snow. Take your dog skiing under canine-friendly conditions, and it will love you forever. Never at a loss for snowballs to chase, even an older dog becomes surprisingly animated in the presence of snow.

Be aware, though, that almost all groomed trail systems prohibit dogs. Those that allow them will probably limit your pet to a few routes. One ski area offers a trail called the Loop de Poop. The name explains one of the reasons dogs are prohibited elsewhere: they like to leave little offerings in the easy-to-squat-on snow of the ski tracks.

Similarly, it doesn't take many dog footprints to ruin carefully laid tracks and earn the ire of both the management and your fellow skiers. Similar concerns may apply on a well-beaten ungroomed route where dozens of skiers have created a path nearly as good as

Dogs love the snow, but be alert to your pet's rest and drinking needs.

© JAN HOLAN

a groomed trail. Take Fido skiing, but plan on taking a lightly traveled route unless you're fortunate enough to live near a ski area with a dog loop.

Do a Photo Outing

When you're first learning to ski, you probably don't want to carry an expensive camera for fear of falling on it. But as you gain skill and confidence, photography can open a new window on the backcountry. Rather than skiing your normal distance, try a shorter trip designed to seek out those intimate moments that make great winter photos: tree limbs fat with snow, a brook winding between three-foot snowbanks, skiers moving single file through falling snow that obscures distant views and gives the impression they are skiing into infinity.

Rick Says

Although skiing with a dog is fun, it requires common sense. Bring something for the dog to drink from and don't go in bitter cold unless you know your dog can tolerate the temperature. Pet stores sell coats and booties for easily chilled animals, but try these out at home before hitting the trail to see if your dog will tolerate them. Also, avoid deep, soft snow, which can be exhausting even for big dogs. You don't want to have to carry your faithful friend back to the trailhead. Finally, consider bringing a leash to control your pet if you meet other skiers. Dog lovers know the difference between an exuberant greeting and a vicious attack, but people who fear dogs often don't.

© DAVID MADISON

You can find beautiful places to ski almost anywhere. Here, an aspen forest.

For padding to both you and the camera in case you fall, wrap the camera in spare clothing and carry it in a backpack. Avoid using a fanny pack—because if you fall you're likely to land on it, hard. Even with a well-protected camera, this isn't the time to explore icy slopes that test your abilities.

The special art of snow photography could be the subject of an entire chapter in an outdoor photography book. Basically, an all automatic point and shoot will bring back decent photos on color print film but will probably disappoint you with slides, which have less exposure latitude. Super-bright snow fools the exposure meter, which tries to tone down that brightness—giving you snow that looks gray rather than white, while trees and people become silhouettes.

If your camera has the flexibility, you can cure this by deliberately overexposing by one or two f-stops—either manually (if your camera has a manual setting) or by dialing the compensation dial to +1 or +2. Shooting a range of exposures in the hopes that one is right also helps.

For photos of your friends, you'll also have exposure problems. The camera will try to expose for the bright snow in the background, and the people will be too dark. In bright sunshine, you'll end up with harsh shadows on their faces.

Again, +1 or +2 on the compensation dial may be the solution. Or, with a manual system or spot meter, move in close, take a meter reading off your friends' faces, then adjust accordingly. Alternatively, you can usually get close to the right exposure by holding your own hand a foot or so in front of the lens and taking a meter reading from it. This assumes, though, that your camera can remember these meter readings when you compose the shot you want.

RICK SAYS

Don't let all this technical photographic talk intimidate you. It's distilled from years of learning from our own mistakes. Snow photography is challenging but rewarding, and a great way to add variety to your skiing. You'll get photos unlike anything most of your nonskiing friends have ever seen, and if you pay attention to the ones that don't come out, as well as those that do, you'll learn quickly.

PAUL SAYS

Two things come to mind when pondering my best cross-country ski photography. The first is to shoot lots of film. The second is to shoot in the morning or late afternoon. Professional photographers refer to these times as the magic hours—although in the North Country midwinter, you get the same low-angle light at midday.

If none of this makes sense to you, your camera may not be sufficiently sophisticated. Read the owner's manual or an introductory book on photography.

Don't limit your photos to sunny days. Cloudy days are lower contrast and may give you better pictures, especially closeups of your friends.

DO A POINT-TO-POINT SKI TREK OR RACE

For many people, nothing builds a sense of accomplishment as much as skiing from one point to another, rather than in a loop.

Typically, the best way to do this is in a citizens' race (open to all-comers), even if you don't like to compete. Many of the participants in these races aren't actually interested in racing—they're taking advantage of the race's support facilities (shuttle service, aid stations, ski patrol) to attempt treks that would be logistically difficult otherwise. The big races have plenty of slow skiers, so you'll probably have company, as long as you're fit enough to go the distance before dark.

Some of these races are quite popular. The Boulder Mountain Tour in Idaho (Galena to Sun Valley) and The Great Race in California (Tahoe City to Truckee) each draw 500 to 900 participants. The American Birkebeiner in Wisconsin (Cable to Hayward) draws over 5,000. Also, some races, particularly east of the Mississippi, have access to private land, allowing routes that are otherwise unavailable. Registration fees vary (and may include substantial late-registration penalties), but expect to pay $25 to $100.

Long races are often called ski marathons, though the low-impact nature of cross-country skiing means they are nowhere nearly as grueling as their running counterparts. But don't enter a long event without several training outings at half the race distance or longer. Cross-country ski areas, ski shops, and cross-country magazines are good sources of information for these various treks.

If mass events and their associated parties aren't your cup of tea, you can set up your own point-to-point tour with a car shuttle. Make sure you have good route information and have a car waiting at the start in case the route doesn't work and you have to backtrack.

ATTEND A SKI FESTIVAL

If you live in a part of the country where there are cross-country ski areas, you may want to attend a ski festival.

Many areas host such festivals, often several times per year. They are the cross-country ski equivalent to small-town harvest festivals or art-and-craft weekends. Often sponsored by equipment companies, they frequently provide opportunities to test the latest equipment at no cost, take reduced-price (or free) ski lessons, participate in citizens' races, and gorge yourself on food, music, sunshine, and the camaraderie of like-minded individuals.

Another prospect is the annual Ski Fest, organized by the Cross Country Ski Areas Association, which represents hundreds of North American ski areas. This event, held on different days at participating ski areas, allows first-timers to try the sport for free by including a beginning lesson, trail pass, and equipment rental in the advance registration price. Contact your local shop or ski center for details.

DO A GOURMET SKI TRIP

Does an opportunity to eat a lot of good food without worrying about gaining weight sound like your idea of heaven? Skiing burns anywhere from several hundred to more than 1,000 calories per hour, depending on how energetically you go at it, so a ski-and-food outing is a natural combination. You can do it yourself or seek a package deal at a cross-country ski area.

If you're doing it yourself, the basic idea is to prepare a multicourse picnic and eat each course at a well-chosen destination, such as a scenic lookout or warming hut. If you're really enterprising, carry a small folding shovel to shape a table and benches from packed snow. Otherwise, carry one or more backpackers' foam sleeping pads (waterproof varieties such as Blue Foam, Ensolite, or Thermarest are mandatory to keep from soaking up moisture) and plop down wherever you like. Turning your skis upside down and sitting on them will also provide a firm sitting platform on soft snow.

Organized outings at cross-country ski areas allow you to let someone else do the preparation. Bear Valley in California, for example, offers a five-course meal scattered along a 10-km route. Appetizers are served at a scenic warming hut, soup and salad at a picnic area, and the main course at another hilltop overlook. A long downgrade leads to coffee and dessert and finally back to the base for champagne and strawberries.

Expect to pay $30 to $40 for the combination of trail pass, food, and guide.

HUT SKIING AND SNOW-CAMPING TOURS

Want to get many of the benefits of a ski backpacking tour with half the effort? Try hut skiing or an organized snow-camping tour. These huts—some are modeled on Mongolian yurts—can be quite warm and comfortable, either as base camps for multiday stays or as way points on a loop. Many national forests provide such huts through concessionaires; some allow you to rent fire towers for the same purpose. Guided tours are particularly appealing, unless you're a fairly advanced skier. For information, contact your local ski shop, the recreation office of the forest you'd like to visit, or the local chapter of an outdoor/environmental group such as the Sierra Club.

Snow camping is another way for your cross-country skiing skills to open new doors to the wilderness. The first time, it's best to go with a group organized by a touring company or outdoor club. Or use a guide service recommended by local ski shops. If you forgo the professionals, make sure you go with

Backcountry huts aren't elaborate, but they help extend the whole skiing experience.

knowledgeable friends or practice a few times within walking distance of a car. We talk more about snow camping in chapter 10 (see page 117).

VISIT A SKI RANCH OR WILDERNESS RESORT

Looking for something a little more posh than a yurt and warmer than a backcountry tent? Many cross-country ski areas have luxurious ski-in lodges, open for overnight stays.

Royal Gorge in California, for example, has a ski lodge ($159+ per day) that features the appealing combination of hot tubs, a pastry chef, ski lessons, and access to hundreds of kilometers of groomed trails. Other ski areas have their own variations on this theme, offering sleigh rides, dogsledding, and food, food, food, along with the typical ski amenities.

CLINICS AND CAMPS

Ski clinics are one-day events designed to help you hone your skills in a particular skiing discipline, such as skating or telemark turns. Camps are multiday events—and you don't have to stay in a tent!

In addition to polishing traditional skills, clinics and camps offer the opportunity to try things you never dreamed of. You can learn to stride like an Olympic champion or practice the ski-and-target-shooting sport known as the Olympic biathlon. You can even learn to ski jump, if you have the nerve.

When you backcountry ski, you might encounter incomparable vistas, such as this half-frozen waterfall in Yellowstone National Park.

PAUL SAYS

There are several ways to find information about ski clinics, camps, tours, or other special events. Ski clubs and ski shops are useful sources of information, and the Cross Country Ski Areas Association maintains a website with links to many of its members' homepages or event calendars. The appendix to this book contains a list of cross-country ski areas, many of which host special events or have overnight accommodations.

Part 2

Cross-Country Skiing 201: Expanding Your Skills

© KARHU

Chapter 7

Ski Skating

© ATOMIC SKI USA

In less than 20 years, ski skating has revolutionized cross-country skiing. Prior to the early 1980s, most people associated skiing with the diagonal stride—anything else was unthinkable. But then, U.S. skier Bill Koch electrified the skiing world by completing the 1982 World Cup using the new marathon skate technique. Using a motion more reminiscent of roller skating than traditional cross-country skiing, Koch not only completed this race series, he won it—demonstrating that "skating," as the technique came to be called, gives you more speed than the diagonal stride. In fact, skating is so much faster that races soon divided into two categories: skating races and "classic" races in which skating is prohibited.

The basic skating concept actually isn't all that new. Generations of skiers have used occasional skating strides simply for a change of pace or to get a better grip on firm, slippery snow. And the familiar uphill herringbone, discussed in chapter 2 (see page 22), is a relative of skating.

What was revolutionary was the idea of committing yourself to doing an entire race (or tour) with no grip wax. As skating evolved, it became obvious that the minor drag of kick wax or the more noticeable drag of a waxless pattern was unacceptable.

The skating revolution soon spawned an entire class of equipment specific to ski skating. This equipment, described in detail in chapter 5 (see page 55), uses skis that are shorter and lighter than traditional skis. Poles are longer than normal, and boots provide exceptionally good ankle support to maximize your ability to push off the edges of the skis—the ski skating substitute for a kick.

Nevertheless, skating won't work well in all snow conditions. In soft, deep backcountry snow, kicking and gliding is still the best mode of locomotion. But other conditions are tailor made for skating. Think of skating whenever you encounter:

- packed snow on groomed trails with wide untracked "skating lanes";

- late-season snow that has been converted into firm pellets of "corn snow" by repeated thaw/freeze cycles;

- crusty snow firm enough that you're not repeatedly punching through it;

- a scant dusting of snow over a frozen lake or golf course;

- those groomed snowmobile trails that permeate so much of the backcountry; or

- any other form of firm, fast-gliding snow.

Getting Started

Skating is arguably an intermediate skiing skill, and your first attempts will be frustrating if you aren't properly prepared. Perfect balance is elusive, even for experienced diagonal-stride skiers, but you can do it if you choose your equipment and snow conditions carefully. Here are some tips to help keep your first skating experience positive.

1. Use the proper equipment; rent skating skis, poles, and boots.

2. Try skating after you've developed good one-ski balance. This means you should be either an intermediate cross-country or downhill skier or proficient at another balance sport such as ice skating, in-line skating, surfing, or water skiing.

3. Pick beginner trails on mostly flat terrain and don't stray too far from the trailhead.

4. Ski on a firm, smooth surface. For backcountry skiers this means hard-packed snow of the type usually found in late spring. For track skiers it means a groomed trail with a separate skating lane devoid of tracks. (Except for the introductory *marathon skate* described below, skating on machine-set tracks is bad etiquette, because a single skater can ruin the track.)

5. Make sure the surface isn't so firm that edge control is limited.

6. Be in good physical condition.

7. Consider taking a lesson from a professional instructor. Lessons are worth the expense (you may be able to find some great beginner deals, particularly midweek) and they'll strongly reinforce the

Paul Says

I can't overemphasize the benefit of being in good cardiovascular shape before making serious attempts to learn skating. Unlike striding, where you can adjust your level of effort to something akin to strolling, even slow-speed skating is aerobically difficult for some—especially when it comes to climbing hills at high elevation in the mountains. But once you've overcome the initial hurdles, you'll discover that skating allows you to ski much faster and farther with the same degree of cardiovascular output.

material presented in this chapter. We recommend that you read this chapter, practice a bit on your own, and then take a lesson. Rereading the chapter after a lesson should help cement what you learned from that lesson and speed your progress.

Poling

In chapter 3, we discussed the double-pole motion, which allows you to propel yourself solely with your poles. For diagonal-stride skiing, double poling is a useful but nonessential skill. For skating, it's mandatory—especially for getting around rolling terrain.

Beginners think of double poling as an arm motion, and they tend to stand stiffly upright as they lever themselves forward with their poles. This is inefficient and exhausting, and it doesn't generate enough oomph to power you up much of a hill. We discussed some of the fine points of double-poling in chapter 3 (see page 34), but it pays to review those now, as well as looking at additional ways to get more power from your double-pole stroke.

Efficient double poling uses several muscles of the upper body in a coordinated effort that transfers most of your body weight onto the poles. It is this transfer of energy and weight that is paramount to strong double poling. By tipping your whole body forward slightly at the ankles, you can ensure that you're doing it properly. As the arms are loaded up with weight, the elbows remain in fixed, comfortably flexed positions. Then, with a push that involves many of the upper body's most powerful muscles, you bend forward at the waist into a deep V, while your hands swing in an arc that has them passing the knees.

Pantomime the hand motion now, referring to the photographs on page 72. Your hands begin at chest height in front of you, then swing low, past your knees. The power for a good double pole comes

Rick Says

I learned to skate (sort of) in a 58-kilometer citizens' race in central Minnesota in the early 1980s—before I'd ever heard anyone apply the term *skating* to cross-country skiing. For about two miles, the course crossed a large frozen lake, during a spring thaw. There was still plenty of ice, but the snow that had once been on top of it had melted into vast, shallow puddles—underlain by ice too solid for double poling. Desperate not to bruise or soak myself in a fall, I skittered around for several minutes seeking a workable method of locomotion, eventually coming up with what would today be viewed as a choppy, shuffling skate that took me efficiently, if not rapidly, to drier surfaces.

Years later, necessity again forced me to work on skating techniques when, frustrated by the incessant *zip-zip-zip* noise of no-wax skis on groomed trails, I attempted to use my Minnesota racing skis (which have to be waxed) in the Oregon Cascades. As will be discussed in chapter 12, waxable skis are difficult to use in the 28° to 35°F temperatures common in Pacific Northwest mountains, because a 500-foot hill can involve enough temperature change top-to-bottom to force you to stop and re-wax, sometimes more than once. On this particular outing, the wax that gave me a good kick at the top of the hill was mediocre halfway down and useless at the bottom. Rather than rewaxing every kilometer or so, I waxed for the hilltop and skated—on over-long touring skis—elsewhere.

Shortly thereafter I took a skating lesson, using proper equipment. I was amazed by how much simpler skating was on the right type of skis.

from three sets of muscles: first the triceps (the muscles at the back of your arms), then the shoulders (the latissimus dorsi, etc.) and abdominal muscles. Of these, the abdominals seem the oddest when you're beginning, because you associate them with doing sit-ups, not with bending forward at the waist. But it's the same motion, and by adding the abdominals to the effort, you can transfer their strength to the poles for more push than you could obtain from the triceps and lats alone. Think of your body as hinging from the waist (not at the knees) with the force of the hinge-swinging motion being transferred to your poles.

Proper forward lean with skate double-poling.

© DAVID MADISON

An effective double-pole stroke uses arms, shoulders, and abdominal muscles.

Double poling ends with a follow-through to the rear, as you gain additional push before the poles lose contact with the snow behind you. At the end of a good follow-through, your pole and arm will form a straight line angled toward the snow behind you. The angle will depend on the vigor of your double poling, which will be affected in turn by your poling tempo and ground speed. If you're poling strongly at high speed, you will have a lot of follow-through. At slower speeds, you will have less.

Before moving on to skating, find a nice flat course about the size of a 400-meter track and practice double poling for several minutes. But don't overly tire yourself—unless you've been working out in a weight room, you may not be good for more than an hour or two of skating practice the first time out.

SKATING STEPS

Once you're reasonably confident that you've mastered the basics of double poling, it's time to move on to the fancy footwork.

If you've ever ice skated or roller skated, ski skating won't feel too alien once you're used to your "skates" being several feet long and to having poles. If you've tried neither of these other sports, ski skating may be a bit harder to learn. Basically, instead of the downward kick of the classic diagonal stride, you'll be do-

ing a sideways push-off from the inside edge of a ski that is sliding away from you at an angle. That means that like the diagonal-stride kick, it's a fairly quick move (otherwise you wind up falling down as your skis run off in different directions). As you do this sideways push-off from one ski, you not only propel yourself forward but also launch your weight away from it, onto the other ski, centering your balance there for an extended glide. The push-off ski quickly loses contact with the snow, and you bring it in underneath you, ready to set back onto the snow for the next stroke.

There are three basic types of skating moves, plus several variations. We will focus principally on the three basics—the marathon skate, the V1, and the diagonal skate—and then briefly discuss three advanced moves. The goal is to help you develop a strong, confident V1 that can carry you across most of the terrain you're likely to encounter—and to develop a hill-climbing method to carry you over anything else. But first we'll start with the easier-to-learn marathon skate.

The Marathon Skate

This is the move popularized by Koch in his World Cup triumph. It's sometimes called a *half-skate* because the skating motion occurs with only one leg, while the other ski rides along in a groomed track.

The marathon skate.

© PAUL PETERSEN

It's one skating move you can do reasonably well on nonskating skis, making it great for a change of pace or for snow conditions when your skis are slipping.

Begin the marathon skate with one ski in the track and the other angled to the outside in the packed snow adjacent to it. To avoid unnecessarily rigid references to "left" and "right," we'll refer to one ski as the "track-bound" ski and the other as the "free" or "angled" ski. It doesn't matter which ski you choose to leave in the track, although most people find it easier to skate with one free ski than the other. To minimize track damage, put the track-bound ski in the groove that keeps the angled one farthest from the track (e.g., if your angled ski is the left one, stand in the left groove). Unlike with other skating moves, you

don't have to worry if your ski tails cross behind you, because the two skis are at different elevations: one recessed in the track and the other safely above it.

Start at a standstill, angling the free ski outward by perhaps 20 to 30 degrees. The ideal angle will depend on such factors as snow conditions, how fast you want to go, the slope, and your desired skating cadence. Pointing the ski out at a broad angle will produce a short, choppy stride that's useful for going uphill but doesn't give you much glide on the level; a shallow angle will give you a long, slow skating rhythm that's great for fast snow or downgrades but might not give you enough push under other conditions. Make sure you plant your poles outside of the angle formed by your skis, to avoid skiing across them—the skier's equivalent of tripping over your shoelaces.

The basic motion combines a sideways push-off from the angled ski with a simultaneous double-pole stroke, for a strong forward push. The other ski merely goes along for the ride, confined to its lane of track. It will keep you going the proper direction—including around corners—while you concentrate on skating and poling.

The double-poling motion is identical to that which you've already practiced, although you'll be forced to plant one pole farther to the side than usual, to keep it away from the angled ski. The asymmetrical pole plant means you won't be able to push equally strongly on the two poles. Don't worry about it. When one arm (or leg) gets tired, you can simply reverse which side of the track you're using for skating and work with the other side of your body.

As was discussed earlier, the skating push-off on the angled ski is very similar to ice skating. To get the ski to bite into the snow, tip your ankle enough for the inside edge to dig into the snow. Remember to push sideways, perpendicular to the edged ski, not backward. As you push off the angled ski, shift your weight onto the track-bound ski, centering it over that ski so it stays flat and glides freely without digging in an edge. If you make this weight transfer correctly, your hip will be directly above the gliding ski.

As you push off and double pole, your body travels forward in the direction of the track-bound ski, while the angled ski runs off in the direction in which it's pointed. You'll probably feel like you're about to do a split, but you avoid that uncomfortable end in exactly the same way an ice skater does: by lifting the angled ski up off the snow and stepping it sideways for another stroke. Time this to coincide with your next double-pole plant for a simple, coupled rhythm in which you push simultaneously with the poles and the angled ski, glide on the track-bound ski, then simultaneously plant your poles and the free ski for the next stroke.

At first, your balance may feel precarious during the recovery interval between skating strokes, when you're briefly gliding on one ski. You'll probably find yourself trying to get the angled ski back on the ground as quickly as possible as an antidote to wobbly balance. But the moment that ski touches, you have to start the next skating stroke, which puts you in a rapid, energy-wasting rhythm. That's okay at first, but as your balance improves, work on slowing down that rhythm by stretching out a long glide on the track-bound ski. With the glide thrown in, the marathon skating rhythm becomes

1. push off on angled ski and poles,

2. glide on track-bound ski, and

3. plant poles and angled ski for next push-off

With practice, that *push, glide, plant* rhythm extends into *push, g-l-i-d-e, push, g-l-i-d-e*, as you simultaneously extend the glide and merge the ski-and-pole plant into the start of the next push-off. Remember: your skating skis are designed to glide far better than touring skis. It makes sense to get as much glide out of them as possible.

The marathon skate is a bit like pushing yourself along on a skateboard, but there are two important differences: your foot is pushing off sideways, not backward, and unlike a skateboard, the track-bound ski is attached to your foot. You can take advantage of this by shifting your weight back strongly onto the angled ski at the start of each skating stroke, thereby setting up the strongest possible skating push-off. If you did this on a skateboard, it would roll off without you. But the track-bound ski must stay attached to your foot, even if you take so much weight off it that your heel lifts away from the ski.

VI or "Offset" Skate

The name "V1" comes from the fact there's only one double-pole move for each complete cycle. This is your all-around, all-terrain skating move. It works on the flats, uphills, and even down gentle downgrades. Better yet, it's not all that hard to learn, especially with a few simple drills. When mastered, it's an elegant side-to-side move that reminds many people of waltzing but that can be twice as fast as the diagonal stride, despite all that zigzagging.

PAUL SAYS

The marathon skate is not only the easiest skating move to learn, but it's also a good drill for learning the V1 and V2 skates. Practice enough to be proficient at skating with either your left or right foot in the track. Try it without poles to further increase your balance and skate stroke effectiveness. Try not to be too "squatty," or bent at the knees—this can become a bad habit that's difficult to correct later.

RICK SAYS

One reason skating is so much faster than the diagonal stride is that both of your skis are always moving forward, even when you're pushing off. In the diagonal stride, the kicking ski must momentarily come to rest as it grips the snow for each kick. That's a limiting factor that puts a cap on your velocity.

Like the marathon skate, the V1 combines a side ways skating push with double-poling. But in this case there's no track and both skis are angled, forcing you to push off first with one leg and then the other while gliding on the nonskating ski—exactly like an ice skater. What differentiates the V1 from other skating moves is that you double pole on every alternate skating stroke. This means you'll alternate between a *strong* side—the ski on which you're gliding while executing both a leg stroke and the double poling—and a *weak* side, on which only the leg stroke occurs, while your arms rest.

The rhythm goes like this: *pole-skate, skate, pole-skate, skate.*

You'll probably find this rhythm to be more natural with one strong-side ski than the other; for the moment it doesn't matter which side you favor. What does matter is the timing of the pole plant. Here's a drill that emphasizes the proper coordination, without forcing you to concentrate too much on one-ski balance:

Stand in place with your skis in a V and holding only your right pole. Raise that pole and your right ski off the ground. All of your weight and balance is now on the left ski. Now, step down on the right side, planting the pole's basket in the snow at the same time the ski touches down. Notice that two things—pole and ski—are hitting the snow together. Pick up the left ski so you're standing on the right one (pole still in contact with the ground), then step back down on the left ski. On that side, only one thing, the ski, lands. Repeating this gives you a rhythm of *two, one, two, one.*

Once you feel comfortable doing this drill standing in place, try moving forward slowly with a little pole push and a gentle skating motion, maintaining that *two, one, two, one* rhythm. A slight downhill slope helps here, particularly if the snow is a bit slow.

The V1 skating rhythm is pole-skate, skate, pole-skate, skate.

Now, pick up your other pole, converting the pole plant into a double pole that is timed to match the landing of the right ski on the snow. The rhythm becomes *three, one, three, one* because now three things (two pole baskets and one ski) are hitting the snow at the same time. Swing your hips back and forth with a slight twisting motion to ensure good weight transfer.

Congratulations: you're doing the V1. But before you're off and running, remember to practice the same drills on the left side so you don't become a one-side skater. To improve your balance, try skating on a smooth, flat or slightly downhill surface without poles, but with your arms making poling movements.

As you gain confidence, keep working on transferring your weight fully to the gliding ski—back and forth, back and forth. At first, this is going to feel too tippy, and you'll have a tendency not to fully commit yourself. But that hesitation is self-defeating; it sacrifices glide by making it impossible to keep the gliding ski flat to the snow.

There are two commonly used indicators of whether you've fully committed yourself to the necessary weight transfer for the V1. One is the motion of your hips. With each skating stride, one hip should wind up centered over the gliding ski—right hip if you're gliding on the right ski, left hip if you're on the left ski. The other indicator is that your toes, knees, and nose momentarily line up vertically over the gliding ski, shifting back and forth as you transfer your weight from one ski to the other. If you want a mnemonic, imagine "Tony," the all-seeing guru of skiing. "Tony knows" equals "toes, knees, nose." As with the marathon skate, try to avoid getting too squatty, or bent at the knees.

Committing yourself to the weight transfer will help you extend your glide by allowing you (with a bit of practice) to keep the ski flatter against the snow. It also allows you to use a narrower V, permitting more forward motion with each stroke. Experts often challenge themselves by noting the tracks left by previous skaters and trying to achieve a narrower V than any of them did. It'll take you a while to get that good, but watching these powerful skaters in motion helps show how much glide can be achieved once you've perfected your balance.

Diagonal Skate

Using the V1 skate, it's possible to skate uphill by shortening your stroke and quickening your tempo. But if the hills get too steep, you'll probably stall out. That's the time for the diagonal skate, which can be thought of as something like a "flying herringbone"—although on the toughest hills "flying" may seem like a misnomer.

The diagonal skate is the simplest hill-climbing move available for skating. It's basically just the old-fashioned herringbone with a bit of glide thrown in. It doesn't even involve double poling. Instead, as in the herringbone, the poles are planted individually, synchronized with the moment the diagonally opposite ski hits the snow. But instead of merely stepping up the hill, you use a forceful skating push-off and weight transfer from each well-edged ski.

To practice, try doing a herringbone *down* a very gentle slope. This will allow you to glide without a lot of effort and without building up too much speed. Practice until you've found the rhythm, then try a gentle upgrade. Take little steps and make quick explosive movements at the ankles to generate the power to glide a short distance on each ski. To get more glide, emphasize the side-to-side movement of your body toward the ski that's currently hitting the snow, using the pole push to help you sway back and forth. As you get better, you can move to increasingly

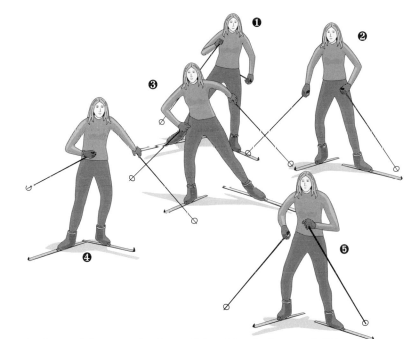

The diagonal skate marries the traditional herringbone and glide.

steep terrain. But you don't have to wait for the terrain to get steep to use the diagonal skate; try it for a break when you're simply feeling tired or for a change of pace on a long outing.

Other Skating Moves

Three other skating moves are frequently used, but they warrant only brief discussion except among aspiring experts. These are *skating with no poles*, *V2 skating* (called the *two skate* in Canada), and the *V2 alternate skate* (the *one skate* in Canada).

Skating with no poles isn't the same thing as the drill of practicing a V1 or marathon skate without poles. It's a fully developed skating motion that doesn't use a pole plant. It's most often used for

powering downhill at faster than gliding speed, although you can use it on flats if your skis are gliding well and you want to rest your arms. Rather than planting your poles to push, you hold them off the ground while swinging your arms freely, both for balance and to help you gain momentum. The arm swing is *cross lateral*, like the diagonal skate, with one arm swinging forward and the other backward. Like an ice skater's speed skating arm swing, it's a fairly forceful motion, although not as forceful as poling.

V2 skating uses two double-poling motions for each complete movement cycle. That is, unlike the V1, where there are two skating strokes for each double pole, the V2 requires you to double pole each time you take a skating stroke with either ski. Furthermore, rather than the *three, one, three, one* pole-and-ski-plant rhythm of the V1, the pole plant for the V2 occurs before the push-off ski hits the snow, while you're gliding on the other ski (with your feet close together). The skating stroke begins just as your hands pass your legs, midway through the poling motion. This move's downside is that it's hard to balance long enough on one ski; it's upside is that once mastered, it's a very fast way to cover flat terrain and even the occasional hill.

The V2 alternate skate combines features from the V1 and V2. The timing of the pole plant is similar to the V2, but like the V1, poling is done only when skating on one side. The move is similar enough to the V1 that, to the untrained eye, the two are difficult to distinguish. The easiest way to tell them apart is by noticing that with the V2 alternate, the poles hit the snow when the feet are together between each skate stroke and start backward before the skating stroke begins to widen the stance. With the V1, the poles hit the snow simultaneously with the ski and move backward with the skating push-off.

Skating without poles.

enough skiing practice to effectively balance on one ski. If this is one of your problems, practice double poling with one ski held up off the ground. Also, while it's important not to squat deeply, some amount of ankle and knee flexion is required at the start of each skating stroke to shift your weight effectively off the edged ski onto the new glide ski.

Finally, proper timing of your pole plant is crucial. Review the descriptions of when the poles hit the snow and how that changes for each of the skating moves discussed in this chapter. Errors in timing may leave you stalling out on uphills or unable to shift your weight completely to the gliding ski.

PAUL SAYS

What's the use of the V2 alternate? It's the easiest way to go really fast on the flats. But it becomes a real dog on uphills, so be sure to get the V1 down pat before you try it.

RICK SAYS

Don't be afraid to experiment with technique as you're learning. It's a good way to discover what works . . . and what doesn't. Watch what other skiers do and try to imitate those you admire. During the halcyon era of the early 1980s, when skating was brand new and nobody really knew what they were doing, some world-class racers came to competitions intending to skate with one style—only to be forced to learn new techniques mid-race from faster competitors. In my own early, untutored skating efforts, I stumbled on the diagonal skate and the V2 long before anyone taught me the V1.

TROUBLESHOOTING

Once you've figured out the basic coordination of movements, difficulty with any skating move usually stems from one of three basic problems.

First, you need good edge control. This means you need to be able to tip your ski to any desired angle between completely flat and strongly onto its inside edge. Flat is important for gliding; total, nonslipping edge engagement is important for each push-off. If the ski slides out to the side, something is wrong—possibly with your equipment. Decent skating skis and tight boots with hinged, plastic cuffs, secured around the ankles, are mandatory.

Second, it's very important to be able to shift your weight all the way back and forth from one ski to the other. Inability to do this is why beginning cross-country skiers can't skate. They simply haven't had

The V2 skate has a poling rhythm that differs from the V1.

© JAN HOLAN

Just as skating has rewritten the book for track skiing, telemark skiing has opened up downhill runs that once were the exclusive domain of alpine skiers. Imported from the Telemark region of Norway, this style of hill descent was popularized in North America in the 1970s. Today it has gained an almost cultlike following. Its hallmark is the graceful telemark turn, in which the skier seems almost to drop to one knee on the mountainside, only to rise again and again in a series of perfectly controlled S-curves.

In this book, we'll generally use the term *telemarking* to refer to this elegant, drop-knee turn. But when other people refer to *going telemarking* they may not be being so precise. Particularly in the United States, *telemark* has come to mean any form of downhill skiing on cross-country (or "free-heel") skis.

Even if skiing at a downhill resort isn't your normal cup of tea, it's useful to take advantage of a ski area's groomed slopes to learn the basics of telemarking. Once you've mastered them, you can carry the same

Chapter 8

PAUL SAYS

There are lots of reasons for taking up telemarking. Experienced alpine skiers may want to try it as a new approach to overly familiar downhill runs. Other people want to practice turns on groomed snow in preparation for wandering into the backcountry. Still others may see telemarking as a challenging way to add a new dimension to their cross-country ski experience.

The dropped-knee telemarking position requires a fluid rising and sinking from turn to turn that not only feels good but *looks* like fun, too. Onlookers are apt to comment on how elegant and difficult it appears, adding, "Gee, are those really cross-country skis?" Frankly, a lot of us get into telemarking just because we're drawn by the combination of grace, power, and control. Also, it's something we cross-country skiers can do that alpine skiers, with their fixed-heel bindings, can't. Sometimes, "different" is good.

RICK SAYS

Where I live in the Pacific Northwest, part of the popularity of telemarking is related to the even greater popularity of mountain climbing. Several famous Cascade volcanoes, including Mt. St. Helens, Mt. Hood, and Washington's 12,200 foot Mt. Adams, have extended slopes that are no steeper than expert runs at downhill ski areas. Each year, hundreds of people climb these mountains in hiking boots, then strap on telemarking skis for fast, graceful descents. But first, they've practiced at downhill areas.

techniques and equipment to the less predictable conditions of backcountry touring, opening up realms of solitude and alpine beauty.

As any downhill skier knows, turns are the easiest way to shed unwanted speed on long downhills—the alternatives being heavy-duty snowplowing, descending the hill at an extremely shallow traverse, or repeatedly falling down. Telemarking is popular because the dropped-knee position puts one tip ahead of the other, effectively giving you longer skis for greater fore/aft turning stability. Also, you can do it in deep powder or other difficult snow conditions in which an attempt to snowplow would stop you so abruptly you'd pitch face forward.

Although the telemark turn can be performed on any free-heel ski setup, for really getting down a mountain in a controlled descent it's important to use the right kind of equipment. This generally requires metal-edged skis with lots of sidecut, sturdy boots with good ankle support, and bindings that are beefy enough to take wicked crashes in stride. See chapter 5 (page 57) for details. When skiing at a downhill ski area, you also need safety straps to secure your skis to your boots in the unlikely event a

binding releases. This not only is important to the safety of any skiers who might be below you, but is generally required by law.

Once you have the proper equipment, you can start learning to telemark. This means you'll learn an arsenal of turns that begin with the already-familiar wedge turn and include step, parallel, and telemark turns.

FIRST POLISH YOUR WEDGE

Let's review wedge-turning skills. Basic athletic stance? Check. Skis in a narrow V? Check. Weight centered over the middle of the feet? Check. Strong steering from the outside foot and knee, complemented by appropriate steering of the inside foot and knee? Check. If you don't know what any of these mean, review the discussions of wedge turns and wedge christies in chapters 2 and 3 (see pages 27 and 36). Now go out and do a hundred of these turns. Then do a hundred more, just for good measure.

Good wedge skills are important to telemarking because they are the foundation on which you're going to build advanced turning skills. Also, the advanced turns are easier to master if you're sufficiently familiar with what you feel and do while completing a wedge turn. So, get your wedge turn down until it's automatic. Make sure you use both your feet and your knees in executing the turn—and don't fall victim to the "dead inside leg" syndrome, in which your inside leg is merely going along for the ride. It will come back to haunt you if you don't cure it now.

While you're practicing, try adjusting your turn radius from medium to long to short. Try going faster and slower. First practice on gentle terrain, then seek out steeper slopes until you're adequately challenged. And don't fret: all of this practice will pay off big-time later on.

THE TELEMARK GENUFLECTION

Once you've mastered wedge turns and wedge christies, the next step is to learn the basic telemark position, which reminds many people of genuflection or a curtsy.

Try it first while stationary on a flat surface. Start with the basic athletic stance (knees slightly bent, skis parallel, feet flat, hands in front, head up), then slide one foot forward and the other backward until the toe of the trailing foot is about a boot-length behind the heel of the other. Dip the rear knee and feel your center of gravity sink lower over the skis. This lowered center of gravity is another reason the telemark position allows for stable, controlled turns—even for hard-core ski mountaineers carrying 70-pound backpacks. Keep your head up (so you can watch where you're going); keep your body upright but not arched backward. The rear knee will be the most heavily flexed, but you'll also be bending the front knee. Except for the unbowed head, if you were to sink all the way down until the rear knee touched the ground, you'd be in a position similar to a Catholic genuflecting before the altar or a medieval knight preparing to be honored by his king.

Now switch leads in a moonwalking-type shuffle. Then try jumping into the telemark position, landing if you can with your weight equally divided between the front and back skis. More specifically, about half of your weight will be distributed evenly across the front foot, while the other half is on the ball of the rear foot. The heel of the rear foot will be slightly raised. When your weight is evenly distributed between the two skis, you'll find that your hips are centered, front to back between your feet.

The telemark position near the top of a telemark run.

© PAUL PETERSEN

Now, try shuffling from one lead foot to the other while gliding straight down a very gentle hill. The goal is to practice the telemark position without worrying about turning or stopping, so make sure the hill isn't too steep. Once you're proficient at this, you can graduate to a gentle descending traverse on a slightly steeper but still shallow downhill. Again, you want to practice the telemark position itself and the art of shifting from one lead ski to the other. If you can maintain your balance, do all of these drills without planting your poles.

TURNING THE TELEMARK

So far you've been telemarking in a straight line. Now you're ready to make your first turn. Lead up to it with a few linked wedge turns down a gentle slope. Then, wedge into a turn and telemark out of it by sinking into the telemark position as you finish the wedge turn, leading with your downhill ski. Do it again, by rising from the telemark position into the wedge position, executing the turn, and sinking back into the telemark position on a new lead foot.

Do it again, and again: rise and sink, rise and sink. It's important to keep the wedge very narrow (i.e., don't let the tails spread too far apart) to make it easier to turn both skis and keep them from winding up in a T-bone position. If you still find your ski tips trying to cross, try doing only a single turn at a time rather than linking them in sequence. To stop between turns, drop into the telemark position

while you're traversing the hill between wedge turns (again, leading with the downhill foot) and twist both of your feet and both knees in the up-slope direction. This should generate a nice round turn until you come to a halt. Reorganize yourself and try another turn, coming to a halt afterward in a similar manner. Try this 10 or 15 times, turning in each direction.

Telemark turns.

Now you're ready to commit to a full telemark turn. Start in the genuflected traverse position with the downhill ski leading. This time, as you rise to the turn, begin guiding and pointing the tips of both skis toward the fall line, without wedging. At the same time, your feet will begin switching leads automatically, so your new downhill foot will wind up on lead when you complete the turn. Be methodical and determined, not backing off as your speed increases through the fall line. Begin the new sinking motion as you continue to twist, point, and coerce your ski tips around the turn. As you sink, think about relaxing into the final part of the turn, twisting and edging appropriately for the snow conditions. If you've taken our advice and practiced a lot of wedge turns, you should have a good feeling for what's needed.

The turn will leave you traversing in the opposite direction as before but leading on the new downhill ski. From this position it's easy to curve into the hillside for a controlled stop between turns—something you'll almost certainly want to do at first.

For the moment, don't worry too much about what you're doing with your poles—you'll probably find yourself planting them at random in hurried efforts to keep your balance. Use them as necessary. As you pick up speed midway through the turn, believe that if you got halfway around it, the same twisting and edging techniques will get you the rest of the way into a nice, controllable traverse. And, for heaven's sake, don't try your first telemark turns on a slope so steep you're terrified of accelerating wildly out of control, downhill.

If you have problems, double-check the basics:

- hips centered between the feet
- body in the basic athletic stance with hands to the front
- weight evenly distributed between the ball of the rear foot and the entire sole of the front foot
- ankles and knees comfortably flexed
- both skis twisted and edged simultaneously, with twisting pressure coming from the knees, feet, and ankles

Think about how your body feels as you're executing a turn. For example, you should feel the big toe of the front foot and the little toe of the rear foot pushing into the snow as the skis' inside edges engage more firmly. Also, imagine you have a flashlight strapped in front of your leading-leg knee. To turn, point that flashlight in the direction you wish to go.

To get your feet and ankles actively involved, pretend there's a cigarette butt under the arch of your leading foot and another under the ball of the rear foot. Try to grind out each of them in the familiar gesture of litterbug smokers. It may not be the most ecologically sensitive analogy for a pristine mountain environment, but it will help you execute a nice, strong turn.

Finally, think of each turn as forming a smooth, round arc like a C instead of a J—or worse yet, an L or Z.

RICK SAYS

It helps to understand the physics of the turning process. Although you tend to think of your skis as straight, they aren't. Instead, they have an hourglass shape, with a comparatively thin waist directly beneath your feet. (On super-sidecut skis, this is exaggerated enough to be unmistakable.) Twisting your skis with your knees and ankles helps force them in the direction you want to go, but it also engages the edges on the side toward which you're turning. Combined with simply tipping the skis with your ankles, this digs in that curving flank to make them want to track in a curve similar to their sidecut, especially if they have metal edges. If you dig in a ski's left edge, it'll curve left; dig in its right edge and it'll go right. The harder the edging pressure you put on it, the sharper the bend. If you don't believe this, coast down a gentle slope and see how much you can turn simply by rocking your ankles. As your telemarking skills improve, you'll find you start a turn by twisting and steering with the skis relatively flat to the snow, but you finish by actively engaging the edges to take advantage of the sidecut to "carve" the last part of the turn.

LINKING TURNS

Once you can make a smooth, comfortable turn, it's time to link two or more together. It's best to start on a very gentle groomed slope that offers a broad, obstacle-free path running directly downhill. Start by gliding slowly down the hill and dropping into the telemark position over and over again. Be sure to switch lead skis each time. Use your poles for balance if you have to. Do about 10 of these lead-switching knee drops; then, between lead switches, start adding the twisting and edging forces you applied earlier when doing single turns. Concentrate on twisting and edging both skis, not just the front one.

As before, you'll come out of each turn leading with the downhill ski, but instead of turning into the hill and stopping, rise and prepare for the next turn. As one turn merges into another, you'll find that linked telemarking feels a bit like the basic diagonal stride, with a turn thrown in with each step. And since you're on a gentle slope with no fear of running away out of control, your first linked turns can be quite shallow, becoming sharper as you gain confidence.

Beware of the number-one nemesis of the beginning telemark turner. Do not lean too strongly into the turn. Repeat after us: *don't lean in.* You're going to have to fight your natural instinct. Bicyclists lean strongly into turns. Water-skiers do the same. Beginning telemarkers shouldn't. Instinct tells us to anticipate what we think will be a high-speed maneuver. But your first telemark turn won't be a high-g turn or anything close to it. If you lean strongly to the inside, you'll just wind up falling over sideways—harmless, but frustrating. As you learn to make faster turns, you will indeed start leaning into them to keep centrifugal forces from toppling you outward, but that's so natural you won't have to think about it. Your instinct will be to lean in far too strongly.

Your other major nemesis is likely to be a tendency to transfer all of your weight to the outside ski as you round each bend. People with downhill skiing experience are particularly prone to this mistake, which can cause you to pitch forward into a sprawling headfirst fall. Avoid it by feeling your weight and hips settle between your feet.

Another error common to beginning telemarkers is a tendency to over-rotate the shoulders and hips as you make the turn. This isn't the best way to generate the turning forces your skis need, although it can be used as a last resort in nasty snow conditions where the skis just don't want to come around. Generally, you want to turn with your feet and knees. Focus on doing this properly while you're on easy terrain. It's mandatory to get the lower body involved when you graduate to quicker turns on steeper terrain. With practice, turning with the lower body will leave your upper body facing somewhat downhill between bends, as your lower body twists back and forth beneath it. This is called *anticipating* the next turn, and it helps make one turn blend into the next. We'll talk about this in more depth when we get to parallel turns in chapter 9 (see page 98).

Once you've linked a few turns, however crudely, it's time to refine your technique by adding some rhythm and the sense that you are flowing smoothly from one turn to the next. As you rise and sink from the telemark curtsy, make the up-and-down movement slow and steady. When you drop down, don't sink to a really low position, as you may have seen experts do, or you may be calling on more strength than you have when it comes to executing the turn.

Proper pole position in a telemark turn.

© PAUL PETERSEN

You can also start thinking about what you do with your poles, rather than just flailing them around to cure wobbly balance. Some people double pole at the midpoint between turns; you'll probably be more comfortable planting the downhill pole at the start of the turn and more-or-less skiing around it as you carve the turn. This is unnecessary on gentle slopes, however, and as with almost any other skiing skill, a good drill is to practice telemark turns without planting your poles. When you do use your poles, make sure you hold your hands low for optimum stability and lowest center of gravity. Keep the inside arm well in front of the body to help keep your weight properly balanced over your skis rather than rocked backward.

As you get better, let yourself run at faster speeds or move onto steeper slopes. Shape a turn more like a C when you want to bleed off some speed. Shape it like an elongated S if you don't want to slow down too much or if the terrain isn't very steep.

TELEMARKING IN POWDER

Telemarking really comes into its own in fine, cold powder, the type of snow that's never seen a thaw and is still as light as thistledown. Carving linked turns through up to a foot of snow like this is one of skiing's finest sensations—one you'll be revisiting in dreams for weeks to come.

Before venturing into powder, make sure your skis are wide enough to float well, without digging in so deeply they plow difficult-to-control, knee-deep grooves down the mountain. Also, make sure they are soft flexing, so they'll come around the turns easily. It's not impossible to ski powder with stiff skis, but because such skis won't turn as quickly, you'll be forced to go faster, in shallower turns.

Since there are no commonly used measures of ski stiffness, familiarity with the equipment is the best way to tell the difference between soft and stiff skis. Ask an experienced friend, an instructor, or a ski shop clerk if your skis are adequate.

On the snow, there are two key ingredients to successful powder skiing. First, make sure you have

Hands are in good position for proper pole use.

© PAUL PETERSEN

ample weight on your rear ski. This is important because powder drags on your feet, making it easy to pitch forward in spectacular "faceplants" that may be entertaining to bystanders but aren't as much fun for the "plantee"—especially when they fill your goggles with snow.

The second key to powder skiing is to avoid leaning too far into the turns. You'll find you want to anticipate a turn and lean inward before you start it. But if the skis don't swing around as quickly as you thought they would, presto—you're on your side, looking like a toppled snowman.

If the powder's really deep or if the base beneath it isn't firm, getting up after a fall can be tricky. As always, before trying to stand, make sure your skis are on the downhill side of your body, parallel to each other and not pointed up- or downslope, so they won't start sliding the moment you put weight on them. Your biggest problem may be lack of a solid surface to push against as you try to stand. Rather than sinking a pole three feet deep in fluff in a vain

Falling in powder can be fun, even for experienced skiers.

© BRUCE INGERSOLL

search for a firm push-off, remember the trick we discussed in chapter 2 (see page 17). Slide off the wrist straps and place both poles flat on the snow on the uphill side, crossed in an X. This creates a platform against which you can push yourself back to your feet with some degree of grace and much less frustration.

Skiing in deep powder, you have two options to help you turn without fighting the snow. One is to let your body rise and sink more aggressively than usual with each turn, "porpoising" in and out of the snow. Properly timed, this aggressive bobbing brings your skis up out of the snow at the start of each curve, momentarily lifting some of your weight off them. You can start turning your skis when they're light, continuing to steer as your returning weight drives them back into the snow. This works well on steep, deep snow and in some snow conditions on more gentle terrain.

The other alternative is to be less aggressive, trying to keep your head at a nearly constant height. Although you still rise and sink slightly through each turn, this more passive approach involves no major up-and-down movement. It works well in medium-depth powder on slopes that aren't particularly steep. Experiment with the two styles and decide which you like better.

PAUL SAYS

You're going to fall occasionally, so as you comb the snow out of your hair or sit down to remove a ski to get lumps of packed powder out of the binding, you might as well learn some of the lingo. A total, spread-eagled sprawl is a *full-frontal faceplant*. Skid a bit, and you can call it a *noseplow*. Tumble, and you can refer to a trip *through the windshield* or *over the handlebars*. A really spectacular wipeout that strews equipment over half the mountainside is a *blowout* or a *yard sale*, but you'd better not get into the kind of steep country that produces these—or be carrying a loaded backpack—when you're learning. And you'll minimize all of this fun by making sure you keep between 40 and 75 percent of your weight on your rear foot!

Telemark Variants for Steep Terrain, Bumps, and Crud

There are three other forms of telemark turning that can prove quite
useful in variable terrain: one-step,
two-step, and hop telemarking.

The one-step turn simply incor-
porates a small step turn at the
start to help you turn more
quickly. While traversing at the
start of the turn, simply pick up
the uphill ski and step-turn (tips
close, tails apart) it to point at a
sharper downhill angle. Now,
stand on it with more than half
your weight. As you start to turn,
drive both skis around the turn by
steering strongly with your feet
and knees. When you do this with
linked turns, the rhythm is *step
and steer, step and steer.*

The two-step turn is for particularly pathetic snow such as the
heavy, wet stuff known on the
West Coast as "Sierra cement" or
"Cascade concrete." You can also
use this turn if you are timid because the slope is too steep or you
find yourself in a large mogul
field. Begin by stepping with the
uphill ski as in the one-step turn.
But rather than relying solely on
steering to get your inside ski
around the bend, transfer all your
weight to the outside ski and step
the inside ski around parallel to it.
This, along with rebalancing your
weight between both skis, com-
pletes the turn. The rhythm for
each turn is *step, steer, step; step,
steer, step.* At a more aggressive
tempo it becomes *step, step, balance; step, step, balance.*

88

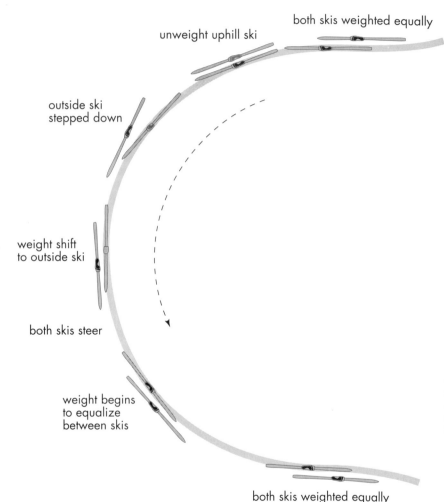

both skis weighted equally

unweight uphill ski

outside ski
stepped down

weight shift
to outside ski

both skis steer

weight begins
to equalize
between skis

both skis weighted equally

Positions for the one-step telemark turn.

When all else fails, the hop telemark can get you out of (or sometimes into) trouble in a hurry. This athletic maneuver is done by jumping up from a telemark traverse position and twisting the skis most of the way around the turn in the air. Switch leads in the air to land in a stable telemark position on the opposite traverse. Needless to say, this is an advanced maneuver. It's favored by steep-terrain skiers, although it can also work in crusty snow that would otherwise lock your skis into a straight line. Jump off both feet, or you won't land on both feet.

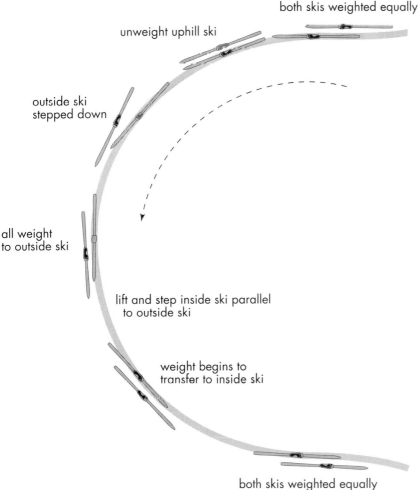

both skis weighted equally

unweight uphill ski

outside ski
stepped down

all weight
to outside ski

lift and step inside ski parallel
to outside ski

weight begins to
transfer to inside ski

both skis weighted equally

Positions for the two-step telemark turn.

Backcountry Skiing

© KARHU

Backcountry skiing doesn't necessarily mean venturing deep into the wilderness. You're drawing on backcountry skills any time you leave the groomed trails, ski slopes, or gentle parklands on which you've practiced your beginning and intermediate skills. "Backcountry" jaunts can range from 15-minute shortcuts between groomed trails to multiday treks through trackless mountains.

Even the simplest backcountry outing opens a realm of skiing different from anything we've discussed so far—one that carries its own mix of rewards and challenges. The rewards are simple: solitude, untracked snow, scenic destinations that few ever visit. The challenges are equally straightforward: untamed snow conditions that can vary wildly over the course of a day's skiing, staying warm and found (as opposed to cold and lost), equipment failures, coping with the risk of injury, and perhaps the need to be savvy about avalanche dangers.

In approaching the backcountry, your first concern should always be safety. When you're far from a trailhead, the basic rule is simple: if you're in doubt about something, don't do it. This isn't the time to experiment with new techniques. And always be on the lookout for untrustworthy snow conditions, such as snow bridges over raging creeks or those difficult-to-climb-out-of (and sometimes surprisingly deep) wells that form around wind-exposed rocks or tree trunks. This chapter will help prepare you for venturing off the groomed trail, but we can't cover all possible backcountry situations. Your greatest allies are caution and your own common sense.

BACKCOUNTRY SNOW

As we've all heard, Eskimos have dozens of words for *snow*. The English language has only a few, but there are lots of useful adjectives.

My most challenging backcountry experience to date occurred within the city limits of Ann Arbor, Michigan, following a snowstorm that dropped three feet of fresh powder. I was a graduate student at the University of Michigan, which at the time had never shut down for snow and was proud of that record. With all means of wheeled locomotion bogged down, I figured I could still make it to class—two miles away—breaking trail on my backcountry skis. It was tough work, but I made it—just in time for the university to concede that the time had come for its first-ever closure.

Whatever else that might say about my excessive dedication as a student, the skiing lesson was simple: One good blizzard can, however briefly, convert city streets into backcountry. There's no better opportunity to practice your skills—and there're few thrills like skiing down the middle of a main thoroughfare when everyone else is stranded.

The best backcountry snow consists of a base firm enough to support your weight but not hard enough to leave bruises if you fall, topped by a couple of inches of fine powder. Like a good groomed trail surface, the base carries you across logs, leaves, rocks, and other obstructions without letting your skis sink so deeply you have to work too hard. The powder gives you a surface to kick or brake against and makes it easy to control edging for turns. It can also provide a nice smooth glide. If you get conditions like this, revel in them. In some parts of the country, such as the Rockies, they're common, but in other areas, such as the West Coast, they're rare gems you'll remember for years to come. Sometimes you can even skate across this type of snow.

Almost as good is *corn snow*, so named because it consists of large, loose grains like kernels of corn. It's produced by repeated freeze/thaw cycles at the end of the season, when new snow isn't burying the old before it can become good corn. Such snow is most common in the Rockies, Sierra Nevada, and Pacific Northwest, where 20-foot snowpacks take months to melt. By the time there's been enough warm weather to produce good corn snow in areas where snow accumulations are lower than about 3 to 5 feet, corn snow is usually accompanied by muddy gaps that spell the end of the ski season.

Skiing on corn snow is a lot like skiing on machine-tended surfaces. It's firm enough to support you and soft enough for your edges to dig in. Turns are strikingly easy, making spring a great time to practice advanced moves if you're fortunate enough to live in corn-snow country. One word of warning, however: those icy kernels have sharp edges. Even if it's warm enough to go without gloves or to ski in a short-sleeved shirt, don't.

Anything up to 6 inches of fresh snow atop an adequate base can also provide good backcountry skiing, and deeper powder can be fun too, although the difficulty of trail-breaking goes up in proportion to its depth. Plan accordingly, and save ambitious outings for snow conditions that provide easier going. Powder that's been exposed to strong winds can form a firm surface that's a lot of fun to ski across, although it tends to be punctuated by stop-you-in-your-tracks drifts. With practice you can learn to spot likely drift locations on the lee sides of ridges, rocks, or other obstructions, and you'll become increasingly adept at avoiding them.

Other types of snow are less user-friendly, although most don't preclude skiing. A deep layer of heavy wet snow can make for tough slogging, as it falls back into your tracks and weighs down your skis. But if it's dense enough, you may be able to ski over it, like so much extra base. Crust can be a nuisance, especially "breakable crust," which collapses under your weight. Skiers have lots of nicknames for these types of snow: *crud, junk, funky conditions, Sierra cement, Cascade concrete,* and a host of other regional variants. It's best to just accept such conditions as part of normal backcountry skiing—the occasional price of admission to the solitary wonderland of crystalline drifts and snow-shrouded trees—and not waste too much energy complaining.

Other than avalanches (see page 111) or blizzards, the only type of snow condition that's likely to be dangerous (as opposed to inconvenient) is ice. Technically, most backcountry "ice" isn't true ice but is firmly packed snow, welded together by a few freeze/thaw cycles. Typically it forms in patches on sun-exposed slopes, but if a prolonged thaw is followed by a long, hard freeze, the entire backcountry can turn into an ice layer that's virtually undentable. Think twice before venturing out into these conditions, and if you do go, use extreme caution. Falling on this type of surface can be like falling on concrete, and if you fall on a hill you might slide all the way to the bottom—or onto a tree trunk or rock.

You should also approach frozen lakes with respect. Don't venture onto them unless you're *sure* there's enough ice to support your weight. In some parts of the country, that never occurs; elsewhere you need to consult with local experts. Even then, you need to know what the weather's been like for the last few weeks. Thin ice may be able to support your skis—but if you fall you might punch straight through it. Sometimes it's hard to tell if a smooth flat surface is a lake or a meadow. Consult your map, and if you're in doubt go around the edge.

More dangerous yet are frozen creeks or rivers. Even in the frigid northlands, moving water can eat holes in the ice, leaving hard-to-locate thin spots. Even the local experts have a great deal of respect for ice-covered rivers. Don't cross them unless someone you're sure you trust shows you a proven route.

Backcountry Skiing Techniques

Backcountry technique is largely composed of catch-as-catch-can variants on skills you've already learned. Wide skis help; metal edges are extremely useful if you're venturing onto steep slopes. Sometimes, the biggest obstacles are logs, briar patches, or dense woods. On other occasions they're deep powder, steep terrain, or creeks. With practice you'll invent your own ways of dealing with these things, but there are a few specific skills that can prove useful.

Breaking Trail

Breaking trail not only serves to get you across untracked snow—it also opens a path for the rest of your party to follow. Experienced trail-breakers leave nice sets of parallel grooves spaced like machine-set track at about the width of their hips. First-timers tend to leave wobbly tracks that typically are too close together, making it difficult for following skiers to maintain good balance.

Paul Says

For obvious reasons, ski parties tend to put the strongest skier in the lead, but the skill difference makes it all the more important for the leader not to set a path that's too challenging for those who will follow. Thinking constantly of the people behind them is one of the ways good nordic guides assure that their clients have a good time. If you use the same approach, you'll find you're always in demand for more adventures. Botch it up regularly, and you'll be looking for new skiing partners.

Good trail-breakers also are thoughtful route-finders, setting a line of track that can be easily followed by the least skilled member of the party. That means not too steep on uphills and not too close to face-whacking tree branches. They make turns in places where everyone in the party can easily follow, and they learn to "read" conditions of snow, wind, and sun to find the best skiing surfaces.

Kick Turn

The kick turn is a nifty way to execute a 180-degree turn in two steps, rather than the incremental V-step method you learned in chapter 2 (see page 28). But it requires limber hips, good knees, and a level of coordination that some people find difficult. Not everyone is physically capable of performing this maneuver.

Try this first on a nice flat surface that's not too slippery, making sure there are no skiers, trees, or

Rick Says

If you're breaking trail in shallow snow through brushy terrain—as in eastern deciduous forests—the biggest difficulty can be from vines, creepers, or briars lurking just below the snow, waiting to wrap around your ankles. To reduce this problem, with each stride lift your skis high enough that the tips ride over the tops of all such foot-grabbers—and don't ski through loops of brush. Lifting your skis this way is slightly harder work, but it's better than having to stop and back up every time your boot snags a vine.

The kick turn.

© JIM CHASE

bushes nearby. Plant your poles behind you, with the baskets about 6 feet apart to provide two stable points of support. Leaning slightly on your poles, lift one foot and kick it forward, up in the air, a bit like a slow-motion football punt, so the ski tail brushes across the snow, coming to rest at the point where the ski tip used to be. You're now in a highly unstable po-

sition with the leg stuck way out in front of you and the ski standing vertically on its tail. Try not to jam the tail down into the snow, or you'll get embarrassingly stuck in this extended position.

Now, pivot the ski on its tail and set it back on the ground exactly where it started, but facing backward. You're now standing with your feet and skis side by side, one facing forward, the other facing backward. (In ballet, this is called the *fifth position*.) This is the hardest part of the turn. It's okay if you can't quite get your foot rotated a full 180 degrees, so long as you get close to it. Now, simply pick up the other ski and swing it around in a sweeping arc until you're facing the direction you want to go, being careful not to clobber your friends with the ski tip or tail. Finally, bring your poles (which should have been far enough behind you and to the side to be out of the way throughout this entire maneuver) into a more normal position. Practice doing this turn without moving either pole until the end. (That's not vital on flat surfaces, but it helps to always have three points of support when doing kick turns on steep hillsides.)

Practice the kick turn a few times on level terrain until you've pretty much got the idea. Even on groomed trail, it's a slick trick for making a quick about-face. But it's especially valuable when traversing a steep hillside, where it's the only reasonable way to turn around.

When you're ready to try the kick turn on a slope, ski onto an appropriate hillside, moving onto a horizontal traverse. Standing perpendicular to the fall line, use your skis to stomp three parallel platforms, at least as wide as the skis. Nothing fancy—you just want somewhere to stand during and after the turn. Now, step your skis onto the upper two platforms and execute the turn so that you rotate away from the hillside. You'll start by kicking and pivoting the lower ski, so it comes back into its original groove. Then rotate the upper ski around, stepping it into the lower platform/groove. On steeper terrain, you'll need to plant both poles on your uphill side before you start the turn and keep them there throughout, so you don't go skittering sideways down the hill. On gentle terrain, you can be sloppier about your pole plant and may even be able to do the turn rotating toward the hill rather than away from it.

Hill Climbing

Uphill traverse. Hill climbing in the backcountry rarely takes the form of herringboning or sidestepping straight uphill. The easiest method is the uphill traverse, in which you simply stride up the hill at an angle, reversing course whenever necessary in a series

More than any other technique discussed in this chapter, the kick turn is the signature maneuver that differentiates backcountry skiers from skiers who spend most of their time in more civilized terrain. Not only does it allow you to reverse course on a steep hillside without careening off downslope, but it can also help you extricate yourself from brushy dead ends. With the kick turn in your bag of tricks, you can confidently ski into unknown terrain, knowing that you can always backtrack if the route doesn't work. Without a kick turn, your only way to turn around may be by taking off your skis.

of switchbacks. This works best in snow that is soft enough to allow your edges to dig in sufficiently to give you a good anti-sideslipping grip. Because you're simply doing the diagonal stride, not sidestepping, this method is typically undemanding, even on long hills. Just choose an angle of attack that allows you to ski diagonally up the hill without slipping. How steep this is will depend on the snow, your energy level, and how much traction you're getting with each stride.

You may find that your uphill pole is too long for comfortable poling. If you're going to be doing a lot of climbing, you may want to invest in adjustable-length poles. Or steal a trick from Little Leaguers faced with over-long baseball bats and "choke up" on the pole by taking your wrist out of the strap and holding it below the grip. To still get a modicum of use from the strap, try hooking your thumb over it from below.

Forward sidestep. Want to climb faster than you can on an uphill traverse? The forward sidestep is a popular method, particularly on firm snow. The trick is to combine a sidestep and an uphill traverse into a single move. First, swing the uphill ski forward while simultaneously lifting it and stepping sideways. Then follow with the downhill ski. It's a lot like sidestepping except that you're also striding forward. The move is easier than the traditional sidestep, because your legs swing forward with each step rather than moving directly sideways, allowing your strong walking muscles to come more fully into play. How much sidestepping you do will depend on how slippery

This ski pole has segments that twist and lock into place to adjust pole length.

The forward sidestep.

your skis are on the particular hill. If you have good grip, you'll be doing mostly an uphill traverse. If your skis are especially slippery, you'll be doing most of the climb with the sidestep.

Climbing skins. Sometimes called *ski skins* or simply *skins*, these simple inventions instantly add an enormous amount of grip to your skis—useful for steep climbs or even for descents on which you really

"Choking up" on your poles allows you to shorten one or both of them.

don't want to start sliding. It's like adding four-wheel drive to your skis. They used to be made from seal skin (hence the name), but are now made of nylon or some other synthetic. Skins are simply a long strip of this material backed by a self-sticking adhesive that temporarily glues the fabric to the base of your skis but can quickly be pulled free when you're done climbing. The business side of the skin has a nap that allows the ski to slide in one direction (albeit slowly) and grip firmly in the other. Make sure you put the proper end in front so the nap is working for you rather than against you. Skins are available in several widths (measured in millimeters); wider gives more gripping surface, but don't get them so wide that they cover the skis' edges.

Hiking. On really steep backcountry climbs, the most efficient means of gaining altitude might be to simply take off your skis and walk. Ski mountaineers often walk up the peak and ski down—particularly appealing on the moderate slopes of big volcanoes. And in late-season skiing you may occasionally be forced to walk across bare patches.

Hiking with skis requires two things: firm snow and a way to carry your skis. There are all kinds of fancy ski carriers designed for use at the trailhead, but most aren't things you're likely to want to carry into the backcountry. One simple, lightweight design has a pair of straps that hold your skis together, with

PAUL SAYS

Climbing skins have uses other than climbing. They're great in deep powder. Trail breaking in two feet or more of new snow is almost impossible without them. They work for walking down hills that exceed your skill level—which with a heavy backpack could mean an otherwise gentle grade. And they're useful to have in your safety kit in case you hurt a knee or ankle and want increased assurance against slipping, to avoid additional injury. Skins go with me on almost every backcountry outing.

a shoulder strap for hands-free walking. Better is a pack designed to carry skis. In the easiest-to-use models, the skis slide though slots behind the side pockets, sometimes with the tails snugging into special pouches. When you carry skis in this manner, the tips rise into the air above your head; strap them together for convenience and to reduce the risk of gouges. If you don't have a Velcro ski strap, a bandanna or duct tape will suffice. Other pack designs

Putting on climbing skins.

require you to strap the skis together and tie them to the pack—possibly beneath straps, which some soft packs have for compressing partial loads. Use your poles as walking sticks.

Downhills

In the backcountry, you have an enormous arsenal of downhill techniques at your disposal. Three of them—taking your skis off to walk down the hill, descending with climbing skins, and the sidestep—need no further discussion. Others are refinements of techniques discussed in earlier chapters. Here's a checklist of turns you may find useful under certain conditions (if they're not already familiar, refer to the descriptions in chapters 2, 3, and 8):

- **Step turn**. This one is mandatory for backcountry skiing because it and the kick turn are the only turning methods you can rely on for tacking downhill in thick breakable crust. You can also use it to finish other types of turns that, for whatever reason, didn't go well.

- **Wedge turn**. By now, this should be second nature, but you may need to modify it for backcountry conditions such as thin crust, deep powder, or firm or icy snow. Try a "monkey wedge" by flexing more deeply at the ankles to effect better steering, edging, and braking. This will also lower your center of gravity, which is particularly important when skiing with a pack. When turning in this lower stance, try to feel your feet, knees, and hips twist and point in the desired direction.

- **Wedge christie**. This is useful whenever snow conditions allow the necessary sideways skidding of your skis.

- **Telemark turns**. These are particularly useful if you have a few inches of powder atop a consistent base.

Other techniques require additional discussion, including one new turning method, the parallel turn. But we'll start with the simplest, the downhill traverse.

Downhill traverse. On a really shallow traverse in slow snow, there's nothing special about this because you'll be kicking and poling as in the normal diagonal

Sometimes it's just easier to walk. Some packs have straps to hold your skis.

stride. But usually you'll be gliding, choosing a traverse angle that allows you to go the desired speed.

We've already discussed proper ways to do this, but they bear repeating, because getting cavalier about them invites a fall. To keep your skis from crossing and for optimum body position, keep the uphill foot slightly forward of the downhill one. Your uphill hand should be in front of your body, not out of sight behind your hip, and a little knee-ankle bend will make it easier to control your edging. Your speed is controlled by the kind of snow you're on and the steepness of your angle of descent. To change the angle, you may be able to wedge turn slightly in the desired direction; in crust or deep new snow, you'll probably need to step turn.

Plan ahead. When the time has come to end your traverse, turn toward the hill or up a little ridgeline to let the terrain do

your braking. Lumps formed by snow-covered rocks, logs, or other terrain irregularities also make great speed bleeders—assuming, of course, that these obstacles are sufficiently buried in snow. As with ascents, long hills are usually descended in a series of linked traverses, forming switchbacklike zigzags. Also, most descent routes are bounded by ridges, canyons, rocks, or woods, forcing you to link traverses regardless of your desired direction. If snow conditions and your abilities allow, you can connect your traverses with steered turns such as the wedge, telemark, or wedge christie. Otherwise, stop and do a kick turn.

If you haven't mastered the kick turn, you may be able to reverse course with the stationary step turn we've previously called V-stepping. This works best if you rotate *toward* the hill. That way, as you pass through the fall line, you're in the herringbone position, from which it is a lot easier to keep from sliding than in a downhill-facing A. But this is a particularly difficult way to link traverses and won't work on all slopes. Taking off your skis will work unless the slope is so icy you can't stand on it, but you run the very real risk of losing a ski down the hill. It's better not to venture onto slopes so steep you get stuck midway down, at the end of a traverse. If this does happen, the best way to extricate yourself may be by sidestepping, either down the hill or back up to gentler terrain, where you can seek another way down.

Perfect High Sierra terrain for a long traverse.

The downhill traverse can take the sting out of many backcountry slopes, as long as you have the patience not to rush it. I once got caught high on a Utah mountainside when late-afternoon freeze-up turned perfect snow conditions to crust and then to ice in only a few minutes. On light-touring skis without metal edges, my only recourse was to tack down the mountain in dozens of shallow traverses. It was a slow way to drop the 1,000 feet to my car, but I made it safely, even coming to enjoy the process before the grade finally tapered into a meadow that offered easy skiing.

Parallel turns. The parallel turn is widely thought of as a downhill skier's move, but you can do it perfectly well on free-heel cross-country equipment. The main difference between it and the wedge christie is that in the parallel turn you don't start by wedging. Instead, you begin with the skis flat and parallel to each other, finishing with them edged toward the inside of the bend. Planting the downhill pole at the end of each turn helps signal the next one, and a significant amount of up-and-down upper-body movement makes the process easier. In most snow conditions, it helps to completely shift your weight to the outside ski as you complete the turn. But this won't work in powder snow, where equal weight distribution is necessary for getting both skis around the bend.

The toughest part of any turn is the moment you swing through the fall line, committing yourself to either completing the turn or rocketing downhill out of control. Most people find that the parallel turn evolves naturally out of practicing higher-speed wedge christies. Confidence helps; timidity and vacillation are the surest ways to find yourself bailing out midway through the turn. To build confidence, try doing a series of bends that don't send you through the fall line but instead follow a sinuous traverse— first bending into the hill, then away from it. Once this feels comfortable you'll be more confident about executing a complete turn.

Also, the pole plant and rising-and-falling rhythm are vital to an easy parallel turn. Properly timed just

Use your upper body to anticipate each parallel turn.

before you initiate the turn, they briefly lift part of your weight off the skis, making them easier to steer. Advanced skiers can exaggerate this into a jump parallel turn, in which the skis are airborne during much of the turn.

Another important trick is to anticipate the turn by keeping your upper body rotated toward the fall line.

I'm most likely to do a downhill traverse when guiding less-skilled friends or clients who can't descend by other methods. Choosing a line of traverse that matches their abilities is the key to a fun outing. Once my companions have learned the basics of traversing, I sometimes indulge my own taste for speed by jumping into the fall line to arc downhill in linked turns, waiting for the rest of my party at the bottom. But even experts are relegated to traverses in breakable crust or when skiing with a heavy pack.

This way, you approach the turn with your upper body wound up in one direction, a bit like a spring. As you turn, the lower body unwinds around the bend and continues twisting in the opposite direction, while the upper body remains more stable, facing downslope. This twisting and untwisting of the body is the same skill you practiced in other types of linked turns, and it makes it simpler for the lower body to steer the skis through each turn.

If you're making the conversion from downhill skis to free-heel equipment, try adding a bit more up-and-down movement to your parallel turns than you're used to and work on centering your weight accurately in the middle of your feet.

ROUTE FINDING AND TERRAIN CONDITIONS

Backcountry terrain comes in a wide variety of flavors, ranging from meadows, pastures, and unplowed roads to hiking trails, forests, and high alpine cirques. Even in the mountains a lot of it is relatively gentle, especially in parklike uplands that mix wide-open meadows, rolling hillsides, and easy-to-skirt islands of trees. In the lowlands, state and county parks sometimes feature similar open terrain on land that was once farmed; picnic areas, campground loops, and play areas can also be combined into surprisingly lengthy ski routes.

Picking a path through the backcountry involves matching your skills to the landscape. The most enjoyable outings induce just the right amount of challenge but not too much adrenaline. No two routes or days are ever identical, but each type of terrain presents its own challenges. Here are a few general considerations to help you plan a trip suitable for your skills, stamina, and willingness to deal with potential obstacles.

Creek Crossings

Creeks come in two types: those that run under the snow, and those whose courses haven't drifted full of the white stuff. The under-the-snow variety range from rivulets you'll never know are there to modest-sized streams. Watch for the gullies that mark their courses and evaluate the snow conditions before

The parallel turn is my favorite for hard and icy snow and for very steep terrain. I also use it to conserve energy on long downhills, and in deep powder I prefer it to the telemark. Just because you're on free-heel equipment doesn't mean you always have to use the telemark turn. To be a truly versatile backcountry skier, at home on all slope angles and slope conditions, you must have the parallel turn figured out.

© PAUL PETERSEN

Jimmy Katz using parallel turns on the 10,000-foot North Sister in the Oregon Cascades.

venturing across. If they're fully snowed over (there are no holes through which you can see splashing water), the weather's been cold for several days, and the gully doesn't drain a large area, it's probably safe to cross (although caution is still advisable). But on a warm afternoon there could be a lot of water under the snow. Always proceed carefully, one skier at a time, at a place where the gully is easy to get into or out of, and be prepared to turn back if you don't like the look of the snow.

Except in very cold climates, larger creeks usually maintain highly visible open channels that block your path with free-flowing water. The best way across is on a bridge—either a footbridge or one for an unplowed road. When planning your route, study the map for likely opportunities. If there's no convenient bridge, you may be able to take your skis off and boulder-hop across, as you would hiking. This is most likely to work in regions with light snowpacks. In heavy mountain snows, the creek is likely to be unreachable, at the bottom of a steep-walled snow canyon. Don't even think of trying to leap across such defiles. Remember also that on warm days, creeks tend to rise in the afternoon; don't get trapped on the far side.

If a creek is uncrossable, you may be able to circle upstream, toward its headwaters, picking off smaller feeder streams one at a time. But in general don't expect to cross major creeks without bridges. And remember, larger streams are dangerous even if they appear to be completely frozen over.

Deciduous Forests

Skiing through the woods can present the ultimate in backcountry touring. Familiar landscapes become new with each snowfall, as twigs fatten with fuzzy layers of snow or stand bare like etched glass against a powder blue sky. But deciduous forests offer substantial challenges, especially if you venture away from marked routes. Terrain undulations will keep you alert, and underbrush and tightly spaced trees may cramp your style on the herringbone or sidestep. Do your first woodland outings on designated ski trails in national forests or state or county parks, where maintenance crews should have cleared away the worst of the brush. Later, you can graduate to hiking trails (typically narrower and steeper, with oddly placed bends and trees). If that becomes too tame, you can move on to off-trail skiing, where you may

have to invent techniques you'll never find in books, such as banking off the roots of trees or Tarzan-style swinging from saplings or branches as you lower or lift yourself through gaps too narrow for the snowplow or herringbone.

Evergreen Forests

Pine and fir woodlands have less undergrowth and often present delightful skiing. But dense fir can produce its own difficulties. The thick foliage of these trees typically catches a lot of snow, holding it for hours or even days. Eventually the trees shed their snow, but their downward-sloping branches deflect it outward, away from the trunk, producing lumpy surfaces that look like waves on a choppy sea. With practice, skiing through this type of terrain is a joyous undulation of rise, drop, and quick turns as you wiggle along the path of least resistance, careening off some snowbanks and bouncing over others. But it's slower going than track skiing, and you must take downgrades with caution.

As the snow slumps off the branches to form these mogul-like snowbanks, it sometimes brings down a lot of twigs, all of which reappear when the snow starts to melt. The best time to ski through such forests is in the first two-thirds of the season, when repeated snowfalls bury each new layer of twigs. Later, as the snow is melting, there can be so many tiny branches that you're constantly skiing over them. You may not want to venture into a fir forest immediately after a heavy snowstorm, however. If you do, be on the lookout for "snow bombs," which occur when a 100-foot tree suddenly sheds enough snow to make a small snowman. They're much more entertaining if you're not the one to get hit. Don't park your car under such trees, either; snow bombs have been known to break windshields.

As with deciduous forests, your best introductions to skiing among the trees are on unplowed roads or marked ski routes. These routes also tend to have bridges or are routed with an eye to avoiding difficult creek crossings. With more experience you can take a topographic map and compass and go wherever the snow allows.

Tree Wells, Cornices, Blow-outs, Mini-Schrunds, and Other Nasties

Wind can do strange things to snow. It can whip around trees or rocks and create steep-sided wells that would be hard to climb out of if you fell in. On exposed slopes, repeated eddies can produce enormous "blow-outs" big enough to swallow two-story buildings, and on ridgelines, cornices (overhanging enbankments of snow) can extend as much as 50 or 100 feet over open air.

Needless to say, you should view all of these as potential death traps and give them wide berths. That means keeping in control skiing downhill, so a hole doesn't suddenly loom before you. On ridgelines where there might be cornices, always ask yourself the simple question "What am I standing on?" If you're not sure of the answer, back away from the edge and use bends in the ridge to scout ahead for possible trouble spots.

A different type of pitfall is created when sun-warmed rocks conduct heat underground, particularly during the prolonged melt-out of heavy alpine snowpacks. This, combined with snow slumping, can create deep crevasses called *bergschrunds* at the heads of snowfields (particularly glaciers). You're not likely to encounter a full-fledged *schrund* unless you're doing serious mountaineering, but you may encounter similar, smaller features or "rotten snow" around sun-exposed rocks that would otherwise be tempting picnic sites. These cracks are usually more nuisance than danger, but it's possible to hyperextend a knee if one leg suddenly plunges hip deep into a hidden hole while you're trying to step from the snow to the rocks. Whenever you see outcropping rocks late in the season, be alert for rotten snow.

One other snow condition, called *sun cups*, bears note only because it's so strangely beautiful. Sun cups form when late-season sun starts to melt uneven holes into the snow surface, particularly on

Skiers on ridgeline, keeping well away from dangerous cornices (background).

© JAN HOLAN

high-elevation, south-facing slopes. Once started, this condition is self-perpetuating as the holes form mini reflecting ovens that concentrate heat at the center. Eventually, sun cups can be 2 or 3 feet deep. They're not dangerous, but it's nearly impossible to ski across them—and difficult enough to walk across them.

For the most part these obstacles are endemic to the mountains of the West, but it pays to be alert for them in the Midwest and New England as well. The high country of the Appalachians can generate all of the conditions familiar to western skiers, and even in the Midwest unstable snowbanks can form along creek embankments or clifftops.

Suncups and rotten snow in the Pamir range.

Fences

Fences can be nuisances or major obstacles, depending on snow conditions and their design. But they needn't stop you, as long as you're sure it's okay to be on the other side. Unless the fence is almost completely drifted over, you're probably going to have to take your skis off. Wooden fences should be climbed adjacent to a post, where the boards are strongest. Metal gates can also be climbed, but do so near the hinge end of the gate to avoid damaging it. For wire fences, including barbed wire, the ideal method of crossing is to have a friend spread two strands of wire apart while you step or crawl between them. Don't try to climb over the fence; you'll beat it down, permanently. If the wire doesn't have enough slack to allow passage, ski along the fence looking for a more suitable place to cross. Patience will usually be rewarded.

Afternoon Ice-Up

We all know that as the sun drops low in the sky, the air temperature generally sinks with it. What's easier to forget is that this can spell a radical change in snow conditions. Wet snow can form crust, and packed wet surfaces can turn to ice. Be aware of this on any day that warms above the freezing mark, and don't stay out too late unless you're prepared to deal with changing conditions. In colder weather, of course, ice-up is no problem, because the snow never melts in the first place.

Ski Ice-Up

Not to be confused with icy trails, this occurs when snow glues itself to the bottom of your skis. It's most common in fresh, wet snow when the air temperature has dropped below freezing but the snow hasn't yet done so. In normal skiing, the friction of your skis on the snow produces a thin layer of water on the base of the ski; when you glide, you're actually gliding on that water, not directly on the snow. In ice-up conditions, that film of water freezes to the snow, causing you to pick up large snowballs. To clear your skis of snow, try standing in place, scuffing them back and forth in your tracks. If that doesn't work, a credit card or pole basket makes a handy scraper, or you can scrape the base of one ski with the edge of the other. To reduce the amount of ice-up, don't expose your skis to cold air by lifting them off the ground during rest breaks. Try to stand on firm snow, or make a firm surface by shuffling your feet occasionally until you've created a platform similar to groomed trail, on which ice-up is less common. Further prevention is possible with proper glide waxing and good ski maintenance, which are discussed in chapter 12.

Skiing at Night

Nighttime skiing is a memorable experience. On snow, even a strong quarter-moon can provide enough light, and sometimes the glow of a nearby city is all it takes for you to find your way. Cross-country ski areas and parks often cater to this by opening their groomed trail systems on full-moon weekends, but you can get similar experiences in the backcountry. Just be aware that route finding is more difficult in dim light, terrain irregularities are harder to spot until you're practically upon them, and clouds can unexpectedly block moonlight.

Skiing with a flashlight is possible but tricky, because carrying it interferes with poling. Headlamps free your arms, and the simplest ones aren't much more expensive than flashlights. The fancier models have adjustable beams. Flashlights and headlamps, however, destroy your night vision for areas outside the narrow beam of light. Sometimes you'll do better skiing cautiously by whatever natural light is available.

Glaciers

Most skiers will never encounter a glacier. But in Alaska, the Pacific Northwest, and the Canadian Rockies, glaciers sometimes form tempting ramps leading deep into the backcountry, particularly late in the season when other routes have melted out. Unless you have mountaineering experience or are in the company of a suitably trained guide, resist the temptation. The moment you set foot on a glacier, even a tiny one, you're engaged in a type of technical mountaineering far beyond the scope of this book. If you're in doubt about whether a particular snow slope is a glacier, consult a map.

SAFETY FIRST: PREPARE FOR THE WORST AND IT PROBABLY WON'T HAPPEN

It's possible to ski for years without having a backcountry mishap, but when an accident occurs it can instantly turn the tamest outing into a rugged adventure. Impossible creek crossings, equipment failure, or a route that won't "go" can also turn even a quick backcountry jaunt into a potentially dangerous expe-

rience. If there's a single rule for backcountry safety, it's this: Think before you try something new. Ask yourself, "What can go wrong in this situation?" and "What can I do if it happens?"

In chapter 10, we review a number of aspects of emergency preparedness, ranging from what to carry in your pack to how to fix (almost) anything with duct tape. But there are a few backcountry safety precautions—and tips for maximizing your enjoyment—that are inherent to all backcountry touring. Here are a baker's dozen of them:

- **Never ski alone.** Yeah, yeah, we know. Everyone says that about every outdoor sport. But if anything goes wrong skiing, you're out in the snow, which you might have noticed is particularly likely to be cold and wet. It's one thing to take a solo spin around a groomed trail system, and quite another to venture into areas where other skiers won't be passing by frequently. This rule is important to instill in children, and the less frequently it's broken by adults, the fewer times the search-and-rescue teams need to be called out. Two people can solve almost any backcountry emergency better together than either could solo.

- **Always tell someone where you're planning to go.** This includes telling them where you're parking your car, what routes you're considering (including all possible options), who's going with you, and your approximate return time. Don't unduly panic your benefactors by being too sanguine about your estimated return time. Allow enough leeway that you can enjoy your trip without feeling in a rush to get back to a phone.

- **Don't suddenly change your mind and go somewhere other than where you said you'd be.** It's amazing how tempting this is for some people. It guarantees that if you need help, the rescue party's going to be in the wrong place. Worse, your car won't be at the expected trailhead, making people think you've gotten out safely and merely forgotten to check in.

- **Allow time for backtracking.** If you're doing a loop trip into unknown terrain, never assume the route will work as planned. A washed-out bridge, unclimbable slope, or lost route may require you to retrace your steps even though you're most of the way around the loop. Even on out-and-back trips it's silly to flirt with being caught by dark unless you're an experienced nighttime skier.

- **Don't ski in avalanche terrain unless you've had avalanche training.** If you simply can't avoid such terrain, then make sure you're carrying the appropriate equipment (avalanche beacons, shovel, and probe poles) and know how to use it. We talk a bit about avalanches in chapter 10 (see page 111), but this book can't substitute for a full-fledged avalanche safety course. Even in flat country, watch out for steep stream embankments or river bluffs that can produce avalanche-style slumps.

- **Avoid getting lost.** This sounds straightforward, but almost anyone can get disoriented if a bank of fog rolls onto an all-white snow slope. Such conditions are called *whiteouts*, and even the most experienced backcountry skiers respect them. Carry a compass and an adequate topographic map and know how to use them. In hill country, altimeters are also extremely useful, particularly in woods or fog. Study the map in advance to familiarize yourself with important landmarks and refer to it regularly to track your progress. Not only will this reduce your chances of getting lost, but good map-reading skills can minimize the risk of making a grueling backtrack after straying off course or boxing yourself into a steep-walled valley. If you're not map-and-compass sophisticated, buy a book or consider taking an orienteering course.

Bad weather and blowing snow are leading reasons skiers get lost. Blowing snow can obliterate your tracks with startling speed, making it impossible to follow them back the way you came if you've ventured more than a little bit into the backcountry. Even without a whiteout, bad weather can make it difficult to locate your position on a topographic map—further increasing the need for good compass skills.

© RICHARD A. LOVETT

More fog could turn moody weather into a dangerous whiteout.

When skiing in unfamiliar terrain, the best approach is to try to find a companion who knows the route or at least the basic lay of the land. In bad weather, stick to terrain that's easy to follow, such as unplowed roads, creek drainages, or ridgelines.

RICK SAYS

Except in the flattest country, it's impossible to over-stress the value of an altimeter as a companion to the traditional map and compass. Unless the barometric pressure is changing rapidly, many pocket altimeters can pinpoint your elevation to within 20 feet, helping you to traverse to an important landmark such as a river valley, a gap between two hills, or a ridgeline. They're also fun toys. I always carry one. GPS devices are also useful, triangulating on a set of military satellites to pinpoint your location (including your elevation) to the nearest 100 yards. They're about the size of a TV remote control unit and can even be programmed to point you back to your car or to any other preselected checkpoint. But they're distinctly *not* for people who don't like complex electronic gadgets. And never let one of these electronic brains substitute for basic map-and-compass skills. If you do, you're never more than a battery failure away from being lost.

Paul Says

Early each winter, I see eager backcountry skiers skiing in terrain that nature simply hasn't yet provided with enough winter padding. The ski damage alone can ruin your day. But the thing that's particularly threatening is doing telemark turns with no knee pads and cracking your kneecap on a rock. Even if you walk away from it, you'll only let yourself do this once. My advice: if you want to get out early in the season, hit a downhill ski area that has snowmaking equipment or carefully manicured runs. Or stick to the groomed tracks. They usually don't have as many underlying rocks and require less snow to be safe.

- **Always carry a pack.** Its size and what you carry in it will depend on the length of your trip, how many people are sharing equipment, and the type of weather you expect to encounter. For light, short tours, you may need only a fanny pack or simple day pack. For more remote conditions, you may need an expedition-caliber backpack. Whatever size pack you carry, use it for extra clothing, food, water, a ski repair kit, and a first aid kit. See chapter 10 (pages 107–11) for a more complete list of recommended equipment.

- **Don't ski in rocky terrain or conditions where there's not enough snow.** Jagged rocks, lurking just beneath the snow, are dangerous to both you and your ski bases. Make sure there's enough snow that you won't hit them if you fall.

- **Don't sandbag your friends.** This is an easy mistake. *You* are in love with the backcountry, can think of no finer way to see it than from cross-country skis, and want to share it with all your friends. So you drag a bunch of beginners into advanced or even intermediate terrain, much to everyone's dismay.

- **When it comes to staying warm and dry, "less" may be "more."** As we said in chapter 1, cross-country skiing is the "warm" winter sport. Your movement creates body heat that's a welcome asset in cold weather. But that asset becomes a liability if you overheat and soak your clothes with perspiration. If you get too hot climbing to a windy ridge-

line, you'll be too cold soon after you get there—and it's a lot harder to warm up again once you're cold. This is why we recommended dressing in layers in chapter 4 (see page 40). But the ability to shed or add layers doesn't do you much good if you don't take the time to manage them carefully. Shed layers or open zippers when you start to overheat, and don't hesitate to reach for a jacket and cap when you take a rest break or move into the wind—before becoming chilled.

- **Check your equipment before you reach the trailhead.** If something needs repair, fix it before you leave home. Just like checking the air in your tires and oil in your car engine before a long trip, checking your gear regularly prior to use is a wise investment of time.

- **Know the strengths and weaknesses of your fellow skiers.** If you're skiing with good friends, you may know these automatically. Otherwise you might need to ask in advance if anyone has an injury that might be exacerbated by skiing, is taking heart medication, or easily becomes altitude sick. Most importantly, you want at least a rough idea of the skill level of everyone in the group. And make sure you're speaking the same language: one person's mountain is another's molehill, and statements like "1,000 feet of climbing in 2 miles" are meaningless to people who've never done anything similar. Clear communication about these things can make or break a trip. We'll talk more about this in chapter 10.

- **Consider carrying a cell phone.** Cellular phones have been getting lighter and lighter, and increasing amounts of the backcountry are within range of cellular services. Although the cell phone is the hallmark of the workaday world that you're trying to

Rick Says

As you're leaving home, don't forget the cross-country skier's mantra: *skis? boots? poles?* You may be able to borrow other gear from friends, but there's nothing like driving two hours to a special ski destination only to discover you left your boots at home.

leave behind by venturing into the backcountry, the ability to dial 911 can be a lifesaver. Being able to call home to tell your check-in people of route changes also gives you more flexibility for spontaneous changes of plans. Our suggestion: leave the thing turned off unless you need it, so you have the benefit of 911 service without the risk of being interrupted. And make sure your cellular service covers your ski destination. Although the technology is changing rapidly, analog services currently have good, long-range coverage; digital or "PCS" services don't.

These pointers are really just a short list to stimulate your thinking. Time and experience will give you a list of your own. Depending on where you ski, you may want to read some books on first aid or avalanche safety or bone up on map-and-compass skills. And never forget to pick up tips from experienced friends. Try not to be the group leader until you are comfortable with the responsibilities that this involves, and above all, remember, as we've said before, that safety comes first, fun second, and technique last.

Chapter 10

Emergency Preparedness

© KAFHU

Being prepared for the challenges winter can throw at you means more than just tossing a few extra items in your car or your pack. It's a state of mind, an attitude that should begin at the planning stage of any winter adventure. For the most part, it's people who are too cavalier about this who get into trouble, finding that they don't have enough clothing or that they have three flashlights but no spare bulbs or batteries. When planning a trip, run through a mental checklist of the things that could go wrong, visualizing how you'd deal with them if they happened. To the extent possible, try to make the equipment you carry serve multiple uses. Your rain jacket, for example, might also function as a windbreaker, and duct tape can fix almost anything—even serving in a medical emergency to help splint a broken bone or bind a wound.

When preparing to be more than a few minutes away from help on even a mild winter day, it pays to be a bit paranoid by conventional standards. "Prepare for the worst and hope for the best" is a mindset that will not only lead to relaxed, confident outings, but

also hone your respect for the winter environment and help keep you out of trouble in the first place.

There are, of course, practical limits to how much you can prepare. Most people won't see a need to burden themselves with tents and sleeping bags on short outings, even if there's a remote possibility these things might come in handy. But emergency bivouac equipment might be necessary on longer jaunts into remote backcountry. One useful trick for determining what you really need and what you can live without is to review the contents of your pack at the end of each trip. Ask yourself what you actually used—and what you nevertheless needed as a cushion against the unforeseen. Anything extra might be excess baggage. If, on the other hand, you found yourself wishing for something you didn't have, note it for future outings.

11 ESSENTIALS

Every outdoor book has its own "10 essentials" list, each slightly different. In the interest of helping you be fully prepared, we have 11. We'll also make other suggestions for your touring kit (see page 109), but except for jaunts at commercial ski areas or other ski-patrolled routes, these are items you should always consider carrying:

- **Extra clothing.** How much extra clothing to bring depends on the length of your trip, your athleticism, and the wildness of the terrain. But remember, if you break a binding only one mile from the trailhead at a well-patrolled cross-country ski area, you can still get mighty cold waiting for the ski patrol.

- **Food.** As with clothing, carry a bit more food than you think you might need. For short outings, a couple of energy bars may be sufficient. On longer trips, you may want to carry two extra bars per person, or some other high-energy snack.

- **Water.** Don't assume you can simply eat snow. Even if it's not contaminated with animal feces or chemicals, eating quantities of snow robs you of huge amounts of body heat as it melts in your mouth. Always carry more water than you actually expect to use; how much more depends on the length of your outing.

- **Map.** The type of map you need depends on the type of outing you're undertaking. On groomed trails, all you need is a simple route map. Similarly, a simple map may suffice for outings on unplowed roads or marked ungroomed trails. For more adventurous backcountry trips, however, a topographic map, which shows elevation contours, is preferred. If you need such a map, make sure you know how to use it. Seek the counsel of a good ski or backpacking shop, ask a skilled friend for advice, or consult the map-reading section of a good backpacking book.

- **Compass.** Even someone with a good sense of direction can get lost in dense forest or fog.

- **Matches (in waterproof container).** Waterproof-windproof matches are particularly useful. You can get them in specialty backpacking shops. Use a butane lighter if you don't have matches.

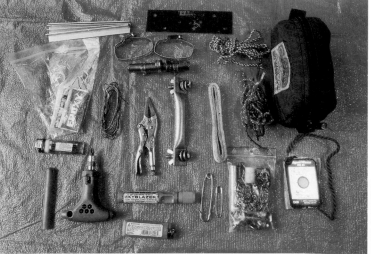

A well-stocked repair kit doesn't have to be large.

© PAUL PETERSEN

- **Whistle.** Three blasts is a universal SOS signal.

- **Signal mirror (to draw help from far away).** It's amazing how well this can work. There are reports of stranded river rafters successfully signaling to commercial jetliners from the bottom of the Grand Canyon.

- **Space emergency blanket.** These inexpensive emergency body wraps are made of a reflective material that looks much like lightweight aluminum foil. Folded, they're about the size of a deck of cards, weigh almost nothing, and work by sealing off drafts and reflecting body heat back toward the user. In an emergency you just wrap the blanket around you, over your clothes.

- **Sunscreen and lip balm**—SPF 15 or better

- **Flashlight or headlamp** (with spare batteries and bulb)

RICK SAYS

You can keep some of the 11 essentials in one nylon travel bag and store it with (better yet, in) your pack between trips. Food, water, clothing, and maps still have to be assembled for each trip, but everything else is in one place, where you're unlikely to forget it.

TRACK SKIING AND NORDIC DOWNHILL

This is the one exception to our suggestion that you always carry the 11 essentials: you won't need the full kit if you stay close to the warming huts and food service areas of commercial cross-country or downhill ski areas. Most such areas have ski patrols and snowmobiles for quick evacuation of incapacitated skiers—generally free to anyone who's purchased a trail pass.

Nevertheless, it helps if at least one person in the group carries a few items in a fanny pack or small day pack, especially on the longer trails. Some of the following you'll recognize from the 11 essentials list. Others, like toilet paper, aren't vital enough to be classified as "essential" but are potentially useful enough that you might want to carry them.

- trail map
- water
- high-energy snack
- sunscreen and lip balm
- Space blanket
- toilet paper
- butane lighter
- duct tape
- adhesive bandages
- Ace bandage
- aspirin or ibuprofen
- ski wax and waxing supplies (as needed, see chapter 12)

Make sure there's room in your pack for unwanted clothing layers once you warm up, or plan on tying them around your waist. Then select trails that aren't too challenging for the weakest skier in your group, taking snow conditions into account. Injuries on groomed trails are uncommon, but the risk increases significantly when people ski terrain that's too difficult for them. Ask the staff about current trail conditions or for recommended loops. Trails are generally rated as *easiest*, *more difficult*, or *most difficult*, but these ratings are relative and vary from day to day

and ski area to ski area. If trails are icy, stick to the easier routes. If conditions are slow, it may be a good day to try trails that normally are beyond your ability.

BACKCOUNTRY OUTINGS

In the backcountry or on unpatrolled roads or trails, you have to be much more self-sufficient. That means a bigger pack, ranging from a large day pack to a well-equipped backpack, depending on the length of your outing and the difficulty of the terrain. Here's a checklist of suggestions for trips of increasing length or complexity.

All trips:
- The 11 essentials (see pages 107–8)
- first-aid kit
- butane cigarette lighter and/or candles
- duct tape
- ski repair kit (see pages 116–17)
- cell phone
- closed-cell foam pad
- pocket knife or multitool
- toilet paper
- waxes and waxing supplies (see chapter 12)

For longer day trips in moderate terrain, add
- spare socks
- additional food, water (at least 2–3 quarts per person), and clothing
- water-purification tablets or water filter

In difficult mountain country, add
- avalanche safety equipment (rescue beacons, shovel, probe poles)
- shovel
- sleeping bag
- bivouac sack (waterproof nylon or Gore-Tex sleeping bag cover)

Let's talk about a few of these in more detail.

Duct tape is an invaluable fix-all. It can mend a damaged boot or help splint ski poles or stout sticks to a broken limb. It can also be used to splice or splint a broken pole into some semblance of usefulness. It's a potential emergency substitute for medical tape. You don't need to carry a full roll of the tape. A few yards is plenty. You can wrap it around a pencil or wooden dowel and keep it in your ski repair kit. Or you may prefer to wind it around your ski pole so you'll have it with you always.

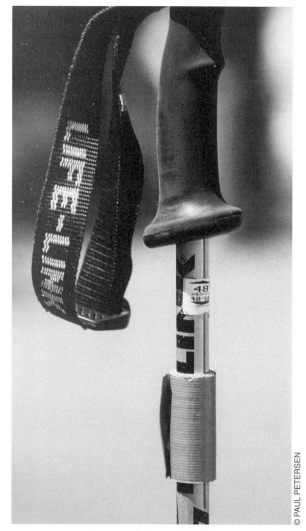

Instead of carrying a bulky role of duct tape, wrap several yards around your ski pole, where it's handy.

Closed-cell foam pads are a type of sleeping pad for backpackers; Blue Foam is one leading brand. Closed-cell foam pads aren't the same as foam mattress pads, which are open-cell foams. The difference is critical: open-cell foams are like sponges—pleasantly soft and squishy, but able to soak up huge quantities of moisture. Closed-cell foams are firmer and stiffer but stay dry. They're also remarkably light, albeit bulky. Sitting on one during a rest break will keep you warm and dry, even in the coldest conditions; it will also spread your weight so you don't sink deeply, even on powder. More importantly, a pad provides a dry, insulated bed for an injured skier, reducing the risk of hypothermia until help arrives.

Foam pads come in several lengths, ranging from about 6 feet to 2-foot squares made solely for sitting. We recommend a relatively long length, particularly if you might want to lie back and do some winter sunbathing on unusually fine days. Bring at least one pad for every two skiers—more if there's any risk of having to do an emergency bivouac (see below). Strap the pad to the outside of your pack to save space inside for other equipment. If you're determined to save bulk on short trips, cut a square of closed-cell foam the shape of the largest compartment of your pack and stuff it into the pack, out of the way against your back. Make sure it's big enough to sit on.

You might want to add a butane lighter to your "essentials" kit. It provides another way to light an emergency campfire, providing a steadier flame than matches. Some people carry candles for this purpose. You can also use a low-temperature flame such as this to heat a car key to help melt it into a frozen door lock. (Don't use the flame directly on the lock to avoid damaging the car.) Some cigarette lighters gradually lose fuel; check yours periodically.

First-aid instruction is beyond the scope of this book, and your first-aid kit should be equipped according to your skills and knowledge of backcountry medicine. At a minimum you should carry

- anti-inflammatory pain killer such as aspirin, ibuprofen, or naproxen sodium (Aleve)

- adhesive bandages

- triangular bandage (for an arm sling)

- any prescription medicines you might need

closed-cell
foam pad

© VERA JAGENDORF

Closed-cell foam pads are handy to avoid getting too cold or wet on the trail.

- Ace bandage

- moleskin (for blisters)

- tiny scissors for cutting moleskin

- nail clippers

- gauze pads

- first-aid/surgical tape (unless you're willing to substitute duct tape)

If you're traveling with children, you might want to add a topical anesthetic/antiseptic such as Bactine for minor scrapes and "boo-boos." And if you're prone to chafing, pack antichafe ointment or powder. To cut weight and volume, pour these products into smaller squeeze bottles that hold only an ounce or so. But beware of the startling ability of some substances to escape from containers, particularly when air pressure changes as you change altitude. For extra safety, double bag containers in resealable plastic bags, and don't rely on twist ties, which can leak.

The ski waxing kit is simply a bag containing the waxing supplies you'll need for the snow conditions you're likely to encounter. Even with no-wax skis, there are a few things you'll want for combating ice-up in fresh powder. We discuss all of these in chapter 12. Ski repair kits are discussed later in this chapter.

If you decide to carry a cellular phone, check at the trailhead to determine if you're in a service area. If you are—or think it might work anyway from ridgetops—put the phone in a plastic bag to protect it from moisture.

The shovel, sleeping bag, and bivouac sack are for regions where you might be spending an unplanned night and need to dig a snow cave. We discuss this later (see page 119). But first let's turn to a ski mountaineering hazard that can be a threat from the moment you leave the trailhead.

AVALANCHES

A full course in avalanche safety is beyond the scope of this book. If you plan to ski in avalanche country, take a seminar, rent a videotape, or read a specialty book. Better, go to the mountains for a one- or two-day avalanche course, which will teach you to recognize avalanche terrain and to use an avalanche beacon (an electronic transmitter worn on the body so searchers can find you quickly) and will train you in avalanche rescue.

Until you've taken such a course, the best way to keep from being caught in an avalanche is to avoid skiing into a potential avalanche path. Here's a partial list of tips. Note that they are rules of thumb, and that *most* does not mean *all*:

- Most avalanches occur during or immediately after a storm. The first 24 hours are the period of highest risk. A less frequent type of avalanche isn't associated with storms and occurs late in the season when the snow is melting.

- Snow falling at a rate of one inch or more per hour is associated with particularly high avalanche hazard.

- Most dangerous avalanches occur on slopes with angles of 30 to 45 degrees. It takes practice to eyeball a slope and estimate the angle with any degree of accuracy, but you can reduce guesswork by making a crude protractor out of your ski poles. Start by holding them in a + shape, crossing at their centers. (If they're adjustable, make sure they're set for the same length.) An imaginary line running through any two adjacent corners is at a

45-degree angle, giving you something to compare to the slope that has you concerned. For a 30-degree reference angle, hold the poles in a sideways T and imagine a line between two of its corners.

- Most avalanche accidents involving skiers are triggered by the skiers themselves.

- Wind increases the likelihood of avalanches.

- When traveling along ridges, watch out for cornices. If you're not alert, you can be standing out over air without even knowing it. Cornices above you can indicate an unstable slope between you and the cornice. The same wind that produced the cornice may have also created crusty slabs that can easily break loose.

- For the same reason, leeward slopes slide more often than do windward slopes. Know the prevailing direction for storm winds, or distinguish windward and leeward slopes by the way the snow has drifted or how trees are bent or encrusted with snow.

- In midwinter, north-facing slopes are far more prone to sliding than are south-facing slopes.

- Avalanches are more likely on open slopes and gullies than on forested slopes. Tree-denuded paths running down the mountainside and fanning out into the valley are "avalanche chutes" where frequent avalanches prune back each year's new growth. The slope at the base may be very gentle, but if there are no trees, be aware that avalanches regularly thunder down from above.

Avalanche safety courses will teach you much more, including the use of avalanche probes to locate buried skiers, how to dig pits in the snow to determine if a slope is on the verge of avalanching, how to find a skier based on her last known position, and

The avalanche path in the middle of this shot was fortunately narrow. The telemark tracks to the right of the chute weave among the trees, which reduces the risk of being in an avalanche path—although this still appears to be a dangerous area. Get avalanche training before you ski in avalanche-prone terrain, such as this.

how to avoid triggering further avalanches while searching for a victim.

If, heaven forbid, a member of your party is involved in an avalanche—or you witness an avalanche disaster to some other party—speed of rescue is vital. Buried skiers' chances of survival drop below 50 percent if they're not located within 5 minutes, so don't waste time going for help. You and anyone else on the scene at the time are the best hope for rescue. A shovel is a vital piece of safety gear in avalanche country. So are avalanche probes; if you don't have one, pull the basket off your pole and use the basketless shaft. Most buried victims are found within 4 feet of the surface.

READING THE WEATHER

Like hikers, bicyclists, sailors, and other outdoor enthusiasts, experienced cross-country skiers are often weather junkies, filling themselves with information from every available source. Some become weather gurus, with an uncanny ability to predict changes not mentioned in the forecast, and many have an almost paranoid sense that nature's out to get them if they let their vigilance slip.

Check the Weather Channel, the local television news, the radio, newspaper, or Internet before leaving home. Or invest in an inexpensive miniature shortwave receiver permanently tuned to the government's network of weather channels, for round-the-clock local reporting. Arm yourself with as much information as you can get so you can better plan clothing, gear, and routes. If you're planning to travel

PAUL SAYS

In an avalanche situation, there are predictable patterns you can learn to recognize. Avalanche training will empower you to make wise route-finding decisions. There are days when frightening-looking slopes are safe and days when they're extremely dangerous. There are days when you simply should not be in the mountain backcountry unless you remain in broad, wooded valleys. Before setting out, collect as much avalanche information as you can. Park rangers, forest rangers, and employees at nearby ski areas or ski shops can provide you with current information. Some mountain states also maintain regularly updated avalanche information hot lines. To find out the hot-line number for your destination, call the local office of the U.S. Forest Service (usually listed under Department of Agriculture) or ask a local ski shop.

COLD-WEATHER DRIVING

Your car is part of your winter survival equipment. Most people who live in snow country winter-prep their cars each fall, but in some parts of the country, particularly the West Coast, city dwellers don't have much reason to do so except for ski trips. Here's a quick checklist of tips:

- Make sure there's enough antifreeze in your radiator for the lowest temperature you might encounter. Diesel-fueled vehicles have additional needs; check your vehicle's owner's manual or ask a mechanic.

- Carry warm blankets or sleeping bags in case of a breakdown or road closure.

- Make sure you have sufficient windshield-washer fluid and that it's rated below freezing. Also, check your wiper blades for wear. If the windshield is wet when you park at the trailhead, swing the wiper arm into the up position to keep the wipers from freezing to the glass.

- Wet parking brakes can freeze to disks or drums, making them difficult to release. Minimize the risk by leaving the brake disengaged if it's safe to do so.

- Tire chains or studded tires are illegal in some parts of the country, mandatory (during storms) in others. Know the law, and practice putting on chains somewhere warm before you have to do it in the snow.

- Make sure you have enough fuel and that your tires have enough air pressure and tread.

- Don't fall victim to the "four-wheel-drive illusion" that causes people to drive such vehicles at far too high a speed. Four-wheel drive improves handling but doesn't help you stop.

to the mountains, remember that sunny weather at home in a broad, lowland valley doesn't necessarily mean sun at the trailhead.

At the same time, never trust too much to a weather forecast. Watch the weather as it develops, so you have an intuitive data bank from which to make your own forecasts, and learn to spot the signs of approaching storms. Know what direction today's weather is moving from and glance that way often, alert for changes. Unless you're on an extended trip, your goal is simply to predict the weather a few hours ahead, not days in advance, making the forecasting job that much easier.

BUDDY SYSTEM

The value of the buddy system is self-evident, but failing to live by it is often a factor when skiers get into serious trouble. Besides providing companionship and allowing you to share equipment, a partner can administer first aid, go for help, and help you puzzle your way out of a predicament.

Employing the buddy system isn't simply a matter of starting out together, then meeting up later at a checkpoint. It means staying in sight or shouting distance of each other for the duration of the outing. If you must ski solo, do so at a commercial cross-country or downhill area, where there's lots of nearby help if something goes wrong.

EQUIPMENT REPAIR

A broken ski, boot, binding, or pole usually doesn't create a life-threatening situation. But it can set you up for a miserable slog on foot, unless you have the proper equipment in your repair kit.

Poles

Your most vulnerable pieces of equipment are probably your poles, which can break, bend, or lose their baskets. You can reduce the risk by trying not to land on them if you fall and by not leaning too strongly on them when standing back up again. If a pole does break, you have two choices: fix it or complete the trip with a single pole.

The easiest way to fix a broken pole is with specially designed metal splints and hose clamps you can carry in your repair kit. Just put one of the metal splints on each side of the pole, attach the clamps, and try not to put too much stress on the pole.

If you don't have pole splints and clamps, you may be able to achieve the same result with a sturdy stick

RICK SAYS

Differences between you and your buddy's temperament, stamina, skiing ability, ability to forecast weather, sense of direction, response to discomfort or potential danger, and awareness of the passage of time will contribute to or complicate your buddy relationship. To the extent that there are rules for such relationships, they wind up having mostly to do with communication. Here are mine:

- **First and foremost, always be honest with your buddy.**

- **Each trusts the other to follow the honesty rule unwaveringly.** This avoids the guessing game of, "Are you really saying what you mean?" The sole exception would be if one of you were to suspect hypothermia, which can cloud the victim's judgment.

- **Make sure you have the same objective before starting an outing.** Are you skiing 6 miles or 16?

On-trail or off? Are speed and distance critical, or is this to be a come-what-may excursion?

- **As a corollary to that rule, agree to commit to that objective unless you mutually decide to change it or conditions (including either partner's physical stamina or injury) require a reassessment.** Midway through a trip, it's okay to say, "I'm feeling lazy today," but not okay to require your partner to concur. Injury, illness, or changing conditions all warrant that you reassess your objective.

- **Recognize that dangers and difficulties are subjective.** If something looks perilous to one partner, it *is* perilous to that person, regardless of what the other believes. Do not pressure each other to attempt routes that your partner doesn't want to do. If that causes disappointment, remember that because you are equals, sometimes the roles will be reversed.

and duct tape. If suitable sticks are scarce, overlap the broken ends of the pole and tape them together. The result will be short but better than nothing.

A lost or broken basket is almost as serious as a broken pole. Ideally, you can carry a spare basket with you, attaching it with creative use of duct tape and/or baling wire. It may be a bit floppy, but it should serve for the remainder of the day. If you don't have a spare basket, you may be able to fashion something suitable with tape, wire, and sticks.

Boots and Bindings

Boots and bindings have two weak points: the point where the boot attaches to the binding and the point where the binding attaches to the ski. For the former, failure means the binding (or the boot's attachment) is broken. Unless you're carrying a spare boot or binding (not likely), duct tape is the answer. Simply tape the boot to the ski with several wraps around both items and head for home by the least taxing route.

In the latter case, the most common failure is for the screws that hold the binding to the ski to pull

© PAUL PETERSEN

Pole splints allow a makeshift fix if your pole breaks.

loose. With the proper repair kit, you can fix this in minutes. What you need is some quick-setting epoxy cement, a screwdriver, and steel wool, a golf tee, or a coffee-stirring stick. You should also carry replacement screws in case you lose the originals. You may be able to substitute a Swiss army knife for the screwdriver, but the ideal tool is a Pozi tip screwdriver, which is slightly larger than most Phillips heads and has eight points instead of four. Most ski shops carry small versions for repair kits. If you can't find one, a Phillips head screwdriver will usually work.

With these tools, the repair itself is simple: stuff the ripped-out screw holes with epoxy, adding the steel wool, golf tee, or stir stick as solid filler. Then, before the epoxy sets, screw the binding firmly back into place and wait for the glue to dry.

Another type of boot/binding failure occurs if a gap opens between the inner sole of the boot and the outer sole that attaches to the binding. Left untreated, this condition can progress rapidly until the outer sole rips completely off the boot, remaining comically attached to the binding but not to your foot. The inner sole will keep your foot from freezing, but unless you have duct tape or good glue, you're walking back to the trailhead.

Skis

Modern skis rarely break, and if they do, the broken piece seldom snaps completely off. This means you can splint it—particularly if the break is near the tip, the most common location. Carry a metal or plastic scraper of the type used for removing grip wax from waxable skis (see photo on page 146) and fashion a splint from it and duct tape.

If a break occurs in the middle of the ski, near the binding, splinting can be more difficult. Get creative with whatever you can dig out of your pack and tape it up as best you can. If worse comes to worse, break off the back half of the ski and tape

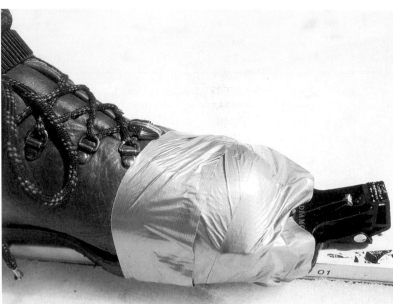

Wind duct tape around your boot and ski if your binding fails.

your boot to the front half for a short scooter-ski that should get you home.

There are many other repair needs that can come up on the trail, ranging from ripped clothing to damaged packs or eyeglass frames. In general, the longer your trip and the more people in your party, the more sophisticated your repair kit needs to be. Here's our list of repair items, in decreasing order of importance.

- duct tape (consider it the twelfth "essential")

- Pozi screw driver or multi-tool, including knife and pliers–wire cutters (for manipulating baling wire)

- quick-setting epoxy (5-minute setting time preferred)

- steel wool, stir sticks, or golf tees

- spare pole basket

- baling wire

- metal or plastic scraper

- 6-inch-long aluminum angle splints (2)

- hose clamps (2)

- safety pins

- needle and thread
- assorted nuts, bolts, and screws
- barge cement (contact cement)

For simplicity, decide which of these items you're going to carry, put them in a nylon ditty bag, and keep it near your skis.

Winter Camping

Winter camping isn't for everyone. Most skiers, in fact, will never try it. But for those who don't mind the long, cold nights, it's the ultimate way to experience the winter environment on its own terms. Don't try it, however, unless you're already an experienced tent camper—ideally a summer backpacker with experience camping in less-than-ideal weather conditions. Winter is particularly unforgiving, and a

Rick Says

There is a special mystique to cold-weather camping—a feeling of awe at the spectacle of nature that seems somehow all the more sharply defined when the temperatures are in the 20s or below. The air has an invigorating tang, the forest is hushed and expectant, and during the evening, above it all, the stars shine brittle and clear.

Astronomers say there are only about 6,000 visible stars—only half of them above the horizon on any given evening. But as you lie on your back beneath the stars, legs and torso snuggled into a warm sleeping bag, tent door unzipped so you can see outside, you know that must be a lie. Only on cold winter evenings can you see so many stars. There seems to be no end to them, shining clear and steady between the dark silhouettes of the trees, whose stark shapes tower beside you until they merge into infinity.

This is the closest most of us can ever come to visiting outer space, camped on a clear, crisp night, far from the smothering bulk of the city atmosphere, with the winter air brisk in our nostrils and our bodies and minds more alive than we would ever have believed possible.

long, February night isn't the time to find out you need a warmer sleeping bag. Even experienced campers would do best to practice first by camping within walking distance of their cars.

To set up camp on snow, first stamp out a flat, cross-hatched platform with your skis, trying to remove as many lumps as possible. Then don't walk on it so you don't pockmark it with boot prints. Your tent should be the "free-standing" type, which doesn't need stakes, and it should be sturdy enough to resist substantial winds. Even so, it behooves you to stake it with extra-long "snow stakes" so it won't roll away in the wind. Insert the stakes into the snow, packing it firmly around them.

You'll need a sleeping bag rated well below your anticipated overnight low temperature and a warm sleeping pad beneath it. When climbing in and out of the tent, try to keep your weight evenly distributed on the pad to avoid making knee holes that will freeze into uncomfortable divots, and brush out any snow that's followed you into the tent. If you get cold at night, check to make sure you haven't rolled off your pad, then try donning a stocking cap. Carry extra closed-cell foam pads for warm seats while cooking or sitting outdoors.

Unless you camp near a stream with easily climbable banks, your most difficult camp chore will be preparing water for the next day. Melt enough snow to make a gallon of water per person—a time- and stove-fuel-intensive task—and don't assume the re-

Paul Says

As an alternative to snow stakes, you can use skis and poles to anchor the corners of the tent when snow camping—even though this does require jamming ski tails into the snow. After all, having your tent blow away is a worse fate than shortening the life of your skis. The little loops that come with the tent to hold stakes usually aren't big enough for this, so I tie short loops of stout nylon cord to them, big enough to accommodate the skis. If it looks as though the wind is going to howl, I further guy-out the tent to buried ski poles, logs, or whatever other anchors are available.

sulting water is safe to drink. Boil it for 5 minutes or pump it through a backpacker's water filter rated to remove *Giardia*. You may have to sleep with the filter to keep it from freezing overnight. Water bottles can also freeze overnight but will usually thaw over the next day in your pack (don't overfill them, which can rupture them). If you want water in the morning, keep one nonleaking bottle with you in your sleeping bag.

For carrying equipment to remote backcountry sites, most skiers prefer *internal-frame* packs to the once-standard *external-frame* variety. Some skiers supple-

ment their packs with sleds, but if you have compact, lightweight equipment, you don't need to carry huge amounts of supplies for a weekend outing.

Most of your equipment will be similar to what you would carry for a same-distance backpacking trip, with a few pounds' extra weight for winter clothes, sleeping bag, sturdier "four-season" tent, extra fuel, and a day or two's extra food in case you get stormbound.

This has merely been a primer on ski camping and backpacking, designed to highlight a few important differences from ordinary backpacking. For more information, consult a good backpacking or mountaineering book such as the classic *Mountaineering: Freedom of the Hills* or Chris Townsend's *Wilderness*

An internal frame pack is the best choice for back-country skiing.

Snow camping at the base of Tower Peak, High Sierra, California.

Skiing and Winter Camping (Ragged Mountain Press). Or seek out experts at your local ski shop or backpacking supply store. And always find out as much as you can about local conditions before venturing into the wilds.

SNOW SHELTERS AND FORCED BIVOUACS

An emergency bivouac is winter camping without a tent or the other equipment you'd bring if camping was the purpose of the trip. Typically, your shelter will consist of a hole in the snow constructed with a shovel and whatever else you may have on hand; you may be forced to substitute your ski clothes for a sleeping bag. Although it's possible to make snug and elaborate snow shelters that are warmer and roomier than most tents, a forced bivouac isn't something most people do for the fun of it.

When people think of snow shelters, many think first of igloos, which are built of snow blocks arranged in a self-supporting dome. Building an igloo requires snow that can be cut into firm blocks, a snow saw, a shovel, patience, and experience. As the Inuit have long known, igloos are superb shelters—but they're not something the average skier will be able to construct in an emergency.

First-time builders can make other types of shelters with reasonable success. The simplest is a snow trench, which is exactly what the name implies. Align it crosswise to the wind, digging with a collapsible aluminum shovel if you have one—a ski, pole, pot lid, backpacker's "poop scoop," ski scraper, sturdy stick, or gloved hands if you don't. Make the trench as narrow as possible and deep enough for the bottom to be nicely sheltered from the wind, piling snow on the upwind side to build your windbreak as quickly as possible. If it's a true emergency, you may be on the verge of panic. Keep calm, and don't work up too much sweat, because your clothes will be hard to dry later.

Roof the trench with a tarp or poncho (if you have one) held down with skis and stout nylon cord secured to nearby saplings or to logs or other anchors buried in packed snow. If you don't have a tarp, use a space blanket, being careful not to tear it. Guying this fragile fabric will be impossible, but you can try

A shovel is valuable in preparing an overnight shelter, but carry one in avalanche-prone terrain even if you don't plan to overnight.

burying the upwind edge in snow to help hold it in place. (This is a good idea with a tarp, as well.) Make sure there's a slope to the roof so condensation runs to one side rather than dripping on you. Punch a couple of fist-sized breathing holes though the snow near the head of the trench to provide critical ventilation.

A similar shelter can sometimes be constructed more easily from the wind-hollowed pits that form at the bases of big trees. Simply enlarge a natural pit to the necessary size and roof it with tree branches, tarps, space blankets, or whatever else is handy.

If you have more time and deep enough snow, you can try building a snow cave, a more elaborate (and warmer) snow shelter. Begin by seeking out a steep snowbank at least 6 feet deep and big enough to make a good cave. If you're in mountain country, make sure the spot is not in an avalanche path.

When you've found a suitable location, dig a vertical door, about shoulder width and a little less than head high. Dig about 3 feet straight back into the slope. Next, convert this door to a fat T by digging sideways slots with their bases at waist height, going about 18 inches to each side. The purpose of these slots is to give you room to toss snow out of the interior of the cave; later you'll plug them with blocks of snow.

Beginning at approximately shoulder height, excavate backward into the snowbank, enlarging the cave

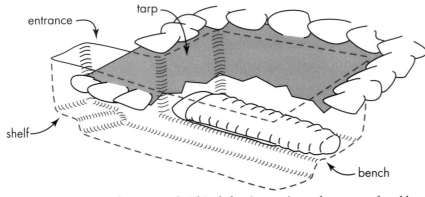

Cut-away view of snow trench. This shelter is roomier and more comfortable than the basic trench described in the text, but the extra width may mean it's not as warm. Note that the sleeping area is on a small shelf, so it's not the lowest (and dampest) part of the trench. There's also a separate entranceway. Although it's hard to see in a diagram, it's important for the roof tarp to slope to a side or corner, so condensation won't drip on you.

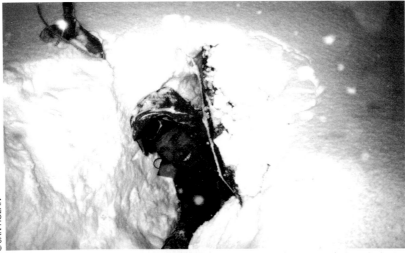

Paul Henrickson emerging from a well-built trench after a snowfall.

as time and the size of the snowbank permit. You're trying to make a platform with an arched ceiling, with the base of the platform at least several inches higher than the bottom of the entrance T's cross-bar. An elevated platform is important because it helps trap warm air inside the cave while preventing cold air from creeping in through the entrance. As you enter or exit the cave, you'll duck through the original door, then climb onto the platform. An alternative design is to extend the original walkway farther back into the cave, constructing elevated sleeping platforms on one or both sides of it. Whichever construction method you use, make sure you leave at least 12 inches of snow above you for ceiling support. Again, ventilation holes are vital.

Snow caves are inherently damp from condensation and slowly melting snow, so try to produce a smooth inside surface that will allow water to run off to the sides rather than drip on you all night long. When you're finished, pack the sides of the entrance T with snow; cut down on drafts through the doorway by partially blocking it with backpacks—but don't cut off all ventilation coming through from this direction.

Trenches or tree-pit shelters are likely to be cold and drafty, and they run the risk of collapsing roofs in snowstorms. But a properly constructed snow cave should maintain an interior temperature slightly above freezing, even in a full blizzard. Your biggest problem will be dampness. To avoid melting your way into soggy hypothermia in this or any other form of snow shelter, each member of your party should have a waterproof sleeping pad, most likely made of closed-cell foam. A good piece of relatively lightweight emergency equipment

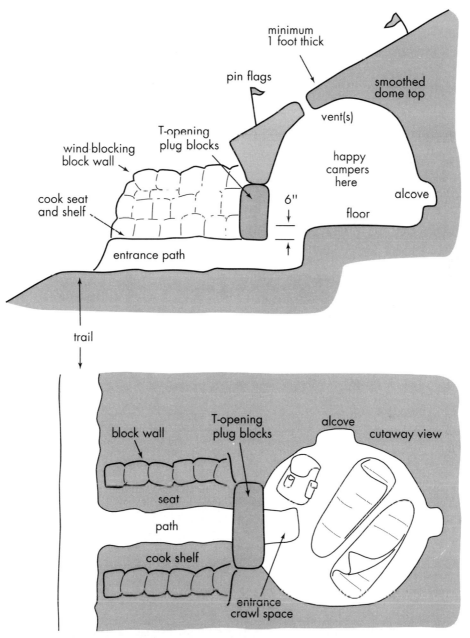

Snow cave. Like the trench shown opposite, this cave is more than a basic survival shelter. But there's no reason not to make your camp comfortable if you have time and energy. Luxury features in this drawing include the wind-blocking wall at the entrance—with its accompanying seat and cooking shelf—the level "trail" providing an easy path to the latrine area, and the gear-storage alcoves in the cave itself. Note that the dome has a nicely smoothed interior surface to prevent drips. The "pin flags" are simply high-visibility markers (tall enough not to be buried in snow) showing the location of the cave so nobody falls through.

Snow caves can be warm and comfortable.

© JAN HOLAN

is a bivouac bag, which is simply a body-sized sack of Gore-Tex or a similar waterproof and breathable fabric that repels moisture and helps retain body heat.

If you can't find a snowdrift big enough for a conventional trench or cave, build the best windbreak you can out of packed snow, branches, and rocks. This may be the only way to make a shelter in the often-shallow snows of the East and Midwest. If you can't pack the snow, you can at least make a big pile of it, with a trench in the middle. Other types of shel-

ter may also be available, such as hollow trees or overhanging cliffs.

As with all outdoor skills, the best way to learn the art of snow shelter construction is to practice under controlled conditions. If this is a skill you want to have in your repertoire, spend an afternoon with a skilled friend digging a cave in a convenient snowbank. You don't have to spend the night in it, but if you do, you'll have a good idea of what clothing and supplies you would need to survive comfortably.

Training and Racing, by John Morton

O nce they've mastered the basics, many skiers think about trying a race. Some are drawn to the collective adrenaline of being part of a crowd of athletes, just as runners are drawn to the New York City Marathon. Some want to see how their skills and stamina stack up against fellow skiers or the clock. Some simply seek the challenge of going the distance in a ski marathon such as Wisconsin's famous 55 km American Birkebeiner. (In running, a *marathon* is run over a precise distance, 26.2 miles, but in skiing it simply refers to a long race, usually from 50 to 100 km.)

Ski races fall into two categories: classic and freestyle. "Classic" means diagonal stride, kicking and gliding. Freestyle races permit any technique, but they're inherently skating races—even accomplished diagonal-stride skiers will find themselves at a major disadvantage. Distances for either type of race can range from as little as 5 km to 100 km or longer (sometimes split over multiple days). Most competitions, referred to as *citizens' races*, are open to all-comers; others may have separate elite and citizen-racer divisions.

Runners with road-racing experience will find ski races a familiar environment, slightly modified for snow. Nonrunners will quickly get the idea. In place of pin-on numbers, racers are sometimes given numbered vests called *bibs*. Water stops and food stops (on longer races) make it unnecessary to carry anything, even in marathon events.

Some race organizers prepare a myriad of parallel tracks at the start so hundreds or even thousands of skiers can begin together. Other competitions spread out the pack by starting skiers one or two at a time at intervals of perhaps 30 seconds. All well-organized races provide ways for skiers to shed warm-up clothing at the start, for transport, if necessary, to the finish. Major events usually provide warming tents, stoves, or bonfires to keep the competitors warm at the start and finish. Point-to-point races typically provide shuttle buses.

There are hundreds of North American races. Ski shops often keep race schedules or maintain bulletin boards for announcements and application forms. These shops are also good sources of information about the size and organizational caliber of races. Regional outdoor magazines usually maintain race calendars.

The need to pay for trail grooming means entry fees may be a bit stiffer than those for running events, often with significant late-registration penalties. Start-of-race parking may be limited, so it's smart to arrive well ahead of schedule.

Performance on race day involves at least six major components: technique, conditioning, nutrition, selection and preparation of equipment, psychology, and to some degree natural talent. Technique is discussed in chapters 2, 3, and 7.

Equipment and waxing are more important in racing than in recreational touring or backcountry skiing. Although many citizen racers find enjoyment and satisfaction competing in both skating and classic events on the same pair of "combination" skis, most racers eventually purchase specialized skating skis and classic skis. Skating skis are shorter, stiffer, and designed to be waxed with gliding wax over the full length. Classic skis are longer and have a distinct wax "pocket" under foot to accommodate the kick wax of the day. Both types of racing skis are lighter and more delicate than recreational nordic skis (see chapter 5).

If you get more serious about nordic racing, waxing will become a significant factor. In elite freestyle events, wax specifically selected for the snow conditions and air temperatures is melted into the skis base, scraped thin, and brushed smooth to create the fastest possible running surface. The same technique is used with classic skis except underfoot, where kick

Before a race, familiarize yourself with the trail map.

wax is applied to allow the skier to propel herself down the track. Waxing is discussed in chapter 12.

Although nutrition is sometimes significant at the Olympic level, it is seldom a deciding factor in citizens' races. And since none of us can alter the talent, or lack thereof, bequeathed to us by our parents, it makes sense to concentrate on the aspects of the sport offering the greatest promise for improved performance: physical conditioning and racing strategy. How deeply you'll want to delve into these topics depends on your racing goals. If your purpose is merely to enjoy the competition in a short race without worrying too much about your result, you may need no special training. If your goal is to complete a ski marathon, you may need to do some longer-than-usual outings in the weeks leading up to the event. Many citizen racers comfortably complete ski marathons by getting out two or three times a week, gradually building up the longer outings to at least half the race distance.

The rest of this chapter explores the basic theory of athletic training and how to apply it to skiing.

The more you know about training, the more efficiently you can use whatever time you choose to invest in it.

PHYSICAL CONDITIONING
Stress and Rest

At its most basic level, physical conditioning is simply a combination of stress and rest. It has long been recognized that if a muscle was given more work than it could comfortably accomplish, then rested, the muscle would respond by growing stronger. Debate surrounds the details of what type of stress, and how much rest, but there is agreement that improved performance results from judicious applications of stress and rest. The key to optimum success is a balance of the two so delicate that it has to be carefully monitored by way of a training plan, a record of actual activities, and later, an evaluation of competition results.

The words *conditioning* and *training* can be used interchangeably to describe physical improvement resulting from an organized program. Physical conditioning can be divided into three categories: endurance (also called distance), strength, and speed. Although there are limitless variations and combinations of the three, it is important to decide which one is the goal of a given workout.

Endurance training. The core of any training plan for nordic racing is endurance or distance training. Distance workouts increase athletic endurance by conditioning the cardiovascular system to operate more efficiently, enhancing the body's capacity to transport oxygen from the lungs to the muscles, where it is used to generate energy. Endurance training can take several forms but should probably comprise at least 60 percent of your annual training. Depending upon the method of training selected—hiking, cycling, skiing, and so on—an endurance workout can last up to several hours.

But if the premium is on duration, then the pace of endurance workouts must be relatively slow. For those lacking electronic heart-rate monitors, a good guideline for pacing a distance workout is the ability to carry on a conversation.

Strength training. The maxim, "Whatever your sport, you'll do it better if you are stronger," appears to be true. It's generally accepted that you can tailor a strength program toward either power or endurance. Football players, gymnasts, and boxers want explosive power and the increased muscle bulk that accompanies dramatic increases in power. This muscle expansion is achieved by lifting heavy weights in relatively few repetitions. A football lineman might bench-press a 250-pound barbell to increase the size and strength of his upper body, but he might lift that weight only three times before exhausting his muscles.

Strength training for endurance favors lighter weights but more repetitions. A runner who wants to add zip to her stride might do leg presses on a weight machine; compared to our example of the football player, the runner might do more repetitions (20 or 25) with lighter weights. Strength training is effective only if the body is allowed to recover, so most strength programs prescribe workouts on alternate days, three times a week.

Speed training. Although cross-country racing requires strength and endurance, the victory still goes to the fastest; we're in the business of building race horses, not plow horses! One reason for those long hours of endurance training is to provide an aerobic base for speed work. Speed work is of shorter duration but higher intensity than distance training.

Interval workouts are the most widely used form of speed training. The concept is to go as fast as or faster than you can in a race, but to do so only for short distances. Remember the basic premise of training, stress followed by rest leads to improved performance? Interval workouts are a microcosm of that training philosophy: each interval workout is a series of short work segments followed by rests. If the idea is to go really fast during the work segments, it is essential that the rest between intervals be adequate to provide recovery. One reliable indicator of when recovery is achieved is when athletes resume chattering with each other.

Pace training is a variation of intervals. If you know how fast you need to ski to achieve your goal but are unable to ski that fast for a full race, shorten the distance until you can perform at the desired rate.

For example, to ski a 15-km race in 45 minutes, I might attempt 1-kilometer repeats at a pace of 3 minutes. The procedure is much like conventional intervals, work alternating with rest. But with pace training, you have a specific target for each work interval. In this example, I would not have succeeded if I skied my first kilometer in 2:53 and my eighth kilometer in 3:25.

One note of caution when skiing interval or pace workouts: snow conditions can play a significant role in your interval times. The Dartmouth College skiers I used to coach trained at 2:30 in the afternoon. Occasionally, even after several difficult intervals, their times on the loop continued to improve, although it was obvious they were getting tired. The snow was getting faster as the sun went down, more than compensating for the fatigue of the skiers. In a situation like that, use your judgment and quit when you've had enough.

Fartlek is Swedish for "speed-play." Unlike running a marathon, where exertion is relatively constant, uphill and down, start to finish, skiing is a series of sprints and recoveries. So the Swedes theorized that a skier should be able to vary the pace frequently, learning to be comfortable with changes in tempo. A *fartlek* workout might go like this: 10 minutes of stretching, followed by a 45-minute run on trails, comfortably cruising the flats and downhills but sprinting hard on all the uphills.

TRAINING PRINCIPLES

We now have the three basic building blocks for any nordic skiing training program: endurance, strength, and speed. But before we begin filling out a training schedule, some other principles deserve comment. Things get tricky here, since a few of these concepts appear to be contradictory.

Consistency

Nothing produces results like consistency. If you want to get good at something, do it every day. In terms of physical conditioning, this means it is better to work out every day, even in small doses, than to rest midweek and beat yourself to a pulp on the weekend. But to avoid overtraining and to ensure proper recovery, elite athletes arrange their training plans so that successive workouts complement each other rather than conflicting. Follow a hard day/easy day rotation.

Even busy individuals rarely miss a meal if they are accustomed to eating three times a day. When training becomes as much a part of your daily routine as eating, then you have established consistency in your program and you will see improvement.

Volume

Closely tied to consistency is the idea of volume. Simply stated, those who succeed at cross-country racing train a lot. Serious nordic racers probably amass more hours actually training than almost any other type of athlete. There is a strong correlation between top international performances and massive hours spent training in the preceding years. If you want to excel in nordic racing, you must be prepared to put in the volume; there are no shortcuts.

Capability

Success in cross-country racing is a long-term investment. Developing the necessary technique and conditioning requires years. If this training is to be productive, it must be progressive and systematic. Most experts agree that a training volume increase of 15 percent per year (for example, in hours of training) is reasonable for promising young racers.

Several years ago, U.S. Ski Team coaches Torbjorn Karlsen and Ruff Patterson wrote "Training Planning for Cross Country Skiers," in which they suggested training levels for various categories of athletes: national team members at 1,000–1,200 hours per year, national team hopefuls at 800–1,000 hours, college skiers at 600–800, national caliber juniors at 400–600 hours, and so on. From the perspective of the U.S. Ski Team, it made perfect sense and was part of a logical progression; but at the college level, for example, the suggested volume of training was simply beyond the capability of most full-time students, both because of the physical demands and the athletes' academic obligations. Any training schedule must be within the capability of the athlete.

Specificity and Variety

The next two principles of training appear to be contradictory: specificity and variety. Specificity suggests that the best way to become a great ski racer is to do a lot of ski racing. All other forms of training are substitutes that fall short. This is a problem for skiers because, unlike world-class swimmers who can be in the pool 365 days a year, skiers are forced by lack of snow to spend considerable segments of the year in alternate forms of training.

In the past decade there has been increased emphasis among national team skiers on summer skiing on glaciers and snowfields from Alaska to the Alps. For those without the means to get on snow in the off-season, roller-skiing has become increasingly important because it is the closest thing to actually skiing without the benefit of snow.

Balancing this principle of specificity is the variety. Mentally, as well as physically, there is great value to a training schedule that includes a healthy component of varied activities.

Such a training schedule promotes spontaneity, generates enthusiasm, and establishes a strong base for more specific ski training later in the season.

The challenge, of course, is to balance these apparently conflicting needs for variety and specificity. It makes sense to emphasize variety for young skiers or those just getting into racing. At the same time, there is an increased need for ski-specific training as the competitive season draws near. Roller-skiing once a week in July might be adequate, but four times a week might be more appropriate in November.

Working on Weaknesses

It's human nature that we prefer to do what we do well. Success in cross-country racing, however, requires a balance of endurance, strength, and speed. Rather than ignoring a weakness, the successful competitor acknowledges the area that needs work and focuses on improvement in that area. One skier might lack upper body strength, another might be timid on downhills, while a third becomes mired in negative self-talk at the start of a race. Very often these shortcomings become the weak link of an otherwise strong chain, preventing significant improvement.

Roller-skiing is an ideal way to keep skiing after the snow is gone. But you might want to add knee pads and a helmet.

Uphills

Races are won on the uphills. A competent racer can ski a typical 15-km course in about 45 minutes. At first glance, we might assume the skier spent 15 minutes on the flats, 15 minutes on the climbs, and 15 minutes tucking the downhills. But obviously, more minutes tick by when the skier is laboring up hills than when he is zooming down descents. It is more likely that 15 minutes were spent on the flats, 5 on the downhills, and 25 on the climbs. Therefore, the greatest potential for improvement lies in the 25 minutes of climb. This suggests that at least 50 percent of your training should be spent on vertical power and endurance. While it's possible to lose a race by falling on a downhill or by riding slow skis, nordic competitors must be strong and confident on the uphills in order to win consistently.

Arms and Legs Together

Cross-country ski racing puts demands on the entire body; arms and legs work in concert to propel the competitor down the track. Under the heading of "variety," we might assume that a distance bike ride would be great for the legs, whereas a Nautilus routine emphasizing the upper body would improve arm strength. That assumption would be true; but when the arms and legs are stressed simultaneously, there seems to be a more significant aerobic impact than in workouts where either arms or legs are stressed separately. This is not to say you should eliminate workouts that focus on just the arms or the legs. But for planning purposes, put a star next to those workouts where arms and legs are stressed together: rollerskiing, hill striding with poles, or hard physical labor. You get an aerobic training bonus from these workouts.

Visualization

It has been proven that the use of mental imagery or visualization, practiced correctly, enhances performance. Examples of visualization are seen throughout the sports world: an alpine skier, leaning on her ski poles at the top of a slalom course mentally running through the gates again and again; a diver poised on the edge of a 10-meter platform, eyes closed, rehearsing his convoluted twists and flawless entry into the water; a basketball player on the foul line, eyes riveted to the rim, imagining the "swish" of the net several times before the ball is ever raised for the shot.

If confidence on fast, icy downhills is a problem, visualization in the summer provides a great opportunity to work on it. Every time you run, bike, or rollerski down a hill, visualize yourself on skis, confident and assertive, gaining time on your opponents.

Warm-Up, Stretching, Cool-Down, and Rest

Much has been learned in the past few decades about stretching the muscles before strenuous exercise. Not only is it possible to perform better when properly warmed up, but the risk of injury due to strained or torn muscles or tendons is dramatically reduced. It's better to stretch after the muscles have been warmed up slightly; a widely accepted approach suggests 10 minutes of light exercise (jogging, skiing, or the activity of the day), followed by a stop to stretch.

Following a tough workout or competition, it's equally important to cool down for a few minutes. Strenuous exercise, especially if it lasts more than an hour, generates lactic acid, which accumulates in the muscles; light aerobic jogging or skiing stimulates the circulatory system to purge the muscles of that lactate. Even after an exhausting competition, 10 minutes of gentle cool-down activity will significantly speed recovery. Watch any major endurance event and you will see the top athletes sprint through the finish line, catch their breath, then walk, jog, or ski a few minutes more before they call it a day.

Another effective method of preventing injury and speeding recovery is massage therapy. Massage has been proven so effective in flushing lactic acid from the body and thus speeding recovery that most World Cup nordic teams have a massage therapist on their support staffs. If recovery time can be reduced, then training volume and intensity can be increased. Massage, whirlpool baths, and saunas have important rejuvenating effects for the serious endurance athlete.

Of course, without adequate rest, no training program can achieve long-term improvement.

METHODS OF TRAINING

What activities do successful ski racers actually do for conditioning? Although training varies considerably among the world's best athletes, it is possible to generalize to some degree. Several popular training methods are listed below, ranked in order of specificity for nordic ski racing.

- **Skiing.** Just as the concept of specificity explains, the best training for ski racing is skiing. Increasing numbers of elite racers and hopefuls congregate at places like Dachstein Glacier in Austria throughout the summer to ski on snow.

- **Rollerskiing.** The next best thing to being on snow is rollerskiing, although there is a danger of developing bad technical habits since rollerskiing is not exactly like skiing on snow. Still, the world's best racers all rollerski extensively during the off season.

- **Ice skating and in-line skating.** Since the advent of freestyle as a cross-country skiing discipline, ice skating in winter and in-line skating in summer have become increasingly popular as training options. V2 ice skating with poles is great for balance, poise, and control. In-line skates are less expensive than rollerskis with boots and bindings, and most skiers would admit they're more fun. However, in-line skates can also encourage technique problems.

- **Hill work with ski poles.** Done properly with visualization, hill work with poles can be remarkably specific to cross-country skiing. By working arms and legs together, you are getting an aerobic bonus in your training.

- **Rowing.** Rowing is surprisingly good training for skiing. An authentic rowing shell with a movable seat provides the benefit of working the arms and legs together, while the delicacy of the shell guarantees some balance development.

- **Hiking.** Hiking in the mountains is perhaps the best method of getting quality distance training, providing excellent vertical training on relatively soft footing.

- **Running.** Although running lacks specificity for skiing, it is the quintessential aerobic exercise and is wonderfully uncomplicated.

- **Cycling.** Cycling can provide excellent aerobic work without the pounding associated with running. Since the skating revolution, the pedaling motion of cycling has become more specific to cross-country skiing. The intervals of sprint and recovery naturally encountered on a mountain bike in hilly terrain are remarkably similar to those of skiing.

Hill bounding with ski poles works both arms and legs, providing good training for skiing.

Mountain hiking provides excellent endurance exercise, and spectacular vistas, such as this one in Seward, Alaska, reward and inspire the spirit.

Several other sports have value as off-season training for skiers.

- orienteering
- rock climbing
- wind surfing
- kayaking
- triathlons
- soccer
- tennis
- swimming

DESIGNING YOUR OWN TRAINING PROGRAM

Regardless of your competitive aspirations, you can design a training plan that will lead to improved results in cross-country ski racing. The first step is to establish your goals. You can't chart a realistic course if you're not sure of the destination.

Goal-Setting

Even if we are not certain of the intermediate steps, a clearly defined goal causes us to make decisions—both consciously and subconsciously—that bring us closer to that goal.

Goals should be appropriate and possible, but not easily within reach. For example, a young skier might first strive to make her high school team, then set her sights on a trip to the Junior Olympics. It's like climbing a ladder: each time you take a step up, celebrate your accomplishment while also looking up toward the next level.

Since success is important for maintaining a positive self-image, give yourself multiple goals: a short-term goal, an intermediate goal, and a long-term goal. The short-term goal should be relatively easy to achieve and thus become a constant source of positive reinforcement. It may be as simple as missing no more than one workout each week. Intermediate goals are farther out in the future, perhaps for a season or even linked to Olympic quadrennials. Fi-

nally, career goals keep everything in perspective. A college skier with aspirations for the Olympic team will make different choices than a classmate who plans to attend medical school following graduation.

A final caution on goal-setting. One of the truly wonderful aspects of cross-country skiing is the ability to regard the course, the snow conditions, and the weather as the primary challenges, allowing us to view other competitors as coadventurers rather than adversaries. You may be racing against the other competitors, but avoid setting goals related to other people. You have control only over your own performance, not anyone else's.

Once you've defined your goals, you must candidly evaluate where you are now. Are you a promising junior racer who has just discovered the fun and excitement of competition? Or are you 44 years old, lured back into the sport because your clothes have become too tight and your cholesterol level has climbed too high? If you've kept a log, and last winter went well, an increase of 15 percent in annual training hours would probably not be excessive.

If you haven't exercised on a regular basis for some time, it's a good idea to consult with your doctor before developing a training program. Anyone earning a living and raising a family should be realistic about the amount of time each day that's available for training. Given your current physical condition, last year's training volume, and your available time, determine a target number of hours for the year's training and racing.

Training Stages

In Rob Sleamaker's book *Serious Training for Serious Athletes*, he talks about five training stages for the year: Recovery, Base, Intensity, Peak, and Racing. Rob assigns each training stage the following time commitments:

Recovery: 4–6 weeks

Base: 16 weeks

Intensity: 16 weeks

Peak: 4–6 weeks

Racing: 8–12 weeks

Look ahead to your next racing season. What do you anticipate will be your earliest competition, and when will the racing be over for the year? If your last major event is scheduled for the second weekend in March, and the first important event is right after Christmas, you're looking at a competitive season of 11 weeks. Work backward through the Peak, Intensity, Base, and Recovery phases, roughing out segments of time that seem reasonable to you.

Now you have the year divided into five training stages. In the illustration, Periodization Distribution Between Training Cycles, Rob shows the percentage of total annual training hours for thirteen four-week training cycles throughout the year.

Your next job is to subdivide these cycles into weeks. Rob advocates a four-week cycle, three weeks of gradually increasing volume and intensity followed by a week of low volume that serves as "R&R" (rest and recuperation). Some very successful competitors simplify this into a three-week schedule: easy week, moderate week, hard week.

Finally, don't forget the hard day/easy day rotation. This can be more complicated than it sounds. Early in your training year, a two-hour distance run might constitute a tough workout, while several months later a mellow, two-hour distance ski could easily be considered a recovery day following a race.

Now start crunching the numbers! Using the two graphs borrowed from Rob's book, break your annual training hours into appropriate percentages for each stage and then into weekly cycles within the stage. Be sure to adjust the suggested percentages to your own situation. These graphs are based on training information gathered from national team athletes and their coaches. What

works for them isn't always feasible for the rest of us.

Once you've determined your weekly targets, you can schedule individual days and specific workouts. This is where the juggling act becomes really challenging, as you try to fit the various pieces of the puzzle together: strength training three times a week, at least one over-distance day, a couple of rollerski workouts, perhaps a local foot race on the weekend, hard day/easy day rotation, specificity, variety, and so on. There is no right or wrong way to develop your training plan—there is only what seems to work for you and what doesn't.

Now that you've established your goals and developed a training plan, you're more than halfway home. All that remains is to keep track of what you've done, and at the end of the season evaluate your results. The easiest way to keep track is in a training log. The purpose of the log is to provide a record of training, racing, and state of mind. If you've had a tremendous racing season, your log will document the training that led to your success. If your race results weren't

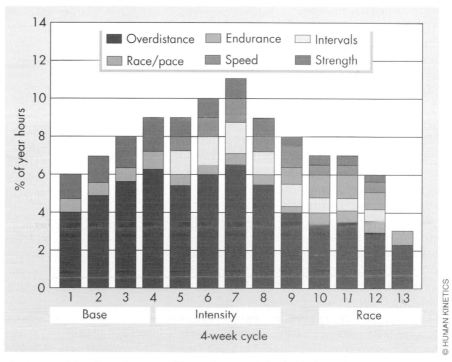

Serious training for endurance athletes. (Source: Rob Sleamaker, Serious Training for Serious Athletes, Human Kinetics. Reproduced by permission.)

what you had expected, the log will contain clues to help you discover the shortcomings in your plan so you can revise it for next season.

If you keep your log simple, you will be more likely to fill it in. It might be helpful to know what your resting pulse was each morning, what you ate each day, and how many hours you slept; but the vital information is: what you did for training, how long it took, and how you felt. If you consistently record these three observations, you'll be well on your way to achieving your competitive goals.

Be sure to review and evaluate your conditioning plan and training log at the end of each season. Were you happy with the winter's race results? If so, what seemed to be responsible for that success? If not, how should you revise your training for next year? The plan and the log are valuable tools only if you use them to improve your program each year.

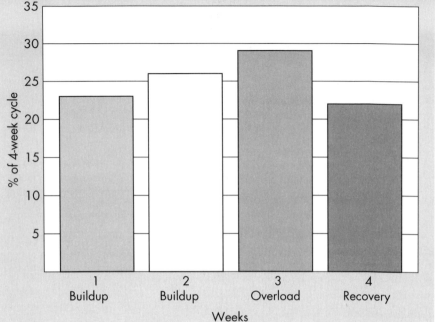

Distribution of training within each four-week cycle. (Source: *Rob Sleamaker*, Serious Training for Serious Athletes, *Human Kinetics. Reproduced by permission.*)

KEEP IT FUN

I've saved the most important aspect of training until last. You must keep it fun! Nordic racing can be a long-term investment requiring years of preparation. The only way to ensure competitive longevity is to enjoy the training. You must look forward to your workouts and enjoy the people with whom you train. When training becomes drudgery, your race results will suffer and soon your competitive career will be over.

On the other hand, if your training instills in you a sense of accomplishment and feeling of self-worth, if it keeps you physically fit, and if it puts you in contact with energetic people who share your enthusiasm, then you probably can look forward to a long and rewarding racing career. Just keep it fun!

RACING

Although success in nordic ski competition is largely dependent upon adequate preparation, you will also benefit from learning a few race-day strategies. These suggestions are loosely grouped as pre-race, during the race, and post-race considerations.

Pre-Race Considerations

Positive self-image. Perhaps the most basic requirement for success in athletic competition is a positive self-image. To be a winner, you must like yourself, be proud of your accomplishments, and be confident that you can achieve your goals. This is not always easy; it seems to be human nature that we often imagine the worst-case scenario rather than the best. While we hope for victory, we picture all the things that can go wrong in vivid detail.

Another assault on our self-image can come from misguided coaches. Until recently, most coaches assumed their primary function was to correct their athletes' faults. Racers constantly received messages such as "You're not going fast enough," "Your weight is too far back," "Your kick is late," "Your stride is too short," "You're too timid on the downhills."

But the most damaging blows to our self-image come from within. This is especially true in the high stress environment of competitive athletics. When we fail to achieve our goals, we often indulge in a level of verbal abuse that we would never tolerate from someone else. The messages we send to our subconscious are critically important to the development of our self-image. We must be on the lookout for negative self-talk and replace it with constructive, positive observations. For example, let's assume I'm driving to a ski race through a heavy snowstorm. It's easy to imagine the following self-talk: "Dammit! Another tricky waxing day, and I probably won't have time to test adequately. Why the hell can't it just be packed powder snow and blue hard wax?"

With self-talk like that, I'll probably start the competition insecure about the wax, and almost certainly I'll be unhappy with my result. But with practice it's possible to approach the same situation from a different perspective, with self-talk like this: "All right, heavy new snow! A wax race! I'm as experienced and capable waxing as anyone out here. This could be a real advantage."

Is there any question which type of self-talk will create the stronger competitive result? Successful positive self-talk takes creativity and mental discipline. It's not lying to yourself; your subconscious can see right through that. Positive self-talk amounts to a change in how you choose to look at the world around you.

If you want to be a winner, you must act like a winner and you must talk like a winner, especially to yourself. A strong, positive self-image is an essential characteristic of every champion.

Visualization. Visualization or mental imagery is a powerful tool for the development of a positive self-image. Your subconscious cannot distinguish between the reality around you and what you imagine. What do you suppose happens when you visualize yourself skiing beside Olympic champion Bjorn Daehlie, matching him stride for stride?

Quite simply, imagery works! Many studies have confirmed its effectiveness, but perhaps the most dramatic one involved basketball. A large, randomly selected group of participants was brought into a gymnasium and tested on their abilities to throw foul shots. Each subject was asked to attempt a certain number of shots, and a percentage score was recorded. Three groups were established, each with an identical cumulative score. Group 1 was sent away with instructions to return in a month. Group 2 was told to practice throwing foul shots an hour a day for the next month. Group 3 was told not to touch a basketball for a month but to visualize shooting foul shots for an hour a day.

When the three groups reconvened a month later, some of the findings were predictable. Group 1 made virtually no improvement over their original test score. Group 2, which had practiced foul shooting for 30 hours, had improved its test score. Group 3 provided the fireworks. In spite of not touching a basketball for a month, Group 3 achieved a test score only slightly lower than that of Group 2, and far higher than Group 1!

You can add excitement and reality to your mental rehearsals if you address all five senses. If you are envisioning an upcoming ski race, be sure to see the brilliantly colorful uniforms of the participating racers, hear the cheering of the crowd, smell the evergreen trees as you glide past, taste the cold crisp air as you inhale, and feel the smooth power of your muscles as you charge up a hill.

Arousal and relaxation. Another aspect of race preparation that deserves attention is the relationship between relaxation and arousal. In our society, we have the general impression that stress is bad. Stress causes high blood pressure, alcohol abuse, and heart attacks. We really mean excess stress is bad. Stress, in appropriate amounts, enhances performance and motivates us to greatness. As a competitive athlete you need to develop a feel for your own optimal state of arousal and learn techniques for controlling excess stress, which can undermine performance.

An effective method of managing excess stress is using relaxation techniques. Your ability to relax, both mentally and physically, is significant in at least three related areas. First, while racing, you must be able to relax for the microsecond between each stride. This is an essential aspect of correct technique, since the power stroke of every stride is followed by a glide phase, and the glide is far more productive if a skier is relaxed. It appears contradictory, but to go faster, nordic skiers must actually relax between strides.

Second, relaxation restores your creative energy. We each embody a certain amount of creative energy; it can be replaced or recharged, but not instantaneously. Energy consumed worrying about world politics, the stock market, or a career promotion is energy that might have made a mediocre workout into an excellent one. And the more excellent workouts you string together, the greater the likelihood that you will have a spectacular race when you want one.

Relaxation's third benefit involves technique improvement. Earlier we discussed the importance of visualization. Studies have shown visualization to be far more effective if done in a completely relaxed physical state. If you really want to improve your basketball free-throw average, visualizing the ball swishing through the net while you are stranded in gridlocked traffic is not going to be as effective as imagining it while lying quietly on your bed, free of outside distractions.

Motivation. For many years motivation seemed to be some type of intangible force that Russian and Scandinavian nordic skiers had in abundance but North Americans seemed to lack. Then at a sports medicine conference sponsored by the U.S. Ski Team, Dr. Rainer Martins helped demystify the concept. "Motivation," Dr. Martins said, "has two components, a feeling of self-worth, and fun." Quite simply, we are motivated to pursue activities that make us feel good about ourselves.

Tips for self-motivation can be very mundane. I love to race but often become bored with the day-to-day drudgery of training. Keeping a basic training log, simply jotting down my workouts every day, becomes good motivation. I hate to see the blank spaces on the calendar that represent skipped workouts.

Few moments in cross-country racing are as exciting as the start of a relay . . .

I've made a habit of entering important competitions well in advance and posting the confirmation of my entry in a place where I see it every day, a constant reminder of why I'm training.

For some folks, a routine cholesterol screening or weighing in on an accurate scale every so often may provide plenty of motivation. And training with a group may be helpful since it can be more enjoyable to exercise with friends a few times a week than to always train alone.

Considerations during the Race

Display confidence. Establish an attitude of quiet confidence at the start of a race. If a rival competitor is

. . . crossing the finish line is one of those moments, too!

frantically changing wax, desperately rummaging through his car for a misplaced racing bib, or sprinting to avoid a late start, it's likely that racer will be vulnerable during the competition. Even if my pre-race preparations are not going as smoothly as I would like, I try never to let my opponents see me rattled. I would rather that they think my wax is perfect, that I had a great warm-up, and that I'm expecting to win (even if I don't actually feel that way). A little good-natured joking with other racers before the start gives the impression that you are relaxed and confident.

Concentration. Coaches in every sport have been pleading with their athletes for decades to "*Concentrate!*" The generally accepted definition of concentration is the ability to focus exclusively on the task at hand, ignoring distractions. Imagine a pitcher throwing strikes while local fans behind home plate frantically wave handkerchiefs in an effort to distract him.

But skiers often become so focused on the track ahead of them that they fail to absorb information that could improve their performance. In certain snow conditions, especially in warm temperatures, as skiers kick and glide down the trail, the tracks become wet and slow. Meanwhile, on the corduroy borders of the groomed surface the snow remains dry, untracked, and significantly faster. Yet one racer after another, concentration etched on their faces, slogs along in the tracks. Don't become so focused on your objective that you aren't concentrating effectively.

Leading and following. On the course, try to give the impression of poise and self-assurance. You may push to the limit, overtaking another racer, but as you pass try to control your breathing and offer encouragement, if only to give the impression you're cruising easily.

When you "track" another skier, break contact quickly. Plan your move in advance and prepare to pour on the power for a couple of minutes after you've passed, just to be certain he or she won't hang with you. Uphills are the best place to pass. If a racer is striding hard up a long hill and another competitor blasts past, it's human nature to think, "Boy, is she tough! If she's that strong on this hill, I'll never stay with her."

Of course, the flip side is knowing that anyone who passes you is probably pushing to the limit and won't be able to maintain that pace for long. If you force yourself to hang with a faster skier for a couple of minutes, especially if you concentrate on relaxing and skiing smoothly, you might discover it's no more difficult to go at a slightly faster pace.

It is usually easier to follow than to lead. Tucked in behind someone, you can watch their steps and try to out-glide them. On the downhills you benefit slightly from drafting the leader.

But an assertive leader can break the race wide open by pulling away at a tactically advantageous location. Twisty-turny sections of a wooded trail are great for this; pour on the coal for a couple hundred meters and you are out of sight. "Out of sight, out of mind" applies here: they may know you are ahead of them, but if you can get beyond their view you have a tremendous advantage.

Sprints and recoveries. Ski racing has one significant similarity to cycling. Although both are endurance sports with competitions often lasting longer than an hour, both sports provide aerobic recoveries on the downhills. Athletes who tend to look at 30- and 50-km races in their entirety are tempted to plod along at a steady pace, especially after they begin to get tired. However, if you study the course profile and envision the race as a series of sprints and recoveries, you'll see small, manageable segments that are more easily digested. Not only are you better able to concentrate on the uphills, where the races are won, but you're more likely to reap the full reward of the restful downhills.

Push over the top. Imagine the crest of each hill about 50 feet over the top. If you continue to push beyond the actual summit, until gravity really takes over, you will gain valuable seconds on every hill.

Use the same approach at the finish line. If you think of the line as the finish, you might subconsciously let up as you approach. Imagine the finish 25 feet or so beyond the actual line, and you'll keep charging right through, saving critical seconds.

Post-Race Considerations

After reaching the finish line, the experienced competitor still has a couple of post-race chores to accomplish before calling it a day.

Rehydrating. Athletes in any endurance event become dehydrated, and cross-country skiers are no exception. The organizers of nordic races usually provide orange slices, water, electrolyte-replacement drinks, and perhaps sweetened tea within a few steps of the finish line. Rehydrating is essential for a quick

recovery, and experienced racers are not shy about getting plenty to drink.

Dry clothes and cool-down. Even in the midwinter cold, cross-country competitors soak their clothing with perspiration during an event. Soon after catching your breath and grabbing a drink, dig a dry shirt and hat from your backpack and immediately replace your wet racing gear. With the dry shirt under your warm-ups, now you can retrieve your skis and head back out on the trail for 15 minutes of easy skiing to stretch and cool-down.

Because nordic ski races often involve interval starts, the results may not be immediately available at the finish line. Skiing a gentle, cool-down loop provides the opportunity to evaluate your race objectively, before putting it in context with all the other participants.

ULTIMATE RACING SUCCESS: LOVE WHAT YOU DO

One final word about ski racing. The most important prerequisite for success is that you enjoy it. True champions sincerely love what they are doing. They develop innovative, creative methods of maintaining their interest and motivation. Quite simply, there is nothing they would rather be doing than skiing.

If you learn to truly enjoy skiing and the training that supports it, you will be very satisfied with your race results. Approach crummy, rainy days and difficult snow conditions as opportunities to exercise your mental toughness. Celebrate your good health, rejoice in a deep blanket of powder snow on a crystal clear day, and let your joy of being in the outdoors infuse everything else you do.

Waxing and Ski Maintenance

Waxing is a North American contribution to the sport of skiing. It began during the California Gold Rush, when miners working the high country of the northern Sierra Nevada took to breakneck downhill ski races as a way to blow off steam and avoid cabin fever during the long winters. In their efforts to plunge ever faster down the mountainsides, they began lubricating their skis with strange mixtures of animal fat, castor oil, and a witches' brew of other secret substances.

Today waxing is, or should be, universal. Any ski will benefit from it, even so-called waxless models. If in doubt, remember what those miners learned more than 100 years ago: If your skis are properly lubricated, they'll go like greased lightning. Waxing also protects the ski's base from damaging oxidation, which can slow you down. Even if extremes of downhill speed aren't your goal, the more slippery your skis are, the less effort you'll have to put into moving along a trail. Who doesn't want that?

Skis can also benefit from periodic tune-ups unrelated to waxing. In this chapter we'll begin by discussing simple waxing methods, then progress to increasingly esoteric methods of ski maintenance designed to coax ever better performance from your nordic boards. We'll also discuss the fine art of grip waxing for waxable skis.

The simplest tasks, such as wiping grit from your ski bases, are ones you can do at the trailhead. Others are best done at home. Some are important for everyone, while others won't matter to the average recreational skier. If a job sounds worthwhile but is too complex for your tastes, there are plenty of ski shops that will be happy to care for your skis' every need.

WAXLESS SKIS

Most skis sold in North America are waxless. They're extremely convenient, and you can indeed just slap them on and hit the trail. But the price you pay for that convenience is that, left untreated, these skis sometimes don't glide well, particularly on colder snow. Many people are startled to learn that their "waxless" or "no-wax" skis actually have to be waxed. The name merely means you don't have to apply grip wax to gain traction. You still have to wax for glide.

The easiest form of waxing is with any of a multitude of liquid, glide-enhancing products such as MaxiGlide, EasyGlide, Zardoz, or Universal Glide Wax. These products are silicone/Teflon lubricants that wipe onto the ski base with a couple quick swipes of a rag or the included applicator. Follow the directions on the product, stroking the wax in a tip-to-tail direction as you apply it to the entire ski base. A little goes a long way, but these lubricants wear off quickly. Use them at the start of every outing and carry a bottle with you in case your skis start to ice up or feel sluggish.

For a longer-lasting wax job and the ability to tune your glide to fit snow conditions, try a solid wax, which we'll call a "rub-on." Typically, these are packaged in blocks like bars of soap and say "glide

© PAUL PETERSEN

When possible, maintain your skis off the trails to minimize down time while skiing.

© SWIX

It takes only a few seconds to apply a liquid glide wax.

wax" or something similar on the package. Just rub the block against the base of the ski. It won't take a lot of pressure—just enough to leave a thin layer of wax. You can then use a ski-waxing cork (see page 142) or rag to buff the waxed ski smooth, but a few hundred yards on the trail will have much the same effect. These waxes are easiest to apply when warm, so don't save this task for the trailhead.

Not all rub-ons work well at all temperatures. If it's very cold (below 15°F), your best bet may be a hard, paraffin-based wax designed for extremely cold temperatures (the package will give the suggested temperature range). If you don't expect such cold temperatures, you may want a wax designed to optimize glide at whatever range of conditions is most likely. There are dozens of options, many containing the latest fast-gliding fluorinated compounds. In slushy, warm, dirty snow, bare skis may offer the best glide, partly because they attract less dirt.

Rub-on or solid glide wax provides a longer-lasting coating.

Better than rub-ons under some conditions are fluorinated pastes, applied much like car wax, with space-age names such as Maxxwax and F4. There are several brands, all designed for a wide range of temperatures. All are at their best for temperatures above freezing but will work adequately down to 20°F. Ask at a ski shop or read package labels to choose one that's right for the conditions you're most likely to encounter. Wipe the paste onto the ski tips and tails, let it dry for a couple of minutes and then buff it to smooth the surface and bond it more strongly to the ski base. Don't use these products on the patterned, grip section of the base, or you'll clog the tread. Use a liquid wax or a rub-on product for this portion of your ski.

The plethora of options shouldn't make you feel a need to buy dozens of glide waxes. Start with one or two broad-range products, then experiment as much (or as little) as you like.

Before each outing, make sure your skis are clean. Nothing slows down a ski like dirt. And, unfortunately, some of the very waxes you use to increase glide are magnets for dirt and grime. If the ski bases are visibly dirty or if you can feel something sticky on them, it's time for a cleaning. Do this with a ski wax remover, available at your local ski store. Don't try substituting paint thinner or other household solvent, which might well dissolve the base. Using the wax remover sparingly, wipe the ski base until it's clean, let it dry completely, then rewax. Always use wax removers in well-ventilated areas and follow any other precautions noted on the label. Note that "well-ventilated" means an area with flow-through ventilation, not just an open window.

HOT-WAXING WAXLESS SKIS

Paste waxes and rub-ons wear off during the course of a few days. For an "average" wax job that lasts longer, you can instead use a "hot-wax" approach that melts the wax into the surface of the ski base. This wax wears off much more slowly.

Hot-waxing is a technique, not a category of waxes. It's done with already-familiar paraffin-based glide waxes. For most people, the main advantage is durability; depending on how much you ski, you may need to hot wax only once or twice a year, with a wax designed for wide-ranging conditions. But hot-waxing also gives the finest possible glide. Performance addicts hot-wax frequently, changing waxes to fit the snow type and temperature.

Most ski shops will hot-wax your skis for a nominal fee, but with the right tools it's usually simpler and faster to do it yourself than to drive back and forth to the ski shop. In addition to the wax, you need an iron, a Plexiglas scraper, and a nylon brush. (A vise to hold the ski immobile is also useful.) Although specialty ski irons exist, you don't need one. A used household iron purchased from a moving sale or secondhand store will work nearly as well. You can use an automobile ice scraper, but you're best off buying one specifically designed for skis; sharp and stiff is good, and thick blades are easier to use than thin ones. The nylon brush need not be a specialty item; a small, inexpensive fingernail brush purchased from a grocery store will suffice.

Wax one ski at a time, turning it upside down and clamping it with the vise, firmly enough to stay put but not so firmly that you crush it. To prevent scratches, pad the vise with an old rag or glued-on felt. If you don't have a vise, recruit a friend to help hold the ski—and don't work in an area where wax drippings would be a household disaster. Pick a glide wax designed for the temperatures you're most likely to encounter (ask for recommendations at your local ski shop). Heat the iron on the *wool* setting. Touch the bar of wax to the iron; the wax should melt but not smoke. If possible, hold the wax and iron above

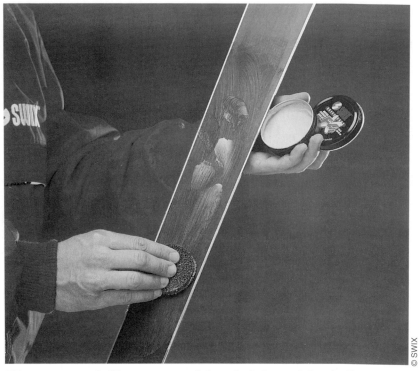

Ski paste wax works like car waxes: rub it on, let it dry, and then buff.

the ski, letting melted wax drip onto the ski base. Otherwise, rub the partially melted wax block quickly against the base, reheating it with the iron when necessary. Repeat this enough times to cover the base with a thorough coating of rough wax. Unless you're waxing skating or telemark skis, do the tips and tails only; don't hot wax the tread pattern or the portion of a waxable ski designed to hold grip wax. Wax the groove or channel that runs down the center of the ski as well. At this point, it doesn't matter if the wax layer is lumpy, but you don't want gaps.

Now, without changing the temperature setting, iron the waxed portion of the ski as you would a piece of clothing. Use the corner of the iron to apply the necessary heat to the center groove. The purpose is to heat the wax and ski base enough to cause the base material to absorb much of the wax. You may even be able to see this happening as the amount of surface wax decreases. Keep the iron moving in slow back-and-forth motions. The ski base should become warm to the touch but not hot. When the wax has

Hot-waxing is easy. Drip melted wax onto the ski and iron it into the base. Scrape off any extra wax and then brush the base smooth.

melted to a liquid, you're done. When you've finished all sections of the ski, set it aside and let it cool for ideally an hour.

Now comes the really messy part (you may want to go outdoors to save your floors and carpets). Using a firm hand on the scraper, scrape off most of the wax that's left *on* the ski. That still leaves plenty of wax *in* the ski base, which is where you want it—where it won't wear off as quickly as it would if you merely rubbed it on. If wax has spilled onto the sidewall of the skis, scrape it off with the scraper, your fingernail, or any other suitable implement. Finally, use the nylon brush in a series of tip-to-tail motions to

smooth off the base for optimum glide. As you'll discover the next time you go out, your tips and tails are now super-slick. To keep the patterned tread of waxless skis from slowing you down, rub it in a tip-to-tail direction with the wax bar (which should now be well-cooled and resolidified, or you'll get too much wax, in big, uneven gobs).

A good hot-waxing can last a hundred kilometers or more of recreational skiing. High-performance skiers will want to re-wax more frequently. If your wax picks up dirt and has to be cleaned with a wax remover, however, you'll have to redo the hot waxing each time you clean. Luckily, the ironed-in wax is less prone to grit collection than are pastes or rub-ons.

Skating Skis

Skating skis have no grip section, because you get grip from your outward push on their edges. Wax the entire ski for glide as you would the tips and tails of waxless skis. As with waxless touring skis, hot waxing gives the longest-lasting wax job, as well as the finest glide especially if you don't mind redoing it for each day's snow conditions. Fluorinated paste waxes are best for last-minute, at-the-snow waxing, when you suddenly discover it's been too long since you waxed and your skis are nearly bare. As we mentioned before, most waxes come in a multitude of varieties, targeted on different ranges of temperature and even humidity. There's a good deal of overlap,

Rick Says

Some people may worry about the potential toxicity of fluorinated paste waxes and rub-ons. The manufacturers assure, however, that the products have been thoroughly tested and that this is not a problem to your health or the environment. The only serious concern comes if these products are overheated during hot waxing, which might cause them to decompose into toxic gases. To minimize

any risk, always work in a well-ventilated room (set up a fan to produce flow-through ventilation) and use the minimum ironing temperature necessary to melt the wax. Swix assures that its waxes are stable up to temperatures of 300°C (570°F), which is far hotter than you'll obtain with proper ironing. Other premium products should be similar.

even within a single manufacturer's product line, so you don't need to buy dozens of waxes unless you're an elite racer. Start with two or three that cover the range of conditions you're most likely to encounter, then buy more as you need them, perhaps at the ski area's concession stand.

WAXABLE SKIS

The waxing of waxable skis is a skill some people spend years perfecting. But don't let that scare you away: the basics are so easy to learn that in most snow conditions even first-time waxers can be on the trail in minutes. All it takes is a small investment in waxes, a few simple tools, and skills you probably learned in kindergarten.

But first it helps to understand the theory of waxing. Like waxless skis, waxable skis divide into two sections: the glide zone and the grip zone. The difference is that there's no tread pattern in the grip zone; grip is provided by the wax, which is designed so the top layer of snow crystals presses into it to provide traction when you kick, then breaks loose when you glide. The wax has to be matched to the snow, which varies in texture with temperature, age, and humidity. Cold fresh snow is composed of very hard, angular crystals. They will dig firmly into a wax that's the consistency of a crayon, giving you good grip. These same crystals, however, will embed too strongly into

a softer wax, causing the ski to ice up when they fail to break loose again. Conversely, warm snow is much softer than cold snow. Hard waxes won't grip because the snowflakes can't penetrate them; softer waxes give the ideal grip.

As snow ages, it loses its multipointed snowflake structure and becomes more like grains of sand, particularly after repeated cycles of freezing and thawing. These granules can be quite hard, but they don't have the points that dig into the waxes used for fresher snow. They require a whole different line of waxes whose hardness still varies with temperature but that, overall, are much softer and applied in thicker layers than the waxes used for fresh snow.

With waxable skis, begin by waxing the tips and tails for glide, as you would for any other ski. The special art of waxable-ski waxing lies in the selection of grip wax; it's often best to do this at the trailhead because you won't be sure what wax you need, or how much you need, until you're there.

A wax kit for grip waxing can be small enough to fit in a wallet-sized belt pack or so complex it fills a carpenter's tool box. Begin at the small end of the spectrum with a limited assortment of waxes plus two tools: a *cork* and a *scraper*. The cork is simply a block of foamy material used for buffing the wax once it's on the ski. Historically, these were blocks of real cork about the size of a child's fist; today the best "corks" are made of a firm, gray foam. The scraper can be the same one you use for hot waxing. Make sure it's plastic, not metal, because removing unwanted waxes takes firm pressure and you don't want to leave gouges in the ski's base. A thick (quarter-inch) plastic wedge is usually best, but in a pinch you could do the job with a credit card—although the card would be unusable afterward (a great budget enforcer). A more complex waxing kit might contain a low-temperature propane torch for hot-waxing in the field or even an iron that plugs into your car cigarette lighter, but ordinary mortals don't need this type of equipment— and a mishandled torch can destroy your skis.

Before you can apply wax, of course, you need to know where to put it. Your skis will probably have markings on the base that purport to identify the *grip zone*, or *wax pocket*. Unfortunately, these are at best approximations, and are probably wrong.

RICK SAYS

Looking for the latest up-to-the minute waxing products and advice? Check your favorite manufacturer's website. Swix Sport USA maintains a particularly extensive site, but other manufacturers are also taking advantage of online technology. You can also find noncommercial webpages with waxing charts. The best of these sites allow you to select the snow conditions you expect to see, click, and view a selection of recommended wax choices from several manufacturers' product lines. Use a search engine to locate the desired manufacturer's homepage, or enter a search that includes the terms *cross-country*, *nordic*, and/or *ski waxes*.

The wax pocket is the portion of the ski's camber that still bows upward when you're gliding on a single ski. If you apply grip wax outside this zone, it will drag when you're trying to glide. If you don't wax enough of the grip zone, you'll need an Olympic-caliber kick to get the ski to grip. There are several ways to locate the grip zone. It's probably about 2 feet long, centered under the ball of your foot. That means it will run from approximately the back of the heel plate to about 8 inches in front of the binding. But its precise location depends on your weight and the camber of your skis. Hold the skis in your hands and squeeze their bases together until the tail gap closes all the way to the back of the heel plate. The remaining gap is more or less the wax pocket. Mark it on the base of the ski with an indelible marker.

The zone you've just marked is your starting point for deciding how much of the ski to wax. You may want to wax a slightly larger or smaller area, depending on the stiffness of your skis. Continuing to hold the skis together, squeeze firmly. If it's fairly easy to close the remaining gap with two hands—or worse, with one hand—then your skis are too soft and will tend to be a bit slow as the grip wax drags. To minimize this, don't wax the entire wax pocket (and consider buying new skis). If you can't close the gap with the full strength of both hands, your skis may not grip well unless you kick athletically enough to force the grip zone to make good contact with the snow. If you don't want to kick that hard all the time, you'll have to wax a few extra inches forward and back of the wax pocket.

If you're skiing with children, let them check the grip zones and camber of their own skis rather than using adult strength to do it for them. Children should be able to squeeze their skis together, or they're going to have trouble getting enough kick.

A more accurate way to measure the grip zone is by standing on your unwaxed skis on a perfectly flat

surface, such as a linoleum floor. With the help of a friend, put a piece of paper under the middle of the ski; then put all your weight on that ski. Slide the paper back and forth. Where it catches toward the tip and tail are the two ends of the grip zone. Mark them—and don't be surprised if the result is a bit different from what you obtained with the squeeze test.

Once you've located the wax pocket, it's time to choose a wax. There are two basic types: *hard waxes* and *klisters*. Hard waxes come in plastic or foil-wrapped cylinders about an inch in diameter and two inches long, somewhat like short, fat crayons. They're about as firm as crayons and are even color coded in a rainbow of shades for easy identification. Klisters come in tubes like toothpaste, have the consistency of glue, and also are color coded. In keeping with the waxing theory discussed above, hard waxes are for newer snow that hasn't gone through multiple freeze/thaw cycles. Klisters are for snow that's been through several such cycles.

Each brand of wax has its own color-coding system with bewildering similarities and differences. We'll use the Swix system here because it comes closest to being the industry standard. In that system, waxes are divided into five major color groups according to the temperature for which they're designed. In order of increasing temperature, they're polar (white), green, blue, violet, and red. For most of these colors, there

Waxing kits generally contain hard waxes, klister waxes, a scraper, an applicator for klister waxes, and a cork. In this kit, the scraper and cork are combined in one tool.

combination cork/scraper

hard waxes

klister spatula

klisters

© SWIX

are intermediate shades called "special" or "extra," designed to fill the gaps. "Special" gives peak performance at the low end of a color's temperature range; "extra" does so at the high end of the range. Thus, Special Red is for conditions at the cool end of the red-wax range, while Violet Extra is for use near the warm end of the violet range. There's not much difference in performance between these or other pairs of adjacent waxes on the temperature chart. All told, Swix has about a dozen hard waxes and nearly as many klisters, with half of them clustered in a seven-degree range centering on the freezing point.

Luckily, beginners don't need a dozen waxes. You can probably start out with as few as three or four. In the Swix line, Special Red, Blue Extra, Green, and Universal Klister will get you through most temperatures you're likely to encounter.

For relatively new snow and below-freezing temperatures, use Blue Extra. Simply remove the end cap on the tube, peel away enough of the metal wrapper to expose the wax, and rub it onto the wax pocket of the ski, avoiding the center groove. It's a lot like the crayon coloring you once did as a child. How much wax you'll use depends on the temperature. If it's particularly cold, put on as thin a coat as possible—just enough so you can see the wax rubbing onto the ski base, looking more white than blue. If the temperature is close to the freezing mark, you'll need to apply several times as much wax. Try to make it smooth

and even, without thick, glide-damaging lumps. When you're learning, that will probably mean applying multiple layers with a light hand, but with practice you'll find that firmer, faster, and longer strokes work better. If you don't know how much wax to put on, err on the side of too little; it's easier to add another layer than to scrape.

Now, take your cork and smooth the waxed surface until it's lump free and shiny—another childhood skill, a bit like trying to erase a stubborn chalk mark from a blackboard. You'll have to rub firmly, but make sure you don't smear wax beyond the wax pocket. When you're done, put on your skis and test them on the snow. If you waxed indoors, your warm skis may slip at first. Ski 100 yards or so to give them time to chill. If they still slip, add more wax. If they stick too much or ice up, you have too much wax or wax of too warm a color. First, with firm pressure, try

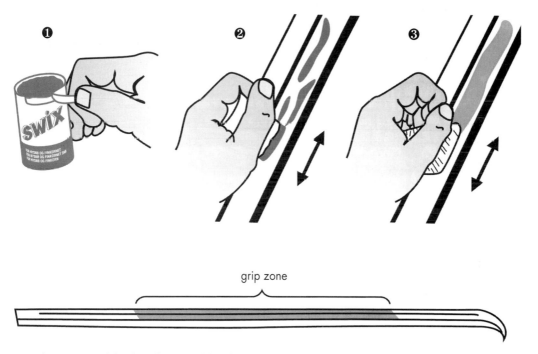

❶   ❷   ❸

grip zone

To apply grip wax, (1) select the wax, (2) rub it on, and (3) cork it smooth.

© SWIX

scraping off some wax with your scraper. Hold the scraper at an angle that causes the wax to roll up into a long, thin cylinder, and use your fingers or a twig to remove the clinging wax rolls from the ski base or your scraper. Again, be careful not to smear wax beyond the confines of the wax pocket. When you're finished, buff the remaining wax with the cork and test the skis again.

If the thinnest layer you can spread uniformly across the wax pocket is still too sticky, perhaps the temperature is so low you need to shift to the green wax. If the temperature is above freezing, start with a thin layer of Special Red and add more until you're getting sufficient grip.

For old, refrozen snow, use the klister. This wax comes out of the tube as a semiliquid; simply squeeze out a bead and draw the nozzle down the ski base, laying down two lines of wax, as thin as possible, one on each side of the center groove. A diagonal pattern or zigzag is best, but not if it leads you to use too much wax. If possible, work indoors; cold klisters are extremely viscous and hard to work with.

Transporting goopy klistered skis from home to the trailhead raises its own problems, however, so the only practical way to work indoors is if there's a convenient warming or waxing hut at the trailhead.

Klisters don't need to be corked, but the two lines of wax do need to be spread uniformly across the wax pocket (avoiding the center groove). To keep from getting tacky wax on your fingers, use the plastic spatula, about the size of a physician's tongue depressor, that comes with the wax.

As with hard waxes, using multiple thin layers is the key; klisters are particularly messy to scrape off if you use too much—and almost impossible to completely remove without a chemical wax remover. The colder the snow, the less klister you'll want.

Waxes, particularly hard waxes, wear off during the course of a day and may need to be replenished. Most often though, you'll find temperature changes will be the reasons for rewaxing. It's not as much of a nuisance as it sounds; with only a modicum of practice you can step out of your skis, scrape or apply wax, cork it, and be back on your way in a couple of

Waxing on the trail.

The plastic scraper is used to remove excess wax from freshly hot-waxed skis.

© RICHARD A. LOVETT

© PAUL PETERSEN

minutes. For recreational skiing, corking doesn't need to be perfect. Often, a few hundred yards on the trail will finish the job of smoothing out your wax.

Rewaxing stops will usually be triggered by a sense that you're slipping a bit when you kick. This means you need to add more wax, probably because the day has warmed up. Start by adding another layer of the wax you're already using. If that doesn't work, it may be time to graduate to a warmer wax, such as Special Red rather than Blue Extra. Because warm-temperature waxes are softer than cold-weather waxes, it's easy to make this change. Just put the new layer of red wax on top of the old layer of blue.

If the temperature drops, you'll find that your skis start to stick or ice up. Cure this first by scraping off some of your wax. If the temperature drops too far, you'll have to shift to a colder, harder wax. As a general rule, hard waxes shouldn't be applied over the top of softer ones; it's difficult to rub a significant amount of the harder wax onto the soft surface. In a pinch, you may be able to dodge this by warming the harder wax under your armpit to soften it, while putting the skis in the coldest, shadiest place you can find. But usually it's better just to scrape off as much of the softer wax as you can, because even if you succeed in applying the harder wax, it will wear off more quickly than normal, leaving you back where you started. Perfect scraping isn't necessary. In the rare event that you travel from hard-wax snow to

Use klister sparingly—you can always add more.

klister snow, you can put the klister on over the hard wax without scraping, but not vice versa—at least not easily.

This simple four-wax system will allow you to ski in a wide range of snow conditions, in any temperature between about 5°F and the upper 40s. But you may find it difficult to get optimum kick under some conditions, particularly at temperatures between 28° and 35°F, where snow changes dramatically with only small changes in temperature. To fine-tune your waxing, you can add more waxes to your kit—both hard waxes and klisters—for the temperatures you're most likely to encounter.

If you're skiing at a commercial ski area or a park with a warming lodge, there's likely to be a prominently posted thermometer telling you a suggested wax—and a shop or concession stand where you can buy it on the spot. If there's no thermometer and you're not carrying one with you, pick up a handful of snow and try to make a snowball. If it packs into a tight ball, you're probably seeing temperatures at or above freezing. If it won't compact at all and you can blow it easily out of your hand, it's well below freezing. If you have corn snow or crust, or the snow shows other signs of repeated freeze/thaw cycles, you need klister. The snowball method may look low tech and crude, but it's preferred by many expert waxers.

And it makes you look like a serious snow guru if you can eyeball the snow, play with it a bit, grunt meaningfully, and pick the right wax. If in doubt, your first guess should err in favor of the colder wax.

The more you learn about waxing, the more you'll relish the speed, kick, and quiet glide of a ski that's perfectly matched to the snow. And that means the more you'll probably want to learn about waxing. Advice is easy to find if you want it. Ski areas typically post the wax of the day or offer free waxing clinics, and other skiers are often willing to share their wisdom. But don't be surprised if not everyone has the same opinion. Waxing remains half science, half art.

PREPPING THE SKI BASE

Beginning skiers tend to take the base of their skis for granted, focusing on waxing as the predominant means of enhancing glide. But there are things you can do *to* the base to enhance the ski's performance before applying wax. Many racers believe that for high-performance skis, these tasks are just as important as choosing the right wax.

The goal is to alter the texture of the ski base to improve its glide. Elite racers often hand over this job to technicians who specialize in stone-grinding

OTHER GRIP-WAXING TIPS

The temperature recommendations that come with each manufacturer's line of waxes are only the beginning of the wax story. Temperature and the age of the snow will get you into the right region of the wax chart, but humidity and many other factors can affect the optimum choice. Here are a few advanced pointers:

- View the wax pocket as a guideline, not a straitjacket. If you're slipping but leery of graduating to a warmer wax, try extending the current wax a few inches beyond the normal wax pocket, particularly toward the tip.

- In deep powder, the soft, cushy snow distributes the force of your kick over a longer-than-normal portion of your ski, making it difficult for a small region of grip wax to make good contact with the snow. Under the same conditions, softer waxes are prone to icing up. The solution may be to use a cold wax, extending it well beyond the standard grip zone.

- With warm, tacky waxes, particularly klisters, wax a slightly smaller region than the normal wax pocket.

- Backcountry skiers seldom need klisters except in late-season corn snow. Track skiers may sometimes find that groomed trail surfaces are composed of finely ground ice produced when grooming machines break up layers of crust. This may look like powder, but it often requires a klister. Check the size of the crystals. If they're more like sand than fresh snow, you'll probably need klister.

- When using klisters on groomed trail systems, stay on the trails. If you venture onto the softer, ungroomed surfaces you're likely to ice up.

- For the same reason, especially when using klisters, don't stand around on soft snow. If you do stop in such snow, scuff your feet slowly back and forth to prevent ice-up.

- In difficult conditions, try mixing waxes. You might apply two waxes simultaneously and mix them on the ski base (easier with klisters than with hard waxes). Or you might put a cold-weather wax on most of the grip zone, with a smaller spot of softer wax in the middle of the zone, where it'll give extra grip when you most need it but is less likely to drag when you don't.

cross-country ski bases, using very sophisticated and expensive (about $20,000) grinding machines. But unless you're aiming for the Olympic team, you can do the job yourself with a few hand tools: a scraper, a *riller*, a brush, and a piece of Fibertex. The scraper shouldn't be the same one you use for hot-waxing; this one needs to be metal, preferably brand-new and sharp. A riller is a specialty tool designed to score the base with numerous parallel scratches. You can obtain nearly as good results with an ordinary metal file. The brush should have stiff brass bristles. Fibertex is like a medium-aggressive pot scrubbing pad, available in ski shops. In the past, skiers used steel wool.

Support the ski with at least two vises. Make sure its base is sufficiently elevated above their jaws that

RICK SAYS

Leaves, crud, and cup wax. A minor drawback to waxable skis is that the wax can pick up loose debris lying on the trail. You'll know if it happens— if you hit a leaf with a gooey kick wax, you'll stop so fast you almost fall on your nose. Similarly, if you take up racing you'll find that at water stops in large races the track becomes littered with discarded drinking cups, producing jokes about the need for "cup wax." Try to step over or around such obstacles, particularly if you're using klister or a warm-temperature hard wax. If one becomes embedded in your wax the only remedy may be to stop and scrape the offending piece of litter out of your wax.

RICK SAYS

You don't have to be an expert skier to be a good waxer. Experienced waxers quickly develop their own favorite tricks just by keeping their ears open for useful ideas. One of my favorites from my days as a middle-of-the-pack citizen racer was to put a cold wax over the top of a soft one. This is particularly useful for dawn starts in half-day or longer ski marathons when you know it's going to warm up quickly, possibly by 20°F or more. The hope is that the outer wax will wear off just about the time you need the softer underlying one. Because timing is everything, a certain degree of luck is involved, but I did this successfully to avoid midrace rewaxing in two runnings of the 55-km American Bierkebeiner. You can even use this trick to put a hard wax over a klister. To get the wax to stick, keep the hard wax warm and pliable while the klistered ski is outdoor-cold. One of my favorite aspects of waxing is learning out-of-the-ordinary solutions to difficult waxing challenges—especially when those solutions actually work.

© SWIX

A riller and a few other tools will enable you to alter the texture of the ski base.

they don't interfere with the riller. Even better than vises is a "ski profile bench" that matches the ski's camber (see photo on page 137).

Begin by making sure your skis are thoroughly cleaned. If you haven't cleaned them already, this is a good time to try an alternative method called "hot scraping" that leaves the base free of both solvent and dirt. To do this, start by choosing a relatively soft glide wax. Using your iron to melt it, drip a substantial amount of wax onto the base, then iron it lightly to form a smooth layer. There's no need to melt the wax into the base as you would for hot waxing. While the wax is still warm, scrape all of it off. The dirt should come with it.

Now it's time to "prep" your bases. With skating skis, you'll be prepping their entire length. For clas-

sical-stride skis, do only the tips and tails, avoiding the patterned tread or the wax pocket. Telemark skis and backcountry skis seldom need their bases prepped. With the ski firmly secured in the vises, scrape the base with the sharp-edged metal scraper. The goal is to remove a thin layer of base material to smooth out irregularities and expose a fresh, porous surface. Work from tip to tail until the base is flat everywhere. Often, the tips and tails of new skis are slightly concave from side to side. You want to eliminate these concavities, allowing the scraper to touch the base across its entire width. In addition, the base may have a slightly wavy texture. Holding the scraper diagonally can help you find and remove such irregularities.

When you're done scraping, stroke the scraped section of the base tip-to-tail a few times with the Fibertex pad to produce an even smoother surface. Next comes the riller. Run that tool down the portion of the ski being prepped, again moving tip to tail. Don't be afraid to press down hard; the goal is to put numerous tiny, parallel grooves into the base. These grooves will break the suction that sometimes develops between ski and snow (particularly in wet snow), giving it extra glide. To deepen the grooves, make several passes with the riller; the warmer the snow you're going to be skiing on, the more pronounced you want the striations to be. If you don't have a riller, you can achieve the same result using the edge of a file, held crossways to the ski. Once the ski is rilled, smooth it a bit with a few lengthwise passes with the brass brush; then finish with the Fibertex to remove loose material and to polish the base for the next step: waxing as usual. For very cold snow, the brush and the Fibertex alone may be sufficient.

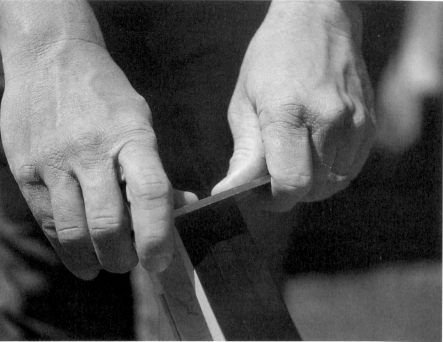

A metal scraper is used to "peel" base material.

© PAUL PETERSEN

Paul Says

The best way to learn waxing quickly is to ski with someone who already knows it. Although we've given lots of tips, a little on-the-spot advice can increase your chances of picking the right wax the first time you try. Even if you go with an expert, don't be too sure the wax that's perfect at the trailhead will be so an hour later. Always carry your cork and scraper, plus the next warmer and colder waxes, just in case conditions changes.

Paul Says

If ski base preparation sounds a bit technical, it is. But it can be done in less than an hour, and if you want to keep pace at the next big ski race, you'd better become good at this or pay a good ski shop to do it for you.

Don't be intimidated by a sense that you're damaging your skis. Many medium-grade and top-of-the-line skis are sold factory tuned and require none of this work when they're new. What you're doing can be viewed as upgrading less expensive skis, restoring an older ski's factory tuning, or retuning the ski for different snow conditions. Furthermore, other than the scraping, which doesn't have to be done frequently, you're not removing much material from the base. You're simply rearranging what's already there, somewhat like a farmer plowing a field. When time and use flatten out the rills—or you need to tune the skis to different snow conditions, you're simply adding a new set of furrows.

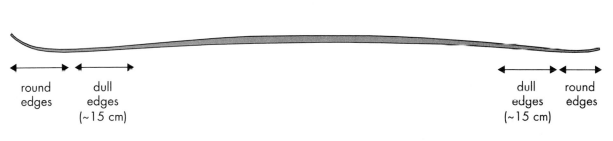

round edges   dull edges (~15 cm)   dull edges (~15 cm)   round edges

The side view of a super sidecut telemark ski shows (lower) the ski's camber and the areas of the tip and tail that should be detuned by rounding or dulling.

METAL-EDGED SKIS

Like any other ski, telemark and backcountry skis need glide wax. If they're waxable, backcountry skis also need kick wax; telemark skis are most often waxed purely for glide, requiring lifts or climbing skins for going uphill. Most people don't bother to rill their bases.

The metal edges require special maintenance. At a minimum, you need an 8- or 10-inch "mill bastard" file, available at any hardware store. You also need a whetstone and, for tuning the edges to top performance, a "file guide" or an "edge-beveling tool." Even brand-new skis may need to be tuned. Otherwise, the edges may be too sharp at the tips and tails. If you don't correct this, they'll tend to grab on turns, hooking you too strongly from one direction to another.

Use the file to round off the edges at the upturned ends of the ski, at tip and tail—the parts that don't touch flat snow. Then, for the next 2 to 3 inches of the tip and 1 to 2 inches of the tail, use the whetstone or a light touch on the file to dull the edges

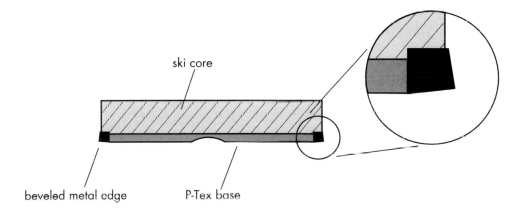

ski core

beveled metal edge   P-Tex base

An edge beveler allows you to file the metal edge to a slightly off-square angle. The bevel is exaggerated in the enlargement to make it easier to see.

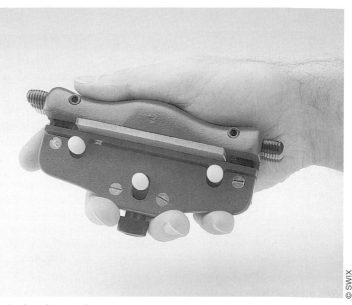

without rounding them. Ski shops call this a *new-ski tune-up* or *dulling the tips and tails.* Sometimes, it's already been done at the factory. To check, run your fingernail over the ski edge to see if it's duller at the tips and tails than in the middle. It'll be obvious if it is.

You may also want to alter slightly the angles of the edges. Most skis come with edges whose bottoms and sides form a 90-degree angle, flat on the bottom and vertical on the sides, but the technical shop manual may suggest a 1-degree or 2-degree "edge bevel." This means the skis will be easier to tilt and turn if the edges, still at a 90-degree angle, are cocked inward 1 or 2 degrees. Because the metal edge is firmly attached, beveling the edge is done not by twisting it, but by shaving off a little bit of unwanted metal on both the bottom and the side, using the edge-beveling tool or the file and file guide.

Edge beveling tool.

A file guide is simply a device used to hold a file at the desired angle. Use it to rasp the metal edges until the file rests flat against them. An edge-beveling tool is a similar device containing a piece of metal-file material positioned at the desired angle. Some are adjustable; others are set to fixed angles. Use it the same way as you would a file in a file guide.

With time, edges become dull and cornering performance suffers. To test sharpness, see if you can shave a small clipping off your fingernail by running it down the edge (being careful not to cut yourself). If you have an opportunity, try this on a factory-sharpened edge to get a sense of how sharp an edge should be. If the edges are dull, sharpen them with the edge-beveling tool or a carefully held file, working evenly from the bottom and the side. Check your progress with the fingernail test.

If your skis hit a rock, or one ski bangs the other's binding, you can get small burrs in the edge. Locate them by running your thumb and forefinger down the bottom and side of the edge. When you find a burr, take it off with the whetstone, holding the stone either flat to the base or parallel to the side of the ski so you don't dull the edge. Don't use a file; burred steel is unusually hard and can damage your file. If you've found one burr, there may be others, so check both skis before or after every outing. Untended burrs not only interfere with performance—they can wreck your scraper.

CUTS AND GOUGES

Deep cuts in the ski base are best repaired at a shop. In the meantime, you can achieve a temporary fix by scraping away any protruding base material and filling the gouge with hot wax. If you're determined to fix your own ski, you need a P-Tex (base material) candle. When lit, the candle drips P-Tex material into the gouge. Initially, the P-Tex will be contaminated with soot from the candle, so collect the drips

File guide with file.

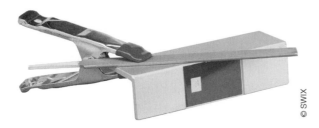

on a metal scraper (positioned next to the gouge) until the melted P-Tex is no longer sooty. Then start dripping clean P-Tex into the gouged area. Let the gouge overfill, then shave off the extra after it's hardened, using a plane, sharp chisel, or carefully wielded pocketknife. Finish with a metal scraper. Beware that a burning P-Tex candle produces odd chemical byproducts. This is a process you definitely want to do with proper ventilation. Check the safety instructions on the label and do as the manufacturer suggests.

PAUL SAYS

Now that you've assured that your skis are in tip-top condition, do yourself a couple of favors. First, check the bindings and make sure there aren't any loose parts or screws. Then, when you transport your skis, don't let the bases bang or scrape against each other, undoing some of your fine work. Use padded ski straps that separate the bases or make your own separators with old socks, held onto the ski with rubber bands.

U.S. and Canadian Cross-Country Ski Areas

The following list was provided courtesy of the Cross Country Ski Areas Association, which has additional information for most of its member areas: visit the Association's website at http://www.xcski.org. The list does not include ski areas that are not members, although you will find marvelous skiing at state parks, local parks, national parks, and other areas not listed here.

CANADA

Alberta

Calgary Ski Club, Calgary AB, T2M 0C2, 403-282-4122, 150 km, skiclub@freenet.calgary.ab.ca

Canmore Nordic Center, Canmore AB, T1W 2T6, 403-678-2400 ext. 104, 70 km

Strathcona Wilderness Center, Sherwood Park AB, T8A 0W9, 403-922-3939, 15 km

Terratima Lodge, Rocky Mountain House AB, T0M 1T0, 403-845-6786, 40 km, www.rmhnet.com/terratima

British Columbia

Caledonia Nordic Ski Club, Prince George BC, 250-564-3809, 55 km

Cypress Bowl Ski Area, West Vancouver BC, V7V 3N9, 604-926-5612, 16 km, www.cypressbowl.com

Hills Health & Guest Ranch, Mile Ranch BC, V0K 2Z0, 802-791-5225, 150 km, www.spabe.com

Mountain Trek Fitness Retreat, Ainsworth BC, V0G 1A0, 800-661-5161, www.hiking.com

Mt. MacPherson Cross Country Ski Area, Revelstoke BC, V0E 2S0, 250-837-7041, 25 km, www.bbcanada.com/1957.html

Mt. Washington Cross Country Ski Center, Courtenay BC, V9N 5N3, 250-334-5705, 40 km, www.mtwashington.bc.ca

Silver Star Mountain Resort, Silver Star Mountain BC, V1B 3M1, 250-542-0224, 85 km, www.silverstarmtn.com

Whistler Cross Country Ski Trails, Whistler BC, V0N 1B4, 604-932-6436, 30 km, parksops@idmail.com

Nova Scotia

Ski Martock, Windsor NS, B0N 2T0, 902-798-9501, 12 km, admin@martock.com

Ontario

Haliburton Nordic Trail Association, Haliburton ON, K0M 1S0, 705-457-1300, 80 km, www.skihaliburton.8m.com

Hardwood Hills Cross Country Ski Center, Oro Station ON, L0L 2E0, 800-387-3775, 36 km

Hiawatha Highlands, Sault Ste. Marie ON, 800-361-1522, 40 km

Highland's Nordic, Duntroon ON, 800-263-5017, 18 km, www.highlandsnordic.on.ca

Horseshoe Resort, Barrie ON, L4M 4Y8, 705-835-2790, 35 km, www.horseshoeresort.com

Stokely Creek Ski Touring, Goulais ON, P0S 1E0, 705-649-3421, 82 km, www.stokelycreek.com

Quebec

Camp Mercier, Chemin Saint-Louis PQ, G1S 1C1, 418-848-2422, 192 km

Carling Lake Resort, Pine Hill PQ, J0V 1A0, 450-533-9211, 20 km, www.laccarling.com

Far Hills Inn Cross Country Ski, Val Morin PQ, J0T 2R0, 819-322-2014, 130 km, www.farhillsinn.com

Gatineau Park, Ottawa ON, K1P 1C7, 800-465-1867, 150 km

Station Mont-Sainte-Anne, Beaupré PQ, 418-827-4561, 225 km

Saskatchewan

Whitetail Resort Ltd., North Battleford SK, S9A 2X3, 306-455-4941, 40 km, www.w2d.com/whitetail

USA Mid-Atlantic and New England

Connecticut

Cedar Brook Farms Cross Country, West Suffield CT 06093, 860-668-5026, 10 km

Pine Mountain Ski Touring, Hartland CT 06027, 860-653-4279, 15 km, beeman@kennametal.ibmmail.com

Winding Trails Cross Country Ski Center, Farmington CT 06032, 860-678-9582, 20 km, www.windingtrails.com

Maine

Carter's Cross Country Ski Center, Oxford ME 04270, 207-539-4848, 85 km

Harris Farm Cross Country Ski Center, Dayton ME 04005, 207-499-2678, 40 km, www.harrisfarm.com

McDougal Orchards Ski Trails, Springvale ME 04083, 207-324-5054, 15 km, mcdorch@gwi.net

Smiling Hill Farm Cross Country Ski Center, Westbrook ME 04092, 207-775-4818, 35 km

Sugarloaf Ski Touring Center, Carrabassett Valley ME 04947, 207-237-6830, 100 km, www.sugarloaf.com

Massachusetts

Bucksteep Manor, Washington MA 01223, 413-623-5535, 25 km

Butternut Cross Country, Great Barrington MA 01230, 413-528-0610, 8 km, bselorch@aol.com

Cranwell Cross Country Ski Touring, Lenox MA 01240, 800-CRANWEL, 11 km, www.cranwell.com

Great Brook Farm Ski Touring, Carlisle MA 01741-0720, 978-369-7486, 15 km

Hickory Hill Touring Center, Worthington MA 01098, 413-238-5813, 25 km, senatj@javanet.com

Maple Corner Farm, Granville MA 01034, 413-357-6697, 20 km

Northfield Mountain Cross Country, Northfield MA 01360, 800-859-2960, 40 km

Notchview Reservation, Windsor MA 01270, 413-684-0148, 17 km, jcaffrey@ttor.org

Weston Ski Tracks, Weston MA 02193, 781-891-6575, 15 km, www.ski-paddle.com

New Hampshire

The Balsams Wilderness, Colebrook NH, 603-255-3400, 75 km

Bear Notch Ski Touring Center, Bartlett NH 03812, 603-374-2277, 70 km, www.harrisoncreative.com/bnski

Bretton Woods Cross Country, Bretton Woods NH 03575, 800-232-2972, 95 km, www.brettonwoods.com

Eastman Cross Country, Grantham NH 03753, 603-863-4500, 16 km, www.eastman-lake.com/winter.html

Great Glen Trails, Gorham NH 03581, 603-466-2333, 40 km, www.mt-washington.com

Gunstock Cross Country, Laconia NH 03247, 800-486-7862, 37 km, www.gunstock.com

The Inn at East Hill Farm, St. Troy NH 03465, 603-242-6495, 10 km, www.east-hill-farm.com

Jackson Ski Touring Foundation, Jackson NH 03846, 800-927-6697, 96 km, www.jacksonxc.com

King Pine Ski Touring Center, East Madison NH 03849, 603-367-8896, 28 km, www.purityspring.com

Loon Mountain Cross Country, Lincoln NH 03251, 603-745-8111, 35 km, www.loonmtn.com

Moose Mountain Lodge, Etna NH 03750, 603-643-3529, www.moosemountainlodge.com

Nordic Center at Waterville Valley, Waterville Valley NH 03215, 603-236-4666, 66 km, www.waterville.com

Nordic Skier, Wolfeboro NH 03215, 603-569-3151, 20 km, www.skinh.com

Norsk Cross Country, New London NH 03257, 603-526-4685, 70 km, www.skinorsk.com

Temple Mountain Ski Area, Temple NH 03084, 603-924-3616, 9 km, www.templemountain.com

Timberland Trails, Conway NH 03818, 800-TRAILS8, 20 km, waltenburg@aol.com

Tory Pines Resort, Francestown NH 03043, 603-588-2000, 20–25 km, www.torypinesresort.com

New Jersey

High Point Cross Country Ski Area, Sussex NJ 07461, 973-702-1222, 16 km, www.xcskihighpoint.com

New York

Art Roscoe Cross Country Ski Area, Salamanca NY 14779, 716-354-9163, 45 km, www.jaconcessions.com

The Bark Eater, Keene NY 12942, 800-232-1607, 20 km, www.barkeater.com

Cascade Cross Country Center, Lake Placid NY 12946, 518-523-9605, 50 km, www.cascadeski.com

Chautauqua County Parks, Ashville NY 14710, 716-763-8928, 5 km

Cunningham's Ski Barn, North Creek NY 12853, 518-251-3215, 40 km

Fahnestock Winter Park, Cold Springs NY 10516, 914-265-3773, 15 km

Friends Lake Inn, Chestertown NY 12817, 518-494-4751, 32 km, www.friendslake.com

Frost Valley YMCA, Claryville NY 12725, 914-985-2291, 36 km, www.frostvalley.org

Garnet Hill Lodge Cross Country Ski Center, North River NY 12856, 518-251-2444, 55 km, www.garnet-hill.com

Lapland Lake Cross Country, Northville NY 12134, 518-863-4974, www.dude-ranch.com/latigo.html

Mohonk Mountain House, New Paltz NY 12561, 914-255-1000, 50 km

Mountain Trails Cross Country, Tannersville NY 12485, 518-589-5361, 35 km

Olympic Sports Complex, Lake Placid NY 12946, 800-447-5224, 50 km, www.orda.org

Osceola Tug Hill Cross Country Ski Center Inc., Camden NY 13316, 315-599-7377, www.tughillregion.com/ski-osceola.htm

Pineridge Cross Country Ski Area, Petersburgh NY 12138, 518-283-3652, 34 km, www.xcski.org/pineridge

Salmon Hills Cross Country Ski Resort, Red Field NY 13437, 315-599-4003, 32 km, www.greatsalmonwilderness.com/salmonhillsframe.html

Whiteface Club, Lake Placid NY 12946, 518-523-2551, 20 km

Williams Lake Hotel, Rosendale NY 12472, 800-382-3818, 15 km

Pennsylvania

Callenders Windy Acres Farm, Thompson PA 18465, 717-727-2982, 6 km

Crystal Lake Ski Area, Hughesville PA 17737, 717-584-2698, 30 km, clski@naccess.net

Hanley's Happy Hill, Eagles Mere PA, 717-525-3461, 40 km

Mystic Mountain, Farmington PA 15437, 724-329-8555, 7.8 km, www.nwlr.com

Vermont

Blueberry Lake Cross Country, Warren VT 05674, 802-496-6687, 30 km

Burke Cross Country Ski Area, Burke VT 05832, 802-626-8338, 60 km, www.burkemtn.com

Catamount Family Center, Williston VT 05495, 802-879-6001, 20 km

Craftsbury Outdoor Center, Craftsbury VT 05827, 800-729-7751, 25 km, www.craftsbury.com

The Equinox, Manchester VT 05254, , 800-362-4747, 38 km, reservations@equinoxresort.com

Grafton Ponds Cross Country, Grafton VT 05146, 802-843-2400, 30 km, www.old-tavern.com/ski

Green Mountain Nordic Center, Randolph VT 05060, 800-424-5575, 30 km, www.3stallioninn.com

Hazen's Notch Cross Country Ski Center, Montgomery VT 05471, 802-326-4708, 30 km, www.pbpub.com/hazensnotch.htm

Hermitage Touring Center, Wilmington VT 05363, 802-464-3511, 35 km, www.hermitageinn.com

Highland Lodge, Greensboro VT 05841, 802-533-2647, 65 km

Hildene Cross Country Ski Center, Manchester VT 05254, 802-362-1788, 22 km, xcski@hildene.org

Mountain Meadows Cross Country, Killington VT 05751, 800-221-0598, 60 km, www.WEBK.com/mtmeadowsxc

Mountain Top Cross Country Ski Resort, Chittenden VT, 802-483-6089, 70 km

Okemo Valley Nordic Center, Ludlow VT 05149, 802-228-4041, 20 km, www.okemo.com

Ole's Cross Country Center, Waitsfield VT 05673, 802-496-3430, 50 km, jthrt@madriver.com

Prospect Mountain Cross Country Ski Center, Woodford VT 05201, 802-442-2575, 35 km

Smugglers' Notch Nordic, Jeffersonville VT 05464, 802-644-8851, 25 km, www.smuggs.com

Stowe Mountain Resort, Stowe VT 05672, 802-253-3000, 35 km, www.stowe.com

Timber Creek Cross Country Ski Area, Wilmington VT 05363, 802-464-0999, 14 km, www.sover.net/~vtcxc./

Trapp Family Lodge, Stowe VT 05672, 800-826-7000, 55 km, www.trappfamily.com

The Viking Nordic Center, Londonderry VT 05148, 802-824-3933, 30 km, www.vikingnordic.com

Wild Wings Ski Touring Center, Peru VT 05152, 802-824-6793, 25 km, www.floodbrook.k12.vt.us/ww/wildwings.html

Woodstock Ski Touring Center, Woodstock VT 05091, 802-457-6674, 60 km, www.woodstockinn.com

USA Midwest
Illinois

Camp Sagawau Nordic, Lemont IL 60439, 630-257-2045, 6 km, mkon6780@aol.com

Michigan

Active Backwoods Retreat, Ironwood MI 49938,
906-932-3502, 30 km, www.michiweb.com/abrski

Boyne Nordican Cross Country Center, Boyne Falls MI
49713, 616-549-6088, 35 km, www.skinordic.org

Cool's Cross Country Farm, LeRoy MI 49655,
616-768-4624, 25-30 km, www.coolxcfarm.com

Corsair Ski Trails, East Tawas MI 48730, 800-558-2927,
56 km, www.tawas.com

Country Village Resort, Ishpeming MI 49849,
906-485-6345, 25 km, www.exploringthenorth.com

Cross Country Ski Headquarters, Roscommon MI 48653,
800-832-2663, 18 km, www.cross-country-ski.com

Crystal Mountain Resort, Thomsonville MI 49683,
616-378-2000, 35 km, www.crystalmtn.com

Garland, Lewiston MI 49756, 800-968-0042, 45 km,
GarlandUSA.com

Grand Traverse Resort, Acme MI 49610, 800-748-0303,
2 km

Hanson Hills, Grayling MI 49738, 517-348-9266, 35 km,
www.hansonhills.org

Hinchman Acres Resort, Mio MI 48647, 517-826-3267,
25 km, www.hinchman.com

Maple Lane Sports, Skandia MI 49885, 906-942-7662,
14 km

Shanty Creek, Bellaire MI 49615-9555, 800-678-4111,
30 km, www.shantyccreek.com

Superior Nordic Training & Recreation Complex,
Ishpeming MI 49849, 906-486-7243, 35 km,
www.exploringthenorth.com

Wilderness Valley, Gaylord MI 49735, 616-858-7090, 56 km

Minnesota

Bearskin Lodge, Grand Marais MN 55604, 800-338-4170,
70 km, www.bearskin.com

Cascade Lodge, Lutsen MN 55612, 800-322-9543, 50 km,
www.cascadelodgemn.com

Giants Ridge Resort, Biwabik MN 55708, 800-688-7669,
60 km, www.giantsridge.com

Golden Eagle Lodge, Grand Marais MN 55604,
800-346-2203, 70 km, www.golden-eagle.com

Gunflint Lodge, Grand Marais MN 55604, 218-388-2294,
80 km, www.gunflint.com

Lutsen Mountains, Lutsen MN 55612, 218-663-7281,
27 km, www.lutsen.com

Maplelag, Callaway MN 56521, 800-654-7711, 53 km,
www.maplelag.com

Pincushion Mountain B&B, Grand Marais MN
55604-9707, 800-542-1226, www.pincushionbb.com

Silver Rapids Lodge, Ely MN 55731, 800-950-9425, 4 km,
www.silverrapidslodge.com

Solbakken Resort, Lutsen MN 55612, 800-435-3950,
32 km, solbakken@boreal.org

Spidahl Ski Gard, Erhard, MN 56534, 218 736 5097,
20 km, dspidahl@runestone.net

West Virginia

Timberline Ski Area, Davis WV 26260, 800-SNOWING,
17 km, www.timberlineresort.com

White Grass Touring Center, Davis WV 26260,
304-866-4114, 35 km, www.whitegrass.com

Wisconsin

Justin Trails Nordic Center, Sparta WI 54656,
800-488-4521, 12 km, www.justintrails.com

Minocqua Winter Park, Minocqua WI 54548,
715-356-3309, 75 km, www.skimwp.org

Nine Mile Forest, Wausau WI 54403-5568, 715-693-3001,
30 km, maheyde@mail.co.marathon.wi.us

North Lakeland Discovery Center, Manitowish Waters WI
54545, 715-543-2085, 19 km, cranq@centuryinter.net

Palmquist's "The Farm," Brantwood WI 54513,
800-519-2558, 35 km, www.northcoast.com/pqfarm/ski

USA Mountain and West

Alaska

Matanaska-Susitna Borough Trails, Palmer AK,
907-745-9690, 25 km

Mineral Creek Ski Trails, Valdez AK 99686,
907-835-2531, 10 km

Arizona

Flagstaff Nordic Center, Flagstaff AZ 86002,
520-779-1951, 40 km

California

Bear Valley Cross Country, Bear Valley CA 95223,
209-753-2834, 70 km, www.bearvalleyxc.com

Camp Richardson Resort, South Lake Tahoe CA 96158,
530-542-6584, 35 km, www.camprichardson.com

Caples Lake Resort, Kirkwood CA 95646, 209-258-8888,
55 km, capleslake@volcano.net

Coffee Creek Ranch, Trinity Center CA 96091,
800-624-4480, 18 km

Eagle Mountain Cross Country Ski Area, Nevada City CA
95959, 800-391-2254, 86 km,
www.eaglemtnresort.com

Montecito-Sequoia, Inc., Los Altos CA 93633,
800-227-9900, 45 km, www.montecitosequoia.com

Mt. Shasta Ski Park Cross Country, Mt. Shasta CA 96067,
530-926-8600, 25 km, www.skipark.com

Northstar Cross Country and Telemark, Truckee CA
96160, 530-587-0245, 65 km, www.skinorthstar.com

Rim Nordic Ski Area, Running Springs CA 92382,
909-867-2600, 12 km, www.rimnordic.com

Royal Gorge Cross Country, Soda Springs CA 95728,
800-500-3871, 164 km, www.royalgorge.com

Tahoe Donner Cross Country, Truckee CA 96161,
530-587-9484, 70 km, www.tahoedonner.com

Tamarack Lodge Resort, Mammoth Lakes CA 93546,
760-934-2442, 45 km, www.tamaracklodge.com

Yosemite Cross Country Ski Center, Yosemite CA 95389,
209-372-8444, 45 km, www.yosemitepark.com

Colorado

Ashcroft Cross Country, Aspen CO 81611, 970-925-1971,
35 km, www.ashcroft.com

Aspen/Snowmass Nordic Ski Trail System, Aspen CO
81611, 970-920-2145, 60 km, rmabello@skiaspen.com

Beaver Creek, Vail CO 81658, 970-845-5313, 32 km

Breckenridge Nordic Center, Breckenridge CO 80424,
970-453-6855, 28 km, www.colorado.net/~nord/

C Lazy U Ranch, Granby CO 80446, 970-887-3344, 25 km,
www.clazyu.com

Cordillera Nordic Center, Edwards CO 81632,
970-926-5100, 12 km, www.cordillera-vail.com

Crested Butte Nordic Center, Crested Butte CO 81224,
970-349-1707, 25–40 km, www.crestedbutte.com

Eldora Mountain Resort, Nederland CO 80466,
303-440-8700 ext. 216, 45 km, www.eldora.com

Frisco Nordic Center, Frisco CO 80443, 970-668-0866,
37 km, www.colorad.net/~nord/

Grand Lake Touring Center, Grand Lake CO 80447,
970-627-8008, 30 km

Grand Mesa Ski Trail System, Cedaredge CO 81413,
800-551-6372, 20 km,
www.coloradodirectory.com/grandmesalodge

High Meadows Ranch, Steamboat Springs CO 80477,
800-457-4453, 15 km, highmeadows@sprynet.com

Latigo Cross Country Ski Ranch, Kremmling CO 80459,
970-724-9008, 50 km

Phoenix Ridge Yurts, Creede CO 81130, 800-984-6275,
5 km, wcrealty@rmi.net

San Juan Guest Ranch, Ridgeway CO 81432,
800-331-3015, 10 km, www.sjgr.com

Skyline Resort, Telluride CO 81435, 888-754-1126, 5 km,
www.ranchweb.com/skyline

Snow Mountain Nordic Center, Winter Park CO 80478,
970-887-2152, 100 km

Trail Mountain B & B, Granby CO 80446, 970-887-3944,
15 km, innsofcolorado.org

Vail Cross Country, Vail CO 81658, 970-479-4390, 15 km

Vista Verde Ranch, Steamboat CO 80477, 800-526-7433,
30 km, vistaverde.com

Whistling Elk Ranch, Rand CO 80473, 970-723-8311,
35 km

Idaho

Bogus Basin, Boise ID 83702, 208-332-5151, 32 km,
www.bogusbasin.com

Galena Lodge, Ketchum ID 83340, 208-726-4010, 56 km

Idaho Rocky Mountain Ranch, Stanley ID 83278,
208-774-3544, idrocky@cyberhighway.net

North Valley Trails, Hailey ID 83333, 208-788-2117,
150 km, mcrofts@micron.net

Sun Valley Nordic Center, Sun Valley ID 83353,
208-622-2251, 40 km, ski@sunvalley.com

Teton Ridge Ranch, Tetonia ID 83452, 208-456-2650,
25 km, atilt@aol.com

Montana

Alice Creek Ranch, Lincoln MT 59639, 406-362-4810,
40 km, alicecrk@linctel.net

B Bar Guest Ranch, Emigrant MT 59027, 406-848-7523,
40 km, www.bbar.com

Big Mountain Resort, Whitefish MT 59937, 406-862-2946,
10 km, www.bigmtn.com

Bohart Ranch Cross Country Ski, Bozeman MT
59715-8288, 406-586-9070, 25 km, cyotl@imt.net

Covered Wagon Ranch, Gallatin Gateway MT 59730,
406-995-4237, 25 km,
www.gomontana.com/coveredwagon.html

Izaak Walton Inn, Essex MT 59916, 406-888-5700, 30 km,
www.izaakwaltoninn.com

Lone Mountain Ranch, Big Sky MT 59716, 800-514-4644,
65 km

Mountain Timbers, West Glacier MT 59936,
800-841-3835, 15 km

Red Lodge Nordic Center, Red Lodge MT 59068,
406-446-9191, 15 km, sylvanpk@wtp.net

Yellowstone Expeditions, Yellowstone MT 59758,
 800-728-9333, 12 km,
 yellowstoneexpeditions@yellowstoneonline.com

New Mexico

Angel Fire Resort Nordic Center, Angel Fire NM 87710,
 505-377-4287, 15 km, www.angelfireresort.com
Capulin Cross Country, Torreon NM 87061,
 505-384-2209, 10 km,
 www.newmexico.com/crosscountryski
Enchanted Forest, Red River NM 87558, 505-754-6112,
 30 km, www.redrivernm.com/enchanted/forest.html

Oregon

Mt. Bachelor Nordic Center, Bend OR 97709,
 800-829-2442, 56 km, www.mtbachelor.com
Mt. Hood Meadows Nordic Center, Mt. Hood OR 97041,
 503-337-2222, 15 km, www.skihood.com

Utah

The Homestead Resort, Midway UT 84049, 435-654-1102,
 12 km, www.homestead-ut.com
Sundance Nordic Center, Sundance UT 84604,
 801-223-4170, 17 km

White Pine Touring Center, Park City UT 84068,
 435-649-8710, 18 km

Washington

49 Degrees North, Chewelah WA 99109, 509-935-6649,
 10 km, www.ski49n.com
Methow Valley Sport Trails Association, Winthrop WA
 98862, 509-996-3287, 200, www.methow.com/~mvsta/
Stevens Pass Nordic Center, Skykomish WA 98288,
 206-812-4510, 25 km, www.stevenspass.com
The Summit Nordic Center, Snoqualmie WA 98068,
 425-434-7669 ext. 3372, 55 km,
 www.summit-at-snoqualmie.com
Sun Mountain Lodge, Winthrop WA 98862, 800-572-0493,
 175 km, www.sunmountainlodge.com

Wyoming

Jackson Hole Nordic Center, Teton Village WY 83025,
 307-739-2629, 17 km, www.jacksonhole.com/ski
Pahaska Tepee, Cody WY 82414, 800-628-7791, 20 km,
 www.pahaska.com
Spring Creek Nordic Center, Jackson WY 83001,
 800-443-6139, 15 km, www.springcreekresort.com
Yellowstone National Park, Yellowstone WY 82190,
 307-344-7901, www.ynp-lodges.com

INDEX